This book is dedicated to my children and grandchildren.

John Hyndman, Jr., Gerald Hyndman, Jeanne Hyndman Barber

Krystal Hyndman, Michael Hyndman, Lisa Hyndman, and Gunter Barber

I hope this book will always be a part of your memories of your grandfather. His children and grandchildren were the most important part of his life. I think that after you read his letters you will see what character and strength he had. He was very proud of his record in the Marine Corps and he was so pleased when his brother Jerry and his own two boys, John and Jerry, chose to follow in his footsteps and be Marines.

Your mother and grandmother,
Lois Hyndman

Cover Design by Gunter Barber, John's youngest grandson.

Second Lieutenant John Hyndman 1946

In addition to the American Theater Ribbon, the Asiatic-Pacific Theater Ribbon (with one battle star), and the Purple Heart shown in the above photograph, Lt. Hyndman also earned the Presidential Unit Citation Ribbon, the Combat Action Ribbon, , the Navy Unit Commendation, and the World War II Victory Ribbon. The Combat Action Ribbon was awarded retroactively to Marine and Navy men who fought in ground combat during amphibious campaigns. See the photograph of John's medals on page 224.

A MARINE IN WORLD WAR II
from
Notre Dame
to
Iwo Jima and Beyond

Letters from

Second Lieutenant John Hyndman, USMCR
1943-1946

*Copyright 2010
by
Lois Hyndman*

ISBN 978-061534125-5

Acknowledgements

Because my mother-in-law, Madge Hyndman, carefully preserved each of these letters and passed them on to me, I was able to put this book together.

A special thanks to those who furnished information on the "Cavaliers at Notre Dame."
Scott Abell   Grant Hall
Mrs. Verlie Abrams   Don Hollar
Tamara Hald   William Kessler and his wife Muriel

Also thanks to John's roommate at Notre Dame, Ralph Hvidsten.

Thanks to Lou Hindbaugh who followed "his lieutenant" from California to Hawaii and onto the beach at Iwo and survived to tell what it was like to be an enlisted man led by John.

To William Parks Johnson who gave me answers to many questions from Boot Camp to Iwo as a fellow Boot, OCS, and fellow platoon leader at Iwo.

To John Murray, James Tout, Mary Margaret Felt Moore and Ann Cowan Van Doren whom John mentions in his letters and who were willing to give personal accounts to me.

A special thanks and admiration for the detailed book on the SOCS 400 by J. Fred Clements and also to Robert Allen for his book on the 1st Battalion, 28th Marines in the Battle of Iwo Jima.

To Margaret Trevitt for sharing her brother, Lester Hutchcroft's letters and her memories of those days before his death on Iwo, even though it was heart rending for her to talk about it even after 60 years.

To John's sister Dorothy Hyndman Rogers who lived through reading the letters and who gave me an account of what it was like to believe her brother was dead for several weeks before she finally found that letter in the mail box and realized he was alive.

To John's brother, Retired. Col. Gerald H. Hyndman, USMC for the "Action Report of Landing Team 128" and insights into John's letters.

To Jerre Allyn for information about the Allyn family and Madge Hyndman's stay with them in California just before John shipped out.

And lastly heartfelt thanks to my editor. Marvin Veronee. He was the perfect person to put this book together as he was at Midshipman's School at Notre Dame in the autumn of 1943. He also landed on Iwo on Green Beach on D-Day and knows first hand what John experienced.

John Spencer Hyndman, Sr.

John Spencer Hyndman, Sr. was born on October 20, 1922. He spent his first fourteen years on a farm near Mayfield, Kansas. When he entered high school at Wellington High School, his family moved to Wellington, Kansas. His first eight years of school was spent in a one room schoolhouse just down the road from the farm. The picture of all the students in the school is on page 4.

Always remember when he is complaining about Notre Dame, that he loved the school, but was in over his head as he had attended the one room school and a small high school in Wellington and had had very little science and math. For some reason, the Marine Corps decided to make an engineer of him and that meant physics, advanced math, etc. His language skills were the very best as shown in his letters. When typing his letters for this book, I found only one misspelled word. (Any mistakes are ones I made when typing.) The misspelled word was khaki and in a later letter he spelled it correctly. I imagine his mother who was a school teacher and stickler for grammar and spelling corrected him. Also remember he had no dictionary or word processor to refer to.

Don Hollar, Bill Busch, Bill Kessler, and John all enlisted in by the Marine Corps Reserves when a recruiter came to Wichita U. in early 1942. They were to finish college and then become officers. In 1943, however, they were called up and sent to Notre Dame to V-12 School. (I am enclosing an article explaining V-12 Schools.) When they went to Kansas City for their physical, examiners told John and Don Hollar they were ten pounds overweight. Because both Don and John were star college athletes in football, basketball, and track at the time, they were very muscular and certainly not overweight. According to Don they ate lettuce for three weeks. John told me that they ate one Milky Way a day and they were able to pass the physical when they returned. John had knee surgery for a football injury the year before and also was flat footed. However, he managed to sneak by the physical. He said that they tested anyone who had knee problems by having them do a deep knee bend. He said that he had not been able to do one since the surgery, but somehow he managed one that day. In all the years I knew him he was never able to do one again. The flat foot test he figured out was done by looking at the bottom of your foot after a day of walking around barefoot during your physical. If your arch area was not dirty you passed. He realized this early in the day and walked on the sides of his feet so his arches would not get soiled. In all the time in the Corps he never had knee or foot problems.

TABLE OF CONTENTS

PART I.   ENLISTED SERVICE - United States   Page

V-12 at Notre Dame University, South Bend, Indiana	1
"The Cavaliers"	60
USMC Recruit Depot, Parris Island, South Carolina	63
Infantry School, Camp Lejeune, North Carolina	87

PART II. OFFICER TRAINING SERVICE - UNITED STATES

SOCS, Camp Lejeune	95
Pacific Coast, Camp Pendleton, San Diego, California	110
Madge Hyndman's Letters from California	118

PART III. OVERSEAS SERVICE

Territory of Hawaii	130
Voyage to Combat	155
Iwo Jima.	165
Army Hospital, Guam & Navy Hospital, Aiea Heights, Oahu	175

PART IV. NAVAL HOSPITAL, SAN DIEGO   197

APPENDICES

Appendix I. SOCS	226
Appendix II. Replacement Draft	231
Appendix III. Action Report of Landing Team 128	235
Appendix IV Personnel Records	254
Appendix V. Notre Dame Cavaliers	267
Appendix VI. Brain Surgery	276
Appendix VII. My Grandpa	278
Appendix VIII. White House Visit, 1985	279
FAMILY PHOTOS	283

BIBLIOGRAPHY   282

INDEX   287

DATES OF SERVICE

Date	Event
July 3, 1943	Left home by train for Notre Dame, South Bend, Indiana
From Oct. 26 to Nov. 7, 1943	Leave home to Kansas
March 1, 1944	Left Notre Dame for Boot Camp
March 3, 1944	Arrived Boot Camp at Parris Island, SC
May 3, 1944	Completed Basic Training at Parris Island
May 3 to July 14, 1944	Infantry School. Camp Lejeune, North Carolina
July 14, 1944 to Sept. 30 1944	Officer Candidate School, Camp Lejeune
Sept. 30, 1944	Commissioned 2nd Lieutenant, USMC
Oct. 1 to about October 7, 1944	Train to Camp Pendleton, California
Nov. 13, 1944	Sailed from San Diego aboard the *USS Callan* to Hawaii
Nov. 1944	Arrived Maui for ten days. Then to Hilo, Hawaii
Jan. 5, 1945	Practice landings on Maui
Jan. 1945	Week in Honolulu, Hawaii
Jan. 27, 1945	Sailed from Honolulu aboard *USS Dickens*
Jan. Feb., 1945	To Saipan via Eniwetok, Marshall Islands
Feb. 19, 1945	Landed on Green Beach, Iwo Jima. Morning of D-Day. As Part of 27th Replacement Draft
March 5, 1945	Took command of 1st Platoon, B Co. 1st Batt, 28th Regiment
March 1945	On line 24 hours. Reserve, back to line.
March 9, 1945	Wounded commanding 1st Platoon.
March 1945	To Guam via Hospital ship, Arrival, March 12, 1945.
March 20, 1945	To Hawaii by air, arrival March 21, 1945.
March 21 to April 26, 1945	In Naval Hospital, Aeia Heights, Hawaii.
March 31, 1945	Wrote letter to his parents saying he was wounded. Received April 6, 1945.
April 13, 1945	Parents received Marine Corps letter.
April 26, 1945	Embarked on *USS Kwajalein* CVE 98.
May 3, 1945	Arrived San Diego Hospital.
June 30, 1945 - July 31	Leave to Kansas.
August 22, 1945	Operation to insert tantalum plate into his skull.
Oct. 23, to Nov. 21, 1945	Leave to Kansas
Nov. 1945 to April 1946	Probably moved to Rancho Santa Fe Convalescent Home
April 1946	Retired as a 2nd Lieutenant, USMCR.
Fall of 1946	Returned to Wichita State University, Kansas

PART I.

Enlisted Man in V-12

at

THE UNIVERSITY OF NOTRE DAME

July 1943 to February 1944

THE V-12 PROGRAM

Their post-Pearl Harbor enlistments didn't immediately put future SOCS members on a train to boot camp. They were all about the same age and the Marine Corps formed them into a cohort of the Navy college V-12 program, which for the Marines was officially designated as Marine Reserve, Class III(d) but commonly referred to as Marine V-12. The V-12 was a wartime Navy and Marine Corps officer procurement plan established to assure the two services of a predictable, controlled source of officer candidates. Even before Pearl Harbor the services were looking at their probable wartime expansion and calculating the number of ships, aircraft, and divisions they would ultimately have to man. In the summer of 1943, when the program was activated, Secretary of the Navy Frank Knox asserted that the armed forces were planning battles that "may have to be fought in 1949." With the draft age being dropped from twenty to eighteen they knew they would have to shelter enough potential officers for later stages of the war.

Many colleges and universities who foresaw financial problems as enrollments dropped with mobilization eagerly sought out the program. The V-12 opened higher education--and commissions--to many trainees who never dreamed of it before the war. Fifteen Marine V-12 went on to become generals, eighteen Navy V-12 ensigns rose to flag rank, and seventeen others who were appointed to Annapolis subsequently became admirals.

On July 1 1943, the V-12 program was activated on schedule, and they took their next step toward the war. All were ordered to active duty as able seamen or private first class. Those not on one of the campuses selected for the program were generally assigned to the one nearest them (therefore Notre Dame for John). *They continued their classes, but with military basic training added on under the supervision of Navy and Marine officers and NCOs. To their puzzlement, the Marine V-12s were required to take some course more related to running a ship, such as physics and mechanical drawing. For the sake of uniformity and continuity, all 131 V-12 schools were put on an academic schedule of three four month terms.*

Failure in one course didn't lead to expulsion but failing two did in the Navy program; the Marines forgave two failures if the student demonstrated improvement and was promising officer material. As the program progressed the screening for leadership qualities became more stringent.

From: *We Few* by James Dickensen.

V-12 SCHOOL[1]

The V-12[2] were college students who were potential Navy and Marine corps officer candidates:

(1) who had been in college when World War II started for the United States on 7 December 1941,

(2) who joined the program as a result of competitive testing in high school, or

(3) were assigned from the field.

The length of their college assignment depended upon their previous college experience. These future leaders had two or more semesters of college when they started into the officer's training track; each one had to meet the requirements of the Marine V-12 program in order to advance to the next step.

At the V-12 schools, besides maintaining a full academic schedule, everyone was in uniform, up at 0530 for PT and close order drill; off-hours were supervised by drill sergeants and frustrated combat ready captains "stuck in some college town."

Military life began in earnest for members of the special OCS class in July 1943 when they were called to active duty from various colleges. Those who survived the academic and discipline standards started to come together in February 1944 when they were shipped to Parris Island for boot camp.

Note: LH indicates a footnote by Lois Hyndman, MV a footnote by the editor, Marvin Veronee.

[1] This is an excerpt from J, Fred Clement's book: *The SOCS 400*. LH

[2] College Students who signed up for the Navy V-5 (naval pilots) or the V-7 program (deck officers) expected to graduate and then be called into active duty and sent to a Midshipman's School for four months of training before receiving their commissions as Ensigns, dubbed by enlisted men as "Ninety Day Wonders." Many college students who already were in college early in the war managed to graduate and then go on active duty. The rest, like John, were in college and had no chance to graduate before all Navy and Marine volunteers were consolidated into the V-12 program and called to active duty on 1 July 1943. MV

MAYFIELD, KANSAS LONG BRANCH ONE ROOM SCHOOL.
About 1933
from left to right

Doris Miller (Dean's twin), Dorothy Armstrong, Anna Marie Ellison, Elizabeth McCreary, Ruth Ann Miller, Kathleen Deffenbaugh, Maxine Deffenbaugh, Geraldine McCammon, teacher (later married Bob Welcher), Orville McCreary (almost hidden), Neal Lauterbach, Lloyd Miller, Eugene Heasty, Bruce McCreary (hidden), Bill McCreary, John Ellison (hidden), JOHN HYNDMAN, David Deffenbaugh,

LETTER 1

Postmarked July 3 ??

Dear Folks,

All is going well except that our train[1] out of K. C. was 6 hours late. It didn't leave until 2:00 A. M. Our Pullman was there, however, waiting to be connected on to the train, so we got on it and went to bed. Now we won't arrive in Chicago until about 4:30 this afternoon. We are going to be awfully late getting into South Bend. May have to stay in a hotel, but I hope not.

We had to stand up all the way to Kansas City.[1] Seat reservations didn't mean a thing. They had sold about 3 reservations, (Just changed pens.)

We have been hearing all kinds of rumors as to how we are going to be handled at Notre Dame. But we don't know anything for sure.

Well, it's awfully hard to write on these bumpy trains, so I'll sign off till I get there.

Love
John

P. S. Better hold off writing to me until I know for sure what my address is. The one I gave you might not be enough.

---

[1] With tire and gasoline rationing, trains and buses became the main means of travel, therefore the overcrowding. MV

LETTER 2

Postmarked July 5, 1943
Sunday Afternoon

Dear Folks,

At last I've found some time to sit down in my room and relax. I've been an awfully busy Marine.

Our train out of Kansas City was so late that we didn't report until 7:30 P. M. Friday. Hollar and the boys who came on the Santa Fe beat us by 3 hours. When we reported too late for chow, they assigned us our rooms, company numbers and laundry numbers. I am in Company B and room 415 Cavanaugh Hall. Hollar is in 405 of the same building and company.

We didn't do anything on Friday nite, but Saturday morning the work began. They got us out at 6 A.M. and we fell in for calisthenics at 6:15. I got dressed in 3 minutes. That's mighty fast! After calisthenics we had 20 minutes to make our beds and get shaved for breakfast. We had to march almost half a mile for breakfast. They gave us a good breakfast, then shortly afterward we had to fall in for drill. And we didn't drill just a little bit, either. We marched and marched and marched for eight hours that day. They did give us time out for a 15 minute swim and noon chow.

After evening chow, we had liberty until midnight, so Hollar and I walked to town (two miles) and went to a show. I developed blisters on my feet and I felt as though I was three inches shorter. One boy in our company passed out while we were standing at attention once. He hit the ground so hard that it sounded like some one had chopped down a tree. Naturally all the boys crowded around him, but he sergeant gave them heck. He said if anyone passed out, to let them lay there and he'd take care of them himself. And if anyone passes out while marching, we aren't to stop, but to walk right over them. Rough Place! But it's mighty easy compared to Parris Island. I still don't know for sure how long I'll be here, but it will probably be either 4 or 8 months.

Tomorrow morning we have to register for classes. Next time I write, I'll know what courses I have to take.

We were measured for uniforms this morning. I had to stand in line about 2 hours before I got in. Our uniforms are going to be good looking, but it's going to take quite a while to get them. Maybe you'd better send me my cords and tennis shoes. Also any polo shirts you can find. If we were going to march much more, I'd have you send some more shoes, but after classes start, we won't do much marching. Lots of studying though. We have to be in bed at 10:00 so there won't be any late studying at least.

Well, I guess there isn't much else to say right now, so I'll sign off. Write soon.

John

Here's my address: Pvt. John S. Hyndman, U. S. M. C. R.
Cavanaugh Hall, Room 415
University of Notre Dame
Notre Dame, Indiana

LETTER 3

Tuesday Evening July 6, 1943

Dear Folks,

It's raining to beat the band outside. We got caught out in it on the way back from chow and got wet as heck.

I was sure glad to get Daddy's letter today. I also got one from Mary Ann[1] yesterday. Those are the only letters I have gotten although I've written to a lot of people. It sure seems good to hear them call out my name when they're passing out the mail.

We sure haven't done very much the last couple of days. I stood in line 2 hours Monday to register, then found out they had me assigned to the College of Engineering. And here I'm supposed to be in Arts and Letters with Geology as my major. So Hollar and I are just waiting around until they decide what to do with us. Pray for me that they don't leave me in engineering, because I just couldn't make it. I'd be in Parris Island as a private before you could blink your eye. Why with all that higher math I wouldn't have a chance. I guess I'll find out tomorrow what's going to happen to me. Classes started for the boys who aren't messed up. But there are quite a few who are in the same boat as Hollar and myself and we'll all get started out behind the rest. Maybe everything will turn out all right. I hope so.

Last nite we had drill for about an hour and we are really getting good. We have a wonderful drill sergeant. He is awful tough, but makes everybody like him. He sure scares to death anyone who makes a dumb mistake. He told one guy that if he didn't be careful, he'd give him a face full of knuckles. Another guy reached up to scratch his head while marching and Sergeant Santos said, " If you raise that arm one more time, I'll come up there and break it off. " Mighty tough.

Hollar and I haven't done a thing all day but sit around in our rooms and go down to the recreation hall and play pool. I got my hair cut down to regulation length which is two inches or less in length. It isn't a regular crew cut, but its still plenty short. Yet it doesn't look bad at all as it is curly enough to still have a wave in front.

I sure wish they'd get our schedules straightened out so we could get busy. Sitting around with nothing to do makes me get a little homesick. We do take our physicals tomorrow so I'll know whether I'm going to be here long or not.

Well, write me soon,

Love John

---

[1] Mary Ann West is the girl he was pinned to when he went into the Marines. Being "pinned" meant that the girl wore your fraternity pin and that meant you were dating no one else. (We also called it going "steady.") LH

LETTER 4

Addressed to Miss Dorothy Jean Hyndman

Postmarked July 14 1943

Tuesday

Dear Dorothy,

I got your letter today and I am sorry that I haven't written sooner, but I just don't have any spare time at all. I am taking a couple of awfully hard courses that take a lot of time. In fact I really don't have enough time and I'm awfully worried about passing Physics. But I did get a good grade in our first test yesterday. There wasn't any way that I could get out of taking these courses. The captain told us that they didn't have us in school to give us a degree, but to educate us to be Marine officers. And if we hadn't ever had any math, physics, and engineering drawing, we must get it here. So I had to take all these at once because I'm going to be here one semester or 4 months. So I guess I'll be going to Parris Island by November 1st. But if I flunk physics, it well be as a buck private. Maybe I will get enough leave between here and P. I. to come home for awhile.

I just got a letter from Mary Ann. She writes me 3 or 4 page letters every single day. Her address is 3614 N. Topeka, Wichita, 15 Kansas. And her phone number is 5-3608. Her phone number at work is 4-1303 at the Magnolia Petroleum Co., First National Bank Building.

Saturday we had liberty all afternoon and evening until midnight. But I didn't leave the campus, as I studied all day Sat. and Sunday too.

I've got to fall out right now.

Love
John

P.S. The food is fair. Good breakfast but a poor noon meal.

LETTER 5

Addressed to Mr. Jerry Hyndman
Postmarked July 21, 1943

Dear Jerry,

How is the money maker of our family getting along? I bet you have more money that you know what to do with. When I was your age, I worked at the pool for 25 cents per morning. Now at 20, I'm working myself to death for $50 per mo. minus deduction for laundry ($5 per mo.), $6.50 for something else, and maybe 1 bond[1] a month. After it is all subtracted I will have about $6 a week to spend. But that is quite a bit here, because I don't have time to spend it.

Apparently one of my letters to you folks got there because I wrote one telling about my physical exam. They hardly looked at my knee, but almost sent me home because of my over bite. Quite a few boys flunked the physical. This kid will probably flunk physics. Gosh it is tough. It takes me more time than I have to put in on it. In Math I'm doing fine though. That is, so far. It'll get harder.

I got a letter from Mary Ann today and she said she had been down to Wellington last week-end.

Well, the bell will ring for lights out in a minute, so I'd better close. I'll send you some picture post cards of Notre Dame in a day or two.

Your big brother
John

War Bond Savings Stamp Book

[1]The bond he is talking about was a savings bond that was sold to finance the war. They cost $18.75 and in ten years they could be cashed for $25. Savings stamps were also sold, mostly to school children. They could buy a stamp for a quarter and paste it into their Savings Stamp Booklet, which contained space for seventy five stamps. MV

Set of Post Cards Sent to Jerry Hyndman.
Note the Six Cent Air Mail Stamp.

The Administration Building

The Library

Notre Dame. 1943.

LETTER 6

Postmarked July 23, 1943

Thursday eve

Dear Folks,

I haven't got much time to write this so I'll have to make it short. I am enclosing an application to Notre Dame which both of you must sign. Then send it back to the address on the letter as soon as possible.

Here it is Thursday nite already and the week is almost over. I can't get used to the way time passes so fast around here. I'll be gone before I know it. The sooner I leave the better I'll like, too. I guess I won't even get to come home before going to Parris Island. The Marines just don't give out furloughs or shore leaves.

I'm beginning to get in pretty good condition now. I feel good all the time and not tired and sleepy like I used to be at Wichita. These regular hours will sure do it for you.

I sure dread tomorrow because we have to start taking shots or vaccinations. We'll all be miserable for a few days I suppose. I've got to get my hair cut again tomorrow, They told me I needed one at inspection this noon. I think I'll get a regular crew cut this time because the way I've got it now it is too long to stay put and too short to comb well. It is unruly as heck.

Say, this physics is getting to be terrible, I can work the daily assignments all right, but they give us a test every day that isn't at all like the other. Of course everyone has a low average which may help. Math is a cinch so far.

Love
John

Set of postcards[1] of Notre Dame Postmarked July 25 and addressed to Jerry Hyndman.

---

[1]These postcards are shown on page10..

LETTER 7

Postmarked July 26, 1943

Sunday Evening

Dear Folks,

Well here it is the last day of July and I have 3 months left at Notre Dame. Our final exams end on Oct. 26 and this is the 25th of July. All that is left is August, September and October. I'll be just barely 21 when I leave for Parris Island. I sure hope I can come home[1] when I finish here, but I guess there is no chance. In fact I'll be lucky if I get home next April as that is when I get my commission. There is 7 weeks at Parris Island, 6 weeks at New River and 8 weeks at Quantico. I'll be a mighty homesick lad by that time.

Well, we get our fatigue suits tomorrow, so my civilian clothes can take a rest. I imagine the rest of our uniforms will get here some time this week. The sooner the better. I'm getting tired of going into town on Saturdays and looking like another civilian. The only bad part is that I'll have to be on my toes and salute and all that sort of stuff, but I won't mind it.

I sure feel carefree tonight because I have all my assignments for tomorrow. In Literature I had to go to the library and read a Greek play and write out a report. I did that Saturday morning, then I worked all math and finished up my physics this afternoon. So all that I'm going to do is review my physics a little and write letters.

We had liberty yesterday so Hollar and I went into town and saw a picture show. It was pretty good, but nothing extra. We also went into a restaurant and bought a $.95 meal with cherry pie for dessert. That was the first pie I've had since I've been here. Sometimes the food here is terrible, but the breakfasts are pretty good. At least we get plenty to eat even if it isn't tasty.

Bill Kessler just came in and asked me about a physics problem. It seems good to be finished and have guys asking me questions for a change. The thing I don't like about physics is studying myself to death just to get a passing grade. Also I don't like the tests where they give you fifteen minutes to work 4 problems. With a little time I could work them all, but instead I have to work so fast that I either get mixed up or make silly mistakes. On our last test I would have had a perfect paper, but I subtracted 15 from 45 and got 20, so naturally I missed one. That's what burns me up. I don't like to be rushed so much.

Well, I'd better close now and write another letter, then review physics.

Love
John

---

[1] John got leave at the end of the semester, October 1943 and never came home again until he had been in the hospital for three months. June 1945. LH

LETTER 8

Postmarked July 29, 1943
Thursday morning

Dear Folks,

I don't have any classes until 11:00 and I have all my homework for today, so I thought I'd better write to you all.

I'm not sure whether I told you about it or not, but we are wearing our fatigue uniforms all the time now. They are a little too hot, but they do fit loose and comfortable. They are a sort of forest green color with a big black Marine insignia on the left pocket of the coat. U. S. M. C. is printed in big black letters just above that. The rest of our uniforms arrived yesterday, so we'll probably be wearing them Monday with neckties and everything. Then the saluting will begin as we will have our overseas caps. You do not have to salute when uncovered, so naturally we haven't done any saluting as yet.

It sure seems good not to have to be on the run every minute. But this is the only day of the week where I can relax just a little. If it wasn't for physics, I'd have plenty of free time. That course has sure got me worried. I'll be tickled to death to get a "D" in it. If I do flunk it won't be because I haven't tried my darndest. Last year a total of 225 students took physics and only 30 passed. That's mainly the fault of the instructors I think. Of course, they aren't to flunk so many service men I hope.

Is Jerry still working at the Safeway and carrying the news too? Yesterday we all had to fill out a blank with our names and home addresses and address of our hometown newspaper. So I guess you'll be reading about me in the news before long. I think Mary Ann is coming up to see me with Don's girl and also Bill Kessler's girl about August 26th or 27th. In fact, Kessler's[1] girl is going to go to school at Purdue which is just a little ways from here.

Well, I'd better close now and study physics.

Love
John

P. S. Do you think you could spare some hangers? I'm going to need them badly.

---

[1] Bill Kessler was dating a girl from Wichita named Carolyn Morris who went to Purdue. Purdue University is in West Lafayette, Indiana, about 90 miles southwest of South Bend. LH

LETTER 9

Postmarked Aug. 2, 1943

Monday afternoon

Dear Folks.

I was sure glad to get Daddy's letter and also Jerry's letter on Sunday morning. In fact, I got 4 letters Sunday, one from Mary Ann and another from Don Jones.

Don is stationed in the College of the City of New York, a big Jewish College just four blocks from Harlem. I guess he is going to be there for some time.

I just got out of Physical Education and am so tired I'm about to drop. In Phys. Ed. this week, we did all kinds of calisthenics for half the period. Then I had to run about a block with Hollar thrown across my shoulder something like I used to do with Dorothy. Of course he had to carry me back. After that we practiced a few hand-to-hand fighting tricks. We learned how to kill a man by hitting a man across the bridge of his nose, also across his temple, and how to break his collar bone with the side of your hand. These Marines are a tough outfit.

Well, I'm pretty happy today because I got a perfect paper on my physics test. I now have an average about 2.8 and average is supposed to be 2.4. I guess I have a strong C grade there, but there is still a long time to go and it doesn't get any easier. We are having a big math exam tomorrow, but I'm not very worried as I understand everything we have covered so far.

I heard some bad news Friday, in that I might be here eight months. But I hope that won't happen to me because eight months is entirely too long to have to stay around this place. I don't want to ever look at another physics book after Nov. 1. And if I have to stay here, I'll have to take more advanced physics and math. They are liable to make an engineer out of me yet.

Well, I'd better close now as I have to finish writing a report for Literature on "Agememnon" by Aeschylus. It's a Greek Tragedy. I'm getting an all around education.[1]

Love
John

---

[1] John graduated with a minor in English. LH

LETTER 10

Postmarked August 9, 1943
Monday Evening

Dear Folks,

I just heard some wonderful news today. I may get to leave here for Parris Island in September instead of November. It seems they are short of officer candidates, so they may take the boys who are scheduled for 1 semester in 2 or 3 weeks from now. Won't that be wonderful! I'll be so glad to get out of here I'll go wild. No more studies and no more books . . . at least for while anyway.

I got a letter from Don Jones today and I guess they are really putting him thru his paces back in New York. It sounds to me like his routine is even tougher than ours. He is taking both chemistry and physics and a more advanced math course than mine.

I got Daddy's letter today with the huge check. I think I can get it cashed all right, but if I can't I'll send it back. Speaking of money, do you suppose you folks could afford to send me some money and take it out of my bonus when it comes? Mary Ann is coming up in 2 weeks and she isn't going to have anything to spare. So I'd like to have some more money with which to show her a good time. I don't have any huge amount of my $50 check minus deductions as it has been 2 weeks since I got it. Please send me as much as you can spare because I'd sure appreciate it.

We are having a meeting tonite which is going to be about the insurance policy we are going to take out. For a $10,000 policy it will cost me $6.75 per month.

It is time to fall out for chow, so I'll continue this letter later this evening. I don't have so many lessons to get tonite.

(Continued) Tonight we filled out application blanks for the insurance policy. They will deduct $6.50 from each pay check.

Here are the answers to the questionnaire:
1. No, I'm very sorry, but haven't written Mrs. Rush. It's so late now I'm ashamed.
2. I don't know for sure about flunking a course, but I don't believe you can.
3. Yes, I have made several good friends although I still run around with the boys from home mostly.
4. My roommate is Ralph Hvidsten, a Swede from northern Minnesota. . . a nice kid, but very quiet and timid. He is younger than I.
5. We were issued 4 summer uniforms, 2 winter greens, two overseas caps, a field jacket and overcoat.
6. Six pairs of socks and six T-shirts. We wear T-shirts for underwear.
7. Yes I do my own mending although I haven't done any yet.
8. I look a little funny with a short haircut. But not much different. A little younger maybe.
9. Do you have an extra iron? If so I might be able to use it. Also the money I told you about before.

Love
John

LETTER 11

Postmark unreadable
Saturday morning

I got your package the other day and the cookies were sure good although I didn't get very many for myself. Every time a boy gets something to eat from home everybody congregates about the room until they get something to eat. The hangers are sure coming in handy because I've got so many clothes. We are going to wear our summer khaki uniforms on liberty this afternoon. It will be the first time we've worn them. I've been studying all morning and haven't had time to borrow an iron to press my trousers and shirt. So I paid a boy with a free period to press mine for me. We have to wear them for inspection before marching to noon chow. Right now I'm writing this letter from my freshman geology class. The teacher talks all hour and doesn't say a thing. He's the worst I've seen by far.

I spent all morning in the library reading Oedipus Rex by Sophocles. It is a Greek tragedy drama. Not a bad play, but it took two hours and a half to read. Every Saturday morning I have to read a play like that and write a report for Readings in Dramatic Literature. Yesterday they had a big list posted with the names of boys who were down in their subjects. My name wasn't on it, so I guess I'm all right so far. Hollar's name was on it for being down in physics, but he's just barely under the mark and will get through it all right, that is if physics doesn't get any harder. Then I'll probably flunk myself.

We took a reclassification test in mathematics the other day. When they get the results they will probably shift the classes around and put the smart ones together. I'm scared to death. I did pretty well and am liable to get in with a class that's too smart for me. Gosh, I hope not because it could get awfully tough. If I ever get through this place, I'll really be well educated. They are really throwing the knowledge at me. I'll learn more in four months here than I did in 3 years at Wichita U. Besides our studies, we are really getting into shape physically. Parris Island will be a lot easier for me too, I'm learning to box, to use judo in hand-to-hand combat, running the half mile obstacle course, learning to swim through burning oil in the ocean, learning how to jump from the deck of a ship into the ocean, how to fill my trousers with air and use them to keep afloat., Then we get calisthenics every morning before breakfast and some more high powered exercise at the beginning of each gym period. They are going to make a muscle man out of me for sure. And my knee has never bothered me in the least, which makes me feel good. I don't believe it will ever bother me.

We got our first pay yesterday. Fifty dollars in cash and I needed it bad. It will be sometime yet before I get my bonus from Stanolind.[1] Yesterday I took a blank down to the First Sergeant to have the Captain sign showing that I've been in the service for a month. Then I'll send it back to Wichita. After that I don't know how long it will be before my money comes through. But I will instruct Stanolind to send the money to you folks. Then you can send me some if I need it. I also want you folks to keep some of it.

Well, it's about time for class to let out, so I'd better close

Love
John

---

[1] John was majoring in geology at Wichita U. when he went into the service. He had a job with Stanolind Oil and Gas in Wichita as a sample boy. Cores were taken from wells when they were drilling a well and they had to be washed and prepared for microscopic study to identify what formation they came from. John did this to supplement his income, as he had a football scholarship, but that only paid room, board, and tuition. LH

LETTER 12

Postmarked Aug. 20, 1943

Thursday morning

Dear Folks,

Well, this is my easy day again and I sure like it. I've already got my physics for tomorrow, so I have two periods this afternoon in which to relax and enjoy life. I just live from Saturday to Thursday to Saturday.

Yesterday I took a math test in which I'm sure I got a hundred. It sure seems good to get your lessons every day and know what is going on all the time. Although I'm not always sure that I know anything about physics. But I've been getting good marks, so I'm not much worried and I don't care what I learn about physics just so I pass and get out of here. I think I told you once that there was a chance that I'd get out of here in September. Well, there is still a chance, but it's pretty slim and I don't expect that much luck. Even if I don't get to leave soon, there is really only 8 weeks of school left. Finals are on October 24 and 25 and there isn't much school work except for review during the week before finals. Then we will probably be sent on to P. I. about Oct. 29 or Nov. 1. I'll be 21 years old when I go to Parris Island. It won't be long before I'll become a man.[1]

Have Jerry and Allen[2] been having a big time? I suppose Jerry has gone up to Augusta by now.

By the way, is Bonnie[3] at Aunt Dott's now? Why don't you send me the address so that I can write them.

I am writing this letter during geology class. In fact, I write a letter almost every time I'm in this class. Say, while I'm talking about geology, I'd sure like to have you send me my geology book entitled "Geomorphology" by Scheck, I think. It's a big thick, new looking book. The book we use here isn't worth a darn.

As I'm running out of borrowed paper and I can't think of anything more to say, I'll close now and listen to the teacher.

Love
John

[1] Parris Island would be Boot Camp, the next stop for all Marines even those going to OCS to become officers. John's reference to becoming a man refers to voting age at that time. LH

[2] Allen is Allen Cobb whose father was Paul Cobb. Paul was the younger brother of Madge Hyndman (John's mother). He lived in Augusta, Kansas and was office manager for a refinery there. He walked with a limp as he had polio as a child. I got to know him well after I married John and he was a fine man .LH

[3] Bonnie is Edna Mae Allyn Cobb, John's grandmother. She was Madge Hyndman's mother. She was widowed at a very young age and raised three children and then worked as a housemother at Southwestern College in Winfield. When she retired she lived in Kansas City with her daughter, Dorothy Murphy, (the Aunt Dott who John mentions in his letters). Aunt Dott's husband died and left her with two very small children, so Bonnie helped her raise them while Aunt Dott worked as personnel manager of Tiche Goettinger, a fancy department store. However, during the war she worked at Remington Arms. Bonnie spent a lot of time in Wellington and she was the sweetest lady I have ever known. Everyone called her Bonnie as that was the closest John could come to grandma when he was just learning to talk. No one ever called her anything but Bonnie again. LH

LETTER 13

Postmarked Aug. 26, 1943

Tuesday Morning

Dear Folks,

Well, here I am back in good old geology class. This is where I keep up my correspondence. It's about the only leisure time around here except for Thursdays and weekends. I had a physics lab for two hours this morning. That's the class I don't like to go to . We do so many silly things and time goes by awfully slow. Then this afternoon I have an hour of physics lecture which makes a total of 3 hours worth of physics every Tuesday. I got my 1st math test back and little Johnny scored a hundred. There were only about 2 in the whole class. So I guess I'm not so dumb in math as I always thought. A little application makes the difference. But I'm not expecting to get such good grades all the way through the course because it will get pretty tough.

Yesterday a deficiency list was posted, but I didn't make the team. Hollar pulled up his physics grade and wasn't on it this time either. But 40% of the Marines at Notre Dame are down in one or more subjects. That's a pretty high average and I guess it is even worse at some of the other schools. I believe it is only what can be expected though because so many boys are having to take courses they aren't prepared to take. An example is myself taking physics and Hollar has a poorer background in math than I do.

Boy, I sure dread this afternoon. We have to take a physical fitness test during Phys. Ed. today. I took one once before and it about killed me. We have to do several different exercises such as pushups and chin-up for endurance. And this time we are supposed to show considerable improvement over the other test. To make matters worse, we have to do it right after eating chow.

We are wearing our khaki uniforms all the time now. They are sure a nuisance after wearing those sloppy fatigue suits so long. In this hot weather we have an awful time keeping our shirts in good shape. We have six shirts which makes 3 for each week. Then of course, I hate to wear a necktie all the time and keep my sleeves rolled clear down at all times. In the evenings it sure seems good to take 'em off and study in my shorts or dungarees. Today noon we are having a big inspection, so after class I'll have to bustle around and see that my shoes are well shined and my face well shaved. We have to get a haircut once a week, so it will be a long time before I get shaggy around the neck like I used to.

Well my old knee has never bothered me a bit. It hurt just once and then never caused me any trouble. One boy in my platoon hurt his knee like I did last fall and they are sending him up to Great Lakes Hospital to have it operated on. I sure feel sorry for the poor guy because it will be a long time before he can get a commission now. And he only had one term here like myself.

I received the check for $35 and sure glad to see it. Now Mary Ann won't have to worry. She is going to arrive here Saturday noon and I'll be awfully glad to see her. It will be very long before I see her again unless I get to come home before going to P. I.

Well, I'd better close now as it is time for the dismissal bell.

Love
John

P. S. Mother, some of your cookies would sure taste good. Hint! Hint!

LETTER 14

Postmarked Aug. 28
Saturday morning

Dear Folks,

Another week is gone and there are only seven weeks of class left and in eight weeks I'll be on my way to Parris Island. I'm counting the days already. I went over to the barber shop and got my hair cut and I wish you could see it. It's been pretty short all the time, but now it's so short you can't even grab a hold of it. After that, Bill Kessler and I went over to the obstacle course and took some pictures. We had on our dungarees without any shirt and with this short haircut, I really looked like a true Marine. We got a picture of me climbing over the wall, vaulting over and fence and also one with my coat on standing at attention. I'll send them to you as soon as they are developed. As soon as we can get a hold of some film, we are going to take some in our good khaki uniforms.

I took another test yesterday which was pretty tricky, but I kind of think I got a hundred. Did I ever tell you that I did get a perfect paper on my last test? This kid has a hundred average in mathematics. Pretty good, eh? I guess all I lacked at W. U. was application. But the instructors weren't nearly as good either.

It sure has been rainy up here lately. We had a rain almost every day last week. And to make things worse, I had swimming in Phys. Ed. this week and it sure was cold. I about froze every afternoon. I think I mentioned one day last week that I was going to have to take a physical fitness test. Well, we took it and it about killed me, but I had an a average of 55 points for each exercise. And they said the average guy should score around 50, so I'm satisfied. I really am in a lot better condition than I've ever been before. Twice a week we have to run about a mile in place of calisthenics and I don't even get winded. I just feel like I could run all day long. I think these regular hours are what's doing it for me. But, I feel good all the time. Never sleepy in class like I did at W. U. and I don't have any desire to lay in bed and sleep in the mornings.

Mary Ann is to arrive in South Bend about 2 o'clock this afternoon. I can hardly wait. I'll have to show her a good time, but that'll be easy to do. We can go to the U. S. O. dance this afternoon. Then there are lots of good shows to see. And I'll show her the Notre Dame campus which is really beautiful when you have time to look around. Most of the time I'm running around like a chicken with its head cut off and never see anything. It sure feels good to have all my grades up so I won't have to worry while she is here. In physics have been getting hundreds almost every time, but I do dread the final exam, because there will be so many things they can ask. In this navy program they teach us so much in so short a time. And I'm afraid that I'll forget everything I ever learned during the first part of the semester. But I will have a pretty good average on the daily quizzes, so I'll have to go pretty low on the final to flunk. Besides they are grading on the curve. But the final is going to last 4 hours which is a mighty long period of time to sit and concentrate.

Well, I've got to stop now.
Love
John

P. S. Don't worry, I'll write Mrs. Rush[1] a "thank you" letter.

---

[1]Mrs. Rush was a dear lady who lived next door to the Hyndmans. She had no children of her own, so she adopted them. John's sister Dorothy said she was always doing things for them. LH

John on the Steps
of Cavanaugh Hall Wearing
His New Winter Greens.

Rolling over the Wall on
the Obstacle Course.

On Campus.

"Walking" the
Parallel Bars.

NOTRE DAME '43

LETTER 15

Postmarked Sept. 5, 1943

Friday nite

Dear Folks,

Well, another week end has come around, but a lot more have to come and go before I leave this place. It seems the Marines are so badly in need of combat engineers that they are switching everybody but philosophy majors.

Hollar went down and talked to the Captain today, but it was to no avail.[1] So Kessler and I aren't even going to try.

We are having a big drill contest tomorrow between companies and the winning outfit will get extended liberty. I kind of think we will win it, anyway we should. Then the best company will drill against the best company of sailors. We are going to wear our winter green outfits which really look good.

I just heard today that we will probably get to come home between semesters for a week. That's the only compensation I have for staying another term. But it will be a lot easier for me to graduate after the war. In fact, I should be able to graduate in one semester. Ten hours of physics will look mighty good on my transcript, and I won't be afraid to take chemistry. You never can tell, I might even decide to major or minor in math or chemistry. A minor in chemistry would be helpful in geology. Don't pay any attention to all this talk. I'm just trying to convince myself that another 4 months around here won't be so bad. I'll live through it though and time does fly awfully fast.

I'd better close now and do an hour's worth of studying.

Here's those questions you wanted answered:

1. Wrist Watch
It was lost in the fraternity house last winter and I could never find it.

2. Pajamas
No need to send them as I'll sleep in sweat clothes. Rooms are plenty warm.

3. Notebook
It was worn out long ago, but I don't need one anyway.

4. Weight. Not sure, around 180, a little more.

5. I wrote Frank Garner and will write to Mrs. Rush this weekend. I've been sewing a lot. You should see me darn socks.

Love
Joh

---

[1] John's worst nightmare came true. He has been notified that he will stay another semester at Notre Dame. LH

LETTER 16

Postmark unreadable Sept. 5
Sunday nite

Dear Folks,

Well, it's almost Monday again with another five day grind awaiting me. But, I've only got five more months left here, so why should I care. I'm going to be a mighty hard person to live with this next term because it irks me so much. Some day my grandchildren are going to ask me what I did in World War II and I'll have to tell them I was stationed at Notre Dame. When they ask me what rank I held, I can say I wasn't a buck private: I was a trainee. Then I can tell them I studied physics and drawing. And if they ask me if I was ever wounded in action, I can explain how I sprained my ankle in phys. ed. class or threw my knee out of joint. I'll really be proud of my part in whipping the Germans and Japs. And then after I had four years of college I didn't have a degree in anything. Just 3 years of geology and one year of physics. Then when I went back to W.U. to finish up I had forgotten all I ever knew about geology. So I had to go back and repeat everything and finally got my degree at the age of thirty five and after seven years of college.

Boy, they weren't kidding when they said the first hundred years are the hardest. What a life! Don't pay any attention to me. I'll get used to it.

It's pretty definite that we are going to get to come home for a week at the end of this semester. So you can be expecting the return of your fighting Marine. I'll expect a big welcome with band and everything at the station. And the mayor should present me with the key to the city after kissing me on each cheek.

You will probably have to send me the money for the train fare unless I can catch a bomber to Wichita. Then it will cost only a dollar—spent for a parachute. That is a privilege given to all servicemen, even the trainees in the college training program.

Well, I'd better stop now before I think of something else to gripe about. Your loving son,
John (the trainee)

Love
John

LETTER 17

Postmarked Sept. 25, 1943

Saturday morning

Dear Folks,

As you can plainly see, I'm writing this on the stationary you sent me. I was surprised to get it, but I sure do like it.

The cookies were also good although I didn't get very many. But I sure like to get 'em. That geology book is going to come in awfully handy, too. The textbook we use here isn't worth a darn.

Well, one more week has gone by and it won't be much longer before I can get out of here. I'm getting awfully impatient now. Mary Ann will soon be going back in another day or two and things get dull again. She has been coming out to the campus every evening from 6:30 till 7:30. We've had a lot of fun and I'll be sorry to see her go.

I'm kind of stiff and sore this week as we have been having combat training in Phy. Ed. We've learned different ways to throw each other and Hollar and I sure tossed each other around. But it is an awful lot of fun. And Parris Island is going to seem a lot easier to us because we'll be in better condition than we would of if we had gone straight there. Also we will know quite a bit about drilling.

Yesterday noon I marched our platoon over to chow, counting the cadence, etc. I was kind of nervous at first, but soon got over it. It's a lot of fun as soon as you get used to it, but there are sure a lot of things to watch out for! I thought I did pretty good. At least I didn't make any mistakes such a turning them the wrong way, etc.

In my last letter I told you I got a hundred in another math test. Well, I didn't, I only got a 91. I copied one problem wrong and made one other silly little mistake like that. It sure burned me up. Well, I'd better close now and study a little.

Love
John

LETTER 18

Postmarked Sept. ?

Well, I have all my studies for tomorrow and 30 minutes left before bedtime. So I thought I'd better write. I'm sure tired tonight because they about worked me to death in Phys. Ed. this afternoon. Then I took a big exam in Literature which covered the last 2 months work. It wasn't so hard, but it did take seven pages to answer five questions. I knew all about it though, so I'll probably get an A or B. Gosh, I hope I can keep up my grades for the rest of the semester. It would sure seem good to come out of Notre Dame with good grades. My poorest grade is in Engineering Drawing so far. I've got a C average in there. The passing grade there right now in physics (on the curve) is 45 and my average is 80. So, I've almost quit worrying about the course. I have a 96 average in math and I got 90 in my mid-term geology exam. That was the highest grade in the class and it sure made me feel good even though I've had the course before. I beat Bill Kessler who has had more geology than I have.

Well, I saw Mary Ann this morning and it will be the last for a long while. That is if I don't get to come home next month which I probably won't.

Tonight we had to fill out a blank in which we marked whether we wanted general line duty or specialized work such as engineering. I preferenced general line duty, naturally. I'd hate to be in any of that specialized stuff.

I got a nice letter from Frank Garner[1] today, so I guess I'd better answer it. I can't remember to call him Uncle Frank or Uncle John. His letter head said John and he signed it Frank. You folks had better let me know before I write. Say, I haven't had a letter from you all for a week. Have you forgotten about your leatherneck son?

I suppose Jerry and Dorothy have started to school by now. Tell Jerry to study his math because some day he'll be awfully glad he did. Everywhere you go they want to know if you've had math and if you haven't, they make you take it. Listen to old John giving advice about studies.

Well, it's time for the bell, so I'll have to stop.

John

---

[1] John Frank Garner was a cousin of Eugene Hyndman (John's father). He was a lawyer in Quincy, Illinois and was mayor of Quincy at one time. He was a bachelor and always came to Wellington for a visit at Thanksgiving. LH

LETTER 19

Postmark unreadable

Sunday Sept. 12

Dear Folks,

Boy, it sure is cold here. I'm afraid I'm going to freeze to death before I get out of here. It's just like December in Kansas only colder. Please excuse the handwriting, but I'm writing while lying in bed. This is the first time since I've been here that I've had time to lay in bed on Sunday. I got up at 7 o'clock and fell in line for morning chow, then I came back to bed. There is no math assignment to get for Monday so all I have to study is Physics.

Hollar and I caught a bus yesterday and went over to Elkhart, (about 18 miles). But it's a worse town than South Bend and we didn't have such a good time.

I talked to one of the sergeants Friday and he said I just as well forget about going home before getting my commission. And I'll be lucky to get home then. We were also told in drill class Friday that we may be sent straight to Quantico and skip Parris Island because they are so hard up for officers. Of course they'll lengthen the period at Quantico, but we'll still get our commissions sooner than originally planned. In a way I hope they work it that way, but I think we'd make better officers if we had a stretch at boot camp behind us. No matter what they do with us, I won't complain as long as I get a commission in the end.

Did you folks send Mary Ann's suitcase up to her?

Well, I'd better close now and write Mary Ann.

Love
John

LETTER 20

Postmarked Sept. 18

Sat. morning

Dear Folks,

Five more weeks to go and I'll be out of this place unless they change their plans and decide to keep us another four months. If that happens, I'll go crazy for sure. I just don't enjoy this life here.

Not that it's so tough, because it isn't, but I hate to spend all my spare time studying physics or some other dumb subject. I don't feel much different than I did at school in Wichita. And it is a lot duller. I just can't feel like a true Marine.

I have shore leave this week end, the first since I've been here and I can leave the campus at 1:00 and don't have to come back till 5:30 Sunday afternoon. Hollar, Bill Kessler and a couple of others got shore leave too, and we are all going to Michigan City. We should have a pretty good time. Anyway, it'll be a relief not to have to race back out to school at 12 P.M. Sat. Or get up at 7 o'clock Sunday morning.

I spent 2 hours in the library this morning reading another Greek tragedy by Euripedes. Did I brag to you about getting an "A", the highest grade in the class in our mid-term exams? Almost 50% of the Marines are deficient in one subject or another.

I'm writing this in geology as usual and the teacher is drawing things on the blackboard. He is so dumb it isn't funny. He is about 65 years old, has grey hair and is almost feeble.

Say, I just learned today that there is a good studio downtown where service men can get their pictures taken free. So the first chance I get I'll go in and have my picture taken. I saw an enlargement of one of the boys and it was really good..

Mary Ann said in her letter this morning that she was going down to see you about next weekend.

I wrote Frank Garner a letter the other day and I'll write Mrs. Rush a letter very soon although I feel like a fool, waiting so long.

I don't have your latest questionnaire here with me, so I'll fill it out in my next letter.

Love
John

LETTER 21

Postmark unreadable
Sept. 20, 1943

Dear Folks,

I don't know what I'm going to do. This morning I found for sure what they are going to do with me and I'm going to stay here until March 1st. The original list had me marked down as a geology major with one term, but geo. was crossed out and Engineering was written after it with 2 semesters instead of one. So I am to be a combat engineer and I don't want to be. Partly because I don't think I can stand it around here, but mainly because I know darn good and well I can't pass the courses I'll get next term.

I can just see me passing Descriptive Geometry and Analytical Geometry along with advanced physics. So I can tell you right now your son will never be an officer. After looking at my college transcript from W. U. I can't see why in the world they would even dream of trying to make an engineer out of me. It's simply out of my line and now I probably won't get my commission just because the Marines get the bright idea they want more combat engineers. We are going to try and get out of it, but I don't imagine there is any chance. So all I can do is stay and try. But if I see that I'm not going to pass, I'm sure going to apply for transfer to Parris Island as a private because there's no use in marking time around this place if I'm going to flunk. It's time to go to class, so pray they will change my status.

Love
John

LETTER 22

Postmarked Oct. 6
Tuesday morning
Dear Folks,

I received Daddy's letter this morning and was sorry to hear that Wellington got beat, but I guess they can't be champions all the time. It does seem funny to see the names of some of the boys in the line-up. I remember them as a bunch of little boys out at the swimming pool.[1]

We sure have a wonderful team at Notre Dame, though. You should have seen them run over Georgia Tech. It was a marvelous thing to watch. Angelo Bertelli is a great football player. I expect Daddy has heard of him. He's sure a funny guy though. He smokes about 10 cigars a day and sleeps the rest of the time.

Well, it was made official yesterday that I'm to be a combat engineer and will be here another 4 months studying advanced engineering courses. And I want to warn my family that they'll better be proud of their son's grades this term, because they certainly won't have anything to be proud of the next time. I don't believe I can possibly pass descriptive geometry although I may scrape through advanced physics (study of electricity) and analytical geometry.

However, I do have one piece of very good news. They have given us leave from the day of our last final until Sept. 6 (probably Nov. 6) at 9 A.M. My last final is physics on Sept. 27 (Oct. 27?) afternoon, and I am going to it with sea bag in hand.

One of the boys told me that if I used Mary Ann's ticket to go home on, I wouldn't save any money because they won't give me a serviceman's rates for a one way ticket. So I am going to cash hers in, then buy a round trip ticket for half fare. I'm not even going to ride in a Pullman. Just catch a train in Chicago on Wed. evening and ride into Wichita the next morning.

I guess I'll have to spend part time in Wellington and part in Wichita. Maybe Mary Ann can stay in Wellington. But I do want to be in Wichita at least a couple of days. Bill Kessler invited me to stay at his home while I'm there. There are a lot of people I want to see. But that can all be planned later.

Well, I'd better close now and study.

Love
John

---

[1] John and Don Jones ran the Wellington swimming pool one summer. LH

LETTER 23

Postmarked Oct. 9 Air Mail Special Delivery[1]
Saturday morning
Dear Folks,

I've got some news for you and I'd like to know what you think of it. I have an opportunity to get in the Navy Air Corps. They are going to be here Tuesday and give physicals to all Marines who are interested, and who have seven semesters of college as of November 1st. Hollar, Kessler and I all qualify and have about decided to do it. We'd get our commissions almost as soon as we would in the Marines. And I know we'd like it a lot better than being engineers in the regular Marines. Then we can transfer to Marines Air Corps after getting our wings. I rather think we'd be required to be Marine pilots since we are going in from the Marines.

Of course, we aren't going to do anything rash until we find out all about the training. If it'll take too long we probably won't join, although we might. This is a long war and I figure I ought to get into something I really like. And I'm sure I wouldn't like the engineers. Besides I might flunk out in the engineers and I'm sure I could make it in the Air Corps since I know my math a lot better. I've got to close now and I am going to call Daddy this afternoon.

John

---

[1] During WWII, very few letters could be sent Air Mail. There weren't enough planes or space on them to carry all first class mail. Special Delivery was an extra service used rarely when a message was very important. First Class letters cost 3 cents. Air Mail 6 cents. Special Delivery perhaps 25 cents. For John to send a letter Air Mail and Special Delivery shows how important he felt this letter and how much he wanted his parents opinion. See Letter 5 for a copy of the air mail stamp John used on the post cards. MV

LETTER 24

Postmark unreadable
Tues. morn
Dear Folks,

I was supposed to meet with the Navy Air Corps examiners this morning, but they are late getting here, so I'll see them this afternoon. I still don't know for sure what I'm going to do. It depends on the kind of deal they present to us. Daddy's letter came this morning and I'm glad to hear that you all have no objections. Kessler's folks want him to stay where he is.

Say, that sure sounds good about the chance to fly to Wichita. I hope it doesn't blowup. If possible, I'd like to have Don and Kessler fly too. Do you suppose that would be possible?

I still don't know which train I'm going to catch. Since so many guys will be leaving at once, the Marine officials are taking care of things. So I'll have to leave when they say so.

It doesn't seem possible that this semester can be so near gone. Physics lab met for the last time today and they've stopped giving us daily tests in physics. Everything is directed toward review. Finals will be tough, but my grades are high enough that I won't have anything to worry about, except physics. Did I tell you I got a hundred in a trig test a couple of weeks ago? We took another one yesterday in trig and I know I didn't get a hundred, but I think I did pretty good. It was the hardest trig test I've taken in all the years I've had the course.

Gosh, I don't know what I want for my birthday. Just wait until I get home and I'll decide then.

It's time to fall out for noon chow, so I've got to close.

Love
John

P. S. I just got back from seeing the Navy boys. When they said it would take us 14 to 18 months, I got up and left. We were to get no credit at all for all our college and would go in like any 17 year old high school boy. So I guess I'm doomed to become an engineer Ho! Hum!

I've got to go to class now.

John

LETTER 25

No postmark on envelope
Approximately Oct. 15
Thurs. morn.

Dear Folks,

It sure is cold here today. We'll have to wear our overcoats before long. How is the weather at home? I'm wondering if I'll need to bring my overcoat home.

Gosh, I can't wait to get home. That's going to be the most pleasant 9 days of my life. I hope nothing happens to cancel my leave, but I'm sure it won't . Although, you never know what they are going to do around here.

Well, I have some news for you and I don't know for sure what you'll think of it. I guess Mary Ann and myself have broken up for good. All the trouble is my fault[1]. I had been writing too many girls and I finally made the sad mistake of addressing a letter to West, which was meant for someone else. Ever since she was here I have slowly been realizing that I have never been really in love with her. So I guess it will be better this way than to let myself get too involved. I know she'll feel terrible for awhile, but she'll get over it and be glad I didn't hurt her later on. So I don't think I'll try to patch things up even if I can. It looks like this kid will never find anyone that he can love enough to marry. Just call me bachelor John. You folks will have to send me quite a bit of money because I'm going to lend Don some money. Now I'll have to keep Mary Ann's ticket and send it to her instead of cashing it in. I expect you'll have to send me $30 to be safe because I've got to buy a barracks cap which costs around seven dollars. I'll be as saving as possible.

I haven't much time left so I'd better close now.

Love
John

---

[1] John said he didn't deliberately send a letter to Nellie Ann Cowan asking her for a date to Mary Ann when he came home on leave. He sent it to Mary Ann by mistake. He said he may have subconsciously made the error as he was ready to break off the relationship. LH

LETTER 26

Postmarked Oct. 20
Tues morning

Dear Folks,

Well, I'm in geology for the last time and I just as well finish it off in the usual way, so I'll write a letter.

I received a letter from Mother yesterday and Daddy this morning. And I'm glad to hear you folks feel like you do about my affair with Mary Ann. I was a little afraid you folks might like her better than I did. Yesterday my fraternity pin[1] came in the mail which was a relief to me. Also I got a box of candy from Cletis Jones which was plenty good. All the boys liked it. I have already written her a thank you letter. Pretty good for me, eh? I have also written Dr. Wallace,[2] which should make you all very happy.

I tried to call you folks long distance Sunday, but I couldn't even get past Chicago. So I guess I'll wait now until I get home. The way I have things planned now, I'm going to catch the 8:15 p.m. train out of Chicago on Tues. the 26th. Then, I'm going to get off in Wichita and Bill Kessler says he will drive me on down home. So be expecting to see me sometime Tuesday afternoon, one week from today. Finals start day after tomorrow and I have one each day except Sunday. Thursday at 8:00 I have the Literature exam, on Friday, at 8:00 I have eng. drawing, Saturday comes math, with a big football game with Illinois in the afternoon. On Monday comes Physics. I'll probably flunk that final. And last comes geology from 11:00 to 12:00 Tuesday. Then I'm making a beeline for the train station.

After enrolling for next semester, I sure dread coming back here. I'm signed up for advanced physics, analytical geometry, surveying, map reading and drawing and last, but not least, literature. I'll have to study my heart out for sure just to pass. And if I flunk I'll never get my commission because they have so many officer candidates that they won't fool around with you. If any of the boys who are supposed to leave this term flunk one course, they get sent to San Diego[3] and lose out on their commissions.

Yes, I got the oranges, candy and gum from you all and it sure was good. Tell Jerry and Dorothy thank you and that I'll be seeing them before long.

Love, John

---

[1] John gave his fraternity pin to his mother and told her to keep it until he got down on his knees and begged for it to give to another girl. In November 1946 he gave it to me. LH

[2] Dr. Wallace was the pastor of their church (Presbyterian). LH

[3] Marine Corps Recruit Depot, San Diego was the site of another Boot Camp like Parris Island. Men in V-12 were assigned to a boot camp when they completed the first part of their military training in college. Which boot camp a man was sent to depended on when a new training session started, Sometimes Parris Island, sometimes San Diego. LH

LETTER 27

Postmarked Oct. 23
Friday nite

Dear Folks,

I am right smack in the middle of finals now. Two are finished with three more to go. I have math tomorrow. Physics, Monday and Geology Tues. I've been studying math since 10 o'clock this morning and it's 8:30 now. It's awfully hard to keep at it when I know I could flunk the final and pass the course. In fact, I could skip the final entirely and pass. But, I'd like to get a real good grade and I think I will. Physics is the course that has me worried. I'm afraid I'll flunk the final because it's going to be awfully hard. And since it counts 40% of our grade, I could possibly flunk the course. Don't be too surprised if I do, but I hardly think I will.

I sent you folks a telegram today to send me a suitcase. Hope you can find one and get it here by Tuesday. We found out last nite that we won't be able to use our sea bags. Also, what has happened to the money? It hasn't arrived yet, and if it doesn't I'll have to do some high powered borrowing in order to get home.

I got candy kisses yesterday and the angel food cake Wednesday. They were both plenty good although neither lasted long. I took the last piece of cake over to my Literature teacher Wed. nite. His final was the next morning. Hollar, Kessler and I are really in good with that professor. He thinks we are quite the stuff.[1]

Well, I'd better close now in order to study a little more before going to bed.

There's a big game tomorrow afternoon with U. of Illinois which I'll naturally see. I'm saving the football programs for Jerry.

Love,
John

---

[1] John said the literature professor had Hollar, Kessler, and him over to his apartment for a bull session. LH

LETTER 28

Postmarked Nov. 7, 1943[1]

Dear Folks,

Your son has arrived safely in the Notre Dame War Theatre. I got checked in at 6:00 o'clock on the nose. Our train broke down somewhere in God's country—Missouri—and we were about three and one half hours late. A 2:30 train out of Chicago got us in South Bend at 5:30. Finally caught a bus and made it in the nick of time.

I have a new roommate[2] as my old one has been sent to San Diego. Can't tell yet what he's like, but he seems OK Out of the original 750 Marines, there are 460 left. And the Captain told us this morning that they are going to be tougher than ever this semester. If anyone even looks like he's going to flunk, he'll get kicked out. So don't be surprised if I go to Diego soon.

Well, I have to go over and enroll, so I'd better close. I'll write again soon.

Love
John

---

[1] There is a two-week gap between Letters 27 and 28 because John went home on leave, his only leave until he returned to the "States" in 1945. LH

[2] John's roommate was Ralph Hvidsten from Stephens, Minnesota. He was even younger than John. He was sent to boot camp at San Diego and then to radar school in Corpus Christi. He said that he never left the states. At the end of the war he was a clerk at Pendleton doing paperwork for the Marines being discharged. After the war he was a potato farmer in northern Minnesota. He is retired and living in Sun City West, Arizona. LH

LETTER 29

Postmark unreadable
Tues. morn
Dear Folks,

Well, the grind is beginning again. There hasn't been much homework yet, but classes are starting and there soon will be. Our physics instructor encouraged us this morning by saying that this second course is easier than the first. We should be able to get a little better grade with the same amount of effort. Math is going to be the hard subject as we will cover both spherical trig and analytical geometry. I haven't been to surveying or map reading yet, but I don't think they will be too easy. I'm afraid I'll have a little rougher time all the way around. And this time we can't flunk one subject and still go to Officer's school. The captain said the trial and error days are over. So I am not too optimistic about ever getting a commission. But it won't be because I didn't try.

It snowed last nite and the ground was white early this morning, but it has warmed up enough for it to change to rain and the snow is all gone. I'm afraid it's going to be a bad winter and I'll never be warm until summer.

Has Mary Ann ever sent my picture back yet? If not, I'll write and ask her for it. Also you'd better send her picture to her.

That vacation at home kind of spoiled me and the next four months in school sure gripes me. I'd give anything to be in boot camp right now like I should be.

Did I tell you in my other letter that we have a celebrity in our midst? Jackie Cooper, the movie star, is one of the Navy boys here at N.D. In fact, I sat across the table from him in chow yesterday morning. He has his hair cut off short and seems to be a regular fellow.

Well, it's time to fall out for chow, so I'll have to stop.

Love
John
P. S. Here's my new address:
Pvt. John S. Hyndman U.S.M.C.R.
Company B, 1st Platoon, Marine V-12 Unit
Notre Dame, Indiana

LETTER 30

Postmarked Nov. 21?
Sunday afternoon Nov. 21

Dear Folks,

It's Sunday and I'm tired. These weekends just don't come around often enough for me. But November is almost over and then I'll just have 3 more months to go around here. We've heard from several boys who got to go on to P. I., and they say it's easier than Notre Dame. They don't have to march very much, because they learned how so well up here. So most of their work consists of rifle training.

I took a test in spherical trig last week, and got a 97 on it. That was about the highest grade in the class. I just can't get over how easy math turned out to be. But physics is still terrible and I'll be lucky to pass it. And that surveying---I'm sure taking it at the wrong time of the year. We just about freeze to death doing our field work. Otherwise, it isn't such a hard course. Mainly because I understand math a little better now.

Yesterday I saw the greatest football game of my life. And I never hope to see a more thrilling one. Notre Dame whipped Iowa Seahawks 14-13. It was their wonderful spirit that did it. They have spirit among the student body like we used to dream about at W. U., but never saw.

Last nite I went to the show and saw "Guadacanal Diary". It was a fine show and it made me feel kind of lucky to be training back here at safe old Notre Dame.

This morning Hollar and I went over to the Knute Rockne Memorial gym and played some basketball. We had a big time, in fact, we are tempted to go out for the Notre Dame varsity. They aren't much of a team, so we could probably make the traveling squad. But, it might cause us to flunk, so we probably won't.

Well, I think I'll lie down and go to sleep. Goodbye.
Love
John

LETTER 31

Postmarked Nov.??
Monday nite
Dear Folks,

Well, they did me dirt today. Never in my life +16 years of school have I met such a dirty dealing, no good teacher. He might just as well have put a hand grenade under my seat and pulled the pin. We had 2 problems in a test Friday (each problem took a page and a half of large paper). I made a little mistake in dividing 328° 25' 42" by two (several seconds) and he took off 50%. So I got a fifty in the test. He did quite a few in the class that way. In fact, he waited until the end of the hour to hand back the papers so we wouldn't have time to complain. Everybody is as mad as a hornet and someone is likely to knock his teeth in. He's a smart-alec civilian who'd just as soon flunk you as look at you. I'm afraid I'm going to lose my temper some day and tell him off good and proper. Then I'd probably get kicked out of class and sent to San Diego. But it sure burns me up to have to take grades like that when I know the stuff so well.

I received the ten dollars today and sure was glad to get it. Saturday night I spent my last cent. Well, we get two days off for Christmas, (Sat. and Sunday) unless they decide to cut it off a little. I wouldn't be surprised if I had to go to physics on Christmas morning.

Say, that furlough bag sounds like a good deal to me. Will I have to wait until Christmas for it? Gosh, I don't know what else I want for Christmas except for handkerchiefs and warm socks.

Well, I can't think of anything else to say so I'll close now.

Love,
John

LETTER 32

Postmarked Nov. 15
Sunday afternoon
Dear Folks,

I received your letter Friday noon and was sure tickled to get it. It's the only mail I've had since I got back. For some unknown reason Boydine[1] never has written to me. She's the girl I dated in Wichita while I was home. It sure puzzles me though, but I don't care very much. What I think happened is that as soon as people found out I was going with Boydine, gossip started flying to her about how dirty I treated Mary Ann. So I imagine she has decided I'm a pretty bad boy to get involved with. It's funny though, that she doesn't at least write and let me in on things. A guy just can't defend himself when he's a thousand miles from home.

Well, last week was pretty easy as classes were just getting started. But from now on things are going to get rough. Not only in an academic way, but in a military way. Demerits are going to fly thick and fast. Our rooms have to be perfect and we can't lie on our bunks until after 4 P.M. In other words, we've got to be on the ball. I'll certainly be glad to get out of this place and go someplace where I can feel like a real Marine.

Mother, I feel awful about forgetting about your birthday. I thought about it while coming back here. They kept us going around in circles, so it completely slipped my mind. But even though it's late, I wish you a happy birthday, Mother. I hope you will forgive me.

Got to work some math problems, so I'd better halt.

Love
John

---

[1] The girl he dated while on leave was Boydine Quiring. I knew her at Wichita U. and she had a reputation for looking for a rich man to marry. LH

LETTER 33

Postmarked Nov. 26
Wed, nite
Dear Folks,

Here your son sits, studying his heart out like always. Physics is driving me mad. The problems aren't so hard now, but I hate to think what they'll be like later on. And math, you should see the problems we have to work. One problem for tomorrow took a page and a half of closely written figures. But I understand it pretty well, so it doesn't bother me much. In fact, I get a kick out of it.

I received Daddy's letter this morning, and I was sure glad to get it. The letters from you folks are the only ones I've had since I've been back. Boydine never has written. Just by that she proved to me that she isn't quite the girl I thought she was. It will be a long time before I'll ever trust a girl. You've got to treat "em rough before they appreciate you. No more of playing the gentleman for me. I was mean to West, but she liked me all the more. Then I treated Joanne Wallace[1] and Boydine Quiring like a gentleman should and look what happened. It's things like that that put age on a kid like me. As far as J. Hyndman is concerned romance is over for the duration.

Well, tomorrow is Thanksgiving and I'll celebrate by going to class six hours. What a life! But we do get turkey for noon chow, which is something. I hope you all have a good time over at Aunt Mabel's.[2] Wish I could be there. For some reason though, I don't mind things around here as much as I thought I would. There's one thing the service does teach you, and that's patience. A guy learns to accept things as they come, and then forget about what might have happened.

Say, they are sure going to treat us fine around here on Christmas. We get all day off since it is Saturday. They are even excusing us from early morning calisthenics on that day. But I'm not even going to count on that.

By the way, do you suppose you could possibly send me five or ten dollars of my money? I'm almost broke and it's 2 or 3 weeks before we get paid. These war bonds cut an awful big hole in your salary. Please send the money soon.

I'm getting so sleepy I can hardly hold my eyes open, so I'm going to hit the sack.

Love
John

---

[1] Joanne Wallace was a girl from Topeka whom John dated when she visited in Wellington one summer while he was in high school. LH

[2] Aunt Mabel is John's father's sister Mabel Casburn. She was a housemother at a girls' dorm at Southwestern College in Winfield, Kansas. LH

LETTER 34

Postmarked Dec. 4
Friday note

Dear Folks,

Well, another weekend is almost here and I'm sure glad. If it wasn't for them, I'd probably go completely crazy around this place. I have a shore leave[1] this time, so I won't have to rush back out at midnight. Also I have a date with a really beautiful girl. I believe she's about the prettiest girl I have ever known. Even better than Boydine. As far as she is concerned, I've forgotten all about her, and am relieved that I found out what she was like so soon.

Has it been cold down home at all? For some reason it has been pretty nice up here. But it seems like on Saturdays that it always turns off cold enough that I have to bother with my overcoat.

I got my grade card today and it averages up to an 88. That makes me feel pretty good. Now, if I just don't ruin my math this time, and I'm likely to with the teacher I have to put up with. We had a surveying test today. It was fairly tough, but I think I did O. K. in it. I hope!

Boy, am I tired tonight. I went over to the gym for an hour after class and worked out on the parallel bars. I'm going to build up my arms and shoulders until I'm strong as a bull. My legs have been developed because of so much basketball and football, so that upper body has been slightly neglected. I'm no weakling or anything, but it sure wouldn't hurt to develop some more muscle.

I got the money O. K. this week. Also I think I forgot, in my last letter to say anything about the Thanksgiving box, but it was sure good. The jelly is gone already, but I still have some of the candy left to suck on. All the boys liked the food, too.

Well, It's time to hit the hay, so good night .

Love
John

---

[1] In the Navy and Marine Corps, men receive liberty, usually in hours and leave usually in days. For example, a Marine might get liberty from his base or ship, go ashore perhaps at noon and be required to return aboard by midnight. The maximum time was 48 hours. Leave was permission to be away from ship or base for more than 48 hours. When men finished training, leave might be given to go home for a week or more. Sometimes, a man received orders requiring him to report to another ship, base, or station on a certain date, with the time in between to count as leave. When a man was discharged, he might be given terminal leave, the amount of leave he had accrued while in service. Compassionate leave might be granted for a man to return home because of a death in the family. Many Sailors or Marines called it shore leave, perhaps a hangover from the time when most men, both Sailors and Marines served aboard ship. MV

LETTER 35

Postmarked Dec. 9, 1943
Wed. nite

Dear Folks,

Since this is the last of the stationary, the letter will have to be short.

Right now your son has one heck of a cold and feels rotten. My nose is stopped up and my eyes burn like heck. But I suppose I'll get over it before long. Hope so, because I can hardly study.

Well, got back my surveying test today and I scored a 94. It sure seemed good after the stinky math test.

You folks said you wanted me to call Christmas. I'll try, but I imagine it will be nearly impossible to get through.[1] Maybe it would be better if I called a few days before or after Christmas. And I hate to have that consist of my Christmas to you all. I think you should send me some of my money so that I can send some presents home.

Did I tell you that Hollar, Kessler and I are going to Chicago for Christmas? We get from Friday till 7 o'clock Monday morning.

Well, I'll have to close now.

Love
John

P. S. What are those pills for that you sent in a box some time ago?

---

[1] In 1943, a serviceman could not pick up the phone and dial home. He had to call an operator who had to get him a line usually after a long wait. In San Diego where there were thousands of Navy and Marine, at a USO or other locations, a man could go in, sign up, and wait until a line was open. As John notes, getting a line on Christmas Day would be almost impossible. In a later letter, John mentions being told that he would have a 12 hour wait. MV

LETTER 36

Postmark unreadable
Friday nite

Dear Folks,

It's Friday and tomorrow is Saturday. That is the thing that always makes me happy. And to make things even better, they have changed the old Saturday liberty plan so that we don't have to report in till 7:30 Sunday evening. And we can go within a 25 mile limit without special shore leave. Things are really looking up around this place. Then I got a 96 in a math test today which brings up my average quite a bit. Everything's going to be fine except for one thing. I heard today that there is a chance that I'll have to stay another semester. It seems that there are more men than they can take at P. I., so we will be taken by ages, and I figure that I'll be right on the border line. And right now I'm not quite sure that being an officer is worth twelve months at Notre Dame plus another six months which is even harder. Of course, I might not even be able to get out of here if I wanted to. But if I could, it would be an awful temptation to apply for transfer to San Diego. Gosh, I don't know what to do. The big thing is that the subjects I'd have to take as an engineer would be too much for me to bite off. Guess I'll just wait till the time comes before I start worrying. And then maybe I won't have to.

I got a Christmas package from Aunt Mabel yesterday which said, "Don't Open until Christmas". Should I write and thank her now or wait till I open it? Also I got the card for your package this evening, and will pick it up tomorrow. It's going to be awfully hard to look at it for the next 3 weeks without opening it up. Guess I won't be needing the bag before Christmas, so I'll wait.

What shall I get Jerry and Dorothy for Christmas, anyhow? It's an awful puzzle. I'm just going in some stores tomorrow and start looking.

My little case of flu has gone now, although I still have a "runny" nose. I finally went to sick-bay yesterday and found out that I really had been running some temperature. So, I was excused from Phys. Ed. until the fever went away. But today I feel fine and ready to go to town tomorrow. I'd die if I felt too sick to leave the base.

Latest rumor: All those who are down in 2 subjects at mid-term will be booted out. You hear more things around this place.

Well, it's about time to hit the hay, so I'd better halt this manuscript. I really have written a lot, haven't I? Pretty good for me, but I felt in the mood tonite.

Love, John

P. S. I forgot to mail this before going on liberty, so I'll mail it Monday morn. Better late than never. Had a good time this weekend, but it passed awfully quick. So another week's grind has begun again. I've already worked my math for tomorrow, but naturally have some other stuff to do. So, good night.

LETTER 37

Postmarked Dec. 11
Thursday afternoon

Dear Folks,

Right this minute your son is freezing to death. I'm sitting in the physics lecture room and it is ice cold in here. I guess that's only natural because it's so bad outside. It snows almost every nite[1] and I don't think it will ever melt. It has been around zero and sometimes below for several days. My ears will never be warm again, or my feet either. But they are going to help us out a little by issuing overshoes and storm caps, whatever they are.

Well, Christmas is almost here—the time has been flying by awfully fast this semester, and the faster it goes the better I'll like it. Wherever I am in the spring, I'll be tickled to death to see some warm weather. I remember when I was a little kid how I always wanted snow and cold weather, well I'm getting it all at once now. And I'm not so crazy about it anymore.

Did I tell you that I got your Christmas package? It sure is hard to keep from opening it, and I'm going to open it before leaving for Chicago next Friday. I also received Daddy's personal gift the other day too. It looked awfully good to me and I'll need it for the trip to Chicago. The vacation will be expensive because we will be there three nights, and the hotel bill is likely to be quite a lot. In fact, I wish you folks would send me some of my own money, about $20 dollars. I really will need it because I had to borrow money last month, so after paying it back, and then lending out quite a bit of this last pay check, I'm not exactly flush. You folks are probably worrying about my spending my money. Well, I have got quite a bit to spend and not much time left at Notre Dame. When I get out of here, I won't be spending very much at all while in boot camp at Quantico. No chance to. Besides we boys have been counting on this trip for a long time and I'd hate to go up there and run out of money. So, pretty please, send the money on to me. I'm going to try to call you while I am in Chicago, so be listening for me.

Say, I got a Christmas card from Juanita Counsell (geography teacher in seventh grade) and I can't figure out how she learned my address. She teaches in Wichita now and I wonder who told her how to write me. Also I got a Christmas card from Don Jones' folks.

My gosh, I'm freezing to death. I'll be glad to get out of here and go back to my nice warm room. I'll put my feet on the radiator and cook them.

Did I tell you about a new deal on weekend liberty? We don't have to come back to the barracks anymore till 7:30 Sunday evening. Also on Wednesdays we may have liberty to go into town after our last class until 7:30 P.M. That only gives me two hours and a half, but it's long enough to go downtown and get something decent to eat. That little bit of freedom kind of relaxes you and makes the week seem shorter., It's something to look forward to anyway. You wanted to know about this good-looking girl I mentioned in one of my letters. Well, she's pretty nice and is a lot of fun. In fact, I have a date with her this Sat. Of yes, I got two letters from Boydine the other day. I almost fainted from surprise. She wants me to forgive her and wants to keep on writing. I don't know for sure whether I will or not. It's time for class to let out and I'll have to go, so I'll close now. Don't forget to send the money soon.

Love
John

---

[1] John thought it got cold in Kansas, but South Bend is subject to the "Lake effect" from cold northwest winds blowing over Lake Michigan which produces heavy snowfalls most winters. The same wind often makes it feel miserably cold and damp. MV

LETTER 38

Postmark unreadable
Monday morning
Dear Folks

Well, counting this week you son has seven weeks left at good old Notre Dame. That is, if they don't do me dirt again, and I wouldn't be surprised at anything anymore. If I should have to stay another stretch, I think I'd go crazy. And if I had to take more advanced engineering courses, I'm sure I couldn't pass. I've reached the limit of my abilities in slide rule subjects. Right now it looks like I'll pass this time, but I can't see my way through calculus, statics, etc.

Received Daddy's letter this morning and am glad to hear about the Hensley boys. It's guys like them that make me feel so bad about going to college where everything is safe. They would make just as good an officer as I, but they didn't have all the opportunities I did. They are over there and I'm here.

So it's really been cold back there? Here all the snow has been melted and it's almost like Spring.

About my trip to Chicago—I'll answer Daddy's questions. We stayed at the Ft. Dearborn Hotel. It was cheap but poor, very poor. Hollar, Ralph Abel from St. Louis went with me. Kessler went to see his girl instead. The man that took us to dinner took us to his house which was out by Wrigley stadium. We stayed there most of the day. Then on Sunday, we went to the game (it was mighty cold) and after that this man Hollar knew took us home to a turkey dinner. After all that the trip wasn't as expensive as I thought it would be

Later today.
I had to stop before to study math, so I'll finish the letter now. Studies have been piling up this past week as we've been having a lot of exams—mid terms you know. We had a tough one in math Friday which I passed. Now I have an 85 average in there which isn't bad considering the bad start I got off to.

How is Daddy's cold by now? I hope it is all right. Tomorrow, I am sending Dorothy's present and the suitcase. Also I will enclose some copies of the "Leatherneck", a Marine magazine which I take. It's pretty good and I imagine you will all enjoy it.

By the way, where is Aunt Mabel now so that I can write and thank her for the handkerchiefs.

Well, I've got to study now for a surveying test, so I'll close
Love
John

LETTER 39

Addressed to Jerry Hyndman
Postmarked Dec. 23, 1943

Dear Jerry,

It is real cold up here now and is snowing to beat the band. We are going to have a white Christmas for sure. It will be plenty deep, too. You should see the new equipment they issued us last week. We got real warm overshoes and also storm caps. The caps are the kind they wear up north—fur with ear flaps and another flap that goes across the face. You can't even tell who a person is when the flap is around the face. So I guess I won't be getting cold this winter, no matter how cold it gets.

Well, only one more day and my Christmas vacation begins. It starts Friday evening and lasts till Monday morning at 7:00 o'clock. I'm heading for Chicago just as soon as I get out of class Friday and not coming back till the last minute Sunday nite. Five boys are all going to stay in the same hotel room, so it won't cost too much. We are going to see a stage show while we are there. Probably "Oklahoma" if we can get in. Also Hollar and I are going out to see his little brother who is in the Navy at Great Lakes.[1]

I got a box of food Wednesday afternoon. For awhile I thought it had been lost or something. But it sure was good. In fact, I ate so much yesterday afternoon and evening that I was kind of sick this morning.

Jerry, I bought you a Christmas present last Saturday, but I checked it at the U.S.O. and forgot to check it out. So I'll have to wait until Friday to pick it up, then you won't get it till after Christmas. I hope you won't mind too much. Tell Dorothy that I'll wait to send hers with yours, both in Mother's suitcase.

How's that black eye coming along? Are you sure that you fell down stairs to get it? I'll bet some little kid biffed you a couple of times. I know if I were going to be home Christmas, I'd beat you up good.

Dec. 28, '43
I wrote the first part of this letter in class then forgot to mail it. And since I've been to Chicago I'll tell you about it. We all had a pretty good time, and hated to come back to school. Hollar and I had the biggest thrill of our lives when we got to see the world series of football---Chicago Bears against the Washington Redskins. They are the 2 best pro football teams in the country with all kinds of All Americans playing for them---Sammy Baugh, Sid Luckman, Bulldog Turner and Bronco Nagurski. Also McEnulty who used to play in Wichita. He got to play a little bit. Boy, it was some game.[2]

I had two good dinners, one Christmas day and one Sunday. On Christmas Day a man walked up to us, asked us if we were from out of town, then invited us out to eat.[3] So we did. Then on Sunday, some people—friends of Hollar's, took us out and fed us a huge turkey dinner. We stayed at their house until eleven o'clock Sunday nite. Then they drove us to the train and we got back to Notre Dame in the

[1]Great Lakes Naval Training Base, located about 40 miles north of Chicago on Lake Michigan, was a boot camp, perhaps the largest in the Navy during WWII. MV
[2]The game they saw was like the Super Bowl today. The Chicago Bears (Sid Luckman QB) were the Western Division champs and the Washington Redskins (Sammy Baugh QB) were the Eastern Division Champs. The Bears won 41-21 at Wrigley Field in Chicago on 26 December, 1943. MV
[3]During the war, people would look for men in uniform on the street to take home for a holiday meal. Some of them had sons overseas and wanted to give a serviceman away from home a family holiday. MV

middle of the nite. I'm still tired. That Chicago is the biggest thing I have ever seen. You just can't imagine how big it is. I saw two big aircraft carriers[1] on Lake Michigan. Then I rode a subway for the first time in my life. It sure does go fast.

I opened up my Christmas box before leaving and everybody really did fine by me. The furlough bag came in handy for the trip to Chicago. Today I got a package from Aunt Dott and Bonnie with a writing kit and stationary. That makes me plenty of stationary. It should last for the rest of my days in the Marine Corps.

Christmas I wanted to call you all, but the operator said it would take about 12 hours to get a call thru. But I'm going to try at 7:30 tomorrow morning. I hope you will all be at home and awake. By the way, where is Aunt Mabel going to be so I can write her a thank you letter for her handkerchiefs.

Well, I've got to study now.

Love
John

---

[1] The aircraft carriers John saw on Lake Michigan while he was in Chicago were the *USS Sable*, IX-81 and the *USS Wolverine*, IX 64 training ships used to teach Navy and Marine Pilots how to land on a carrier, which was a much different skill from landing on an airfield with long runways. The Navy trained nearly 18,000 pilots flying offshore of Chicago. The *Sable* and *Wolverine* were converted excursion steamers much smaller than the Navy's large carriers. These makeshift flat tops were a challenge to pilots in training. MV

LETTER 40

Postmarked Jan. 7, 1944
Tuesday morning

Dear Folks,

I just finished my physics test, and the worst part of the day is over. It is now about ten o'clock and I don't have another class until 9:15. For me this is a wonderful day. It's one day in the week I don't mind at all. Of course physics mars it a little, but not too much.

Well, I've been here 6 1/2 months and hate it more everyday, but I guess I can stand another 4 or 5 weeks. Finals begin exactly one month from Thursday. When they are over with, this will be one happy boy. I'll sure be glad to get to Parris Island, although after I've been there for awhile, I'll probably wish I was back in school. They've changed the time in P.I., so we'll have to stay 5 months instead of 8 weeks. A boy who just finished boot camp was back here the other day. Physically, he says it's not so bad, but putting up with the drill instructor is the hard part. If you let what they say effect you, they would drive you crazy. Also, he said the bed bugs were terrible. He put a towel around his face, socks on his hands, and slept with his clothes on. And when you first get there, they practically shave everyone's head. So my hair is going to be clipped about the time it gets like it used to be. It sure grows slow.

I got a letter yesterday from Boydine[1]—six pages long. Apparently she figures she is a queen or something. Well, little Johnny just won't jump at all when she whistles. I learned that a long time ago from Joanne Wallace.

Boy, am I stiff and sore today. I went over to the gym late last nite and high jumped. This morning I could hardly get out of bed. Every muscle I have hurts.

This surveying has me very worried. I'm going down to see the captain about it first of next week. Hollar went down about it some time ago because he has been flunking it all along. And I'm not even down in it now, but sure as the world will be. Hollar explained to the captain that the course was just too much for him—he hadn't had enough math or anything. So the captain told him not to worry about it. Now I'm going down. I don't want to go to San Diego just because I didn't go talk over my trouble with the Captain. I saw that happen last semester to more than one boy. Well, It's time to close now and do some work.

Love
John

P. S. Mother, your suitcase should have arrived by now as I sent it.

---

[1] Letter pretty well finishes off Boydine Quiring. John was good at reading people. LH

LETTER 41

Postmarked Jan. 16, 1944
 Sunday evening

Dear Folks,

And so another week end has come and gone. If it weren't for Saturday and Sunday, I'd go crazy for sure. If next week is as bad as last I'll give up the ghost. Never have I gone through such a discouraging and miserable five days. Sat., Sun., Mon. and Tues., I studied all the time for a surveying test. Then I flunked it. I don't know what was the matter—guess the stuff is too much for me. It's a good thing I got a ninety-four on my other test,. So my average is still passing. But don't think I'm not worried about my final grade in there. Then to add to all that, I heard more rumors to the effect that I might have to stay another semester. The only decent thing that happened was a hundred in a math exam. Don't think we are not really getting deep into that stuff. Not only do you have to know geometry, but you have to remember every little thing about algebra and trig.

Here's a little bit of news I heard last week. A group of 125 boys[1] entered Quantico three months ago, and seventeen finally graduated. The Marines are really particular, or they just don't want any more officers. Personally, I'm not too much on a commission anymore. It's going to be mighty hard to get. And my being young will go against me, I'm afraid.

How's everything been going at home? Is it still as cold as it has been? Up here the weather has been pretty nice. I can't understand. They say it isn't normal at all. But as long as it stays this way it'll be OK with me.

Well, it's time to study, so good night.

Love
John

---

[1] The usual rumors, or scuttlebutt as Marines and sailors say, was flying and none of it was true. LH

LETTER 42

Postmarked Jan. 17, 1944
Friday nite

Dear Folks,

One more week gone and the end draws nearer. I'm counting the days now. Hope they don't spoil things for me and keep me around for another semester. That would be the last straw.

They are having a big ball tonite for the Marines and sailors. But I couldn't think of any South Bend girls worth spending three and a half to dance with. So, I'm staying in to write letters.

You asked me about Boydine. Well, there isn't much to say. She didn't have much of an excuse, but she wrote two letters and a Christmas card asking me to write. So I answered. But I kind of burned her ears and told her what I thought about it all. She never answered and I don't give a hoot! She proved to me in quick order that she's not the girl I'm looking for. Believe me, it's going to be hard to find one that'll suit me.

The deficiency list came out yesterday but I wasn't on it. In math, I've gotten hundreds on the last two tests and my average has climbed to ninety two. So I should be set there. But I'm awfully dense in this surveying and I'm scared to death of what my final grade will be. Everything else is OK Hollar and I are leading the class in Mapping.

Your son was a bad boy and gathered ten demerits last week. They have been missing sheets and pillow cases lately, so one day last week they went thru our rooms. In my drawer they found an old rag which I had torn off of a sheet. Altogether about one hundred boys got stuck with the same thing. In addition to the demerits we all have to get up at 5:45 and scrub the drill house floor from 6 to 7. Ho hum. That'll be great sport. Well, I've got to press my uniform, so I'll close now.

Love
John

LETTER 43

Postmarked Jan. 25. 1944
Sunday nite

Dear Folks,

Well, here I go again. Another week-end has flashed by with five more days of drudgery in the offing.

Saturday morning I got three letters from you all. One from Jerry, one from Mother and the money from Daddy. And don't think I wasn't glad to get that money.. I've been flat broke for a week. Saturday nite I had a date with a little brunette named Doris Odor—not pronounced like it looks. We just spent the evening at her house, listening to the radio, talking to her folks—they're nice—and raiding the ice box. Then this afternoon, I took her to the show. Last week she took me to a swell formal dance. Really had a good time, too. She's very nice girl—quiet, but not too quiet. Reminds me of Joanne Wallace, only she has more personality. I intend to date her quite a bit before I leave. Got to enjoy myself during the next month because there won't be anymore week-end liberties for a long while. Of course, after I've been in Quantico for awhile, they'll give us a few week-ends in Washington, D.C. But it'll be quite some time before I'll get to Quantico.. As far as that goes, I may never be there. I wouldn't be surprised if they sent me west next month. And if they say I'm too young to leave for Parris Island, I may volunteer for the trip to San Diego. In some ways I think I'd rather be a private anyway. I'm beginning to wonder if a commission is worth all the sweat and worry. It's just the spirit of competition that makes guys want a commission anyway. If so and so can do it, so can I.

There's sure a lot of guys around here who don't care about being a 2nd Lt. In fact, they're having trouble with boys sneaking out at nite. Last week two boys went over the hill to Chicago and were caught. They're being shipped out Monday. But all that shows how much the boys dislike this place. It's enough to make a nervous wreck out of anyone. Especially if they are scheduled to stay 5 or 6 semesters. This place has done me a lot of good and I've learned a lot. But I've had four years of college and <u>I don't want another minute.</u> They are liable to give me some more, too.

I better study now, so good night.

Love
John

P. S. Tell Dorothy I'm glad she liked her gloves. And tell Jerry that I had an awfully nice billfold for him. It's too bad they lost it for him at the U.S.O.[1]

---

[1] The U.S.O. or United Service Organization provided many services to men in uniform. They helped make telephone calls, organized dances, provided a place in major train and bus stations where service men could meet and tell goodbye to their families, and much more. MV

LETTER 44

Postmarked Jan. 28. 1944
Tuesday nite

Dear Folks,

I'm happy! Just learned tonight that it's Parris Island for me in March. A Lt. Colonel in the Marines, who is one of the big shots from Washington, said that all engineers who are scheduled to leave will leave. And he also implied that anyone in Engineering has a much easier road to a commission than general line duty officers. So for the first time, I'm glad I'm an engineer. And I'm in the most important branch of engineers, Combat Engineers. The colonel said they rated first above communications and ordinance engineers. He left me more or less breathless, because I had almost conceded the fact that I would be here another term. Another thing he did was to kill some of the foul rumors that have been going around. We will be in Parris Island only 7 or 8 weeks instead of the 13 that everybody has been saying. Three weeks on the rifle range, and as he put it, 9 weeks of hardship. That totals 7 weeks. Then if we don't go direct to Quantico, we spend from 2 to 8 weeks at New River. That I don't mind, because it is awfully good training. The sergeants around here say that it is the toughest training camp in the country. Well, it's time for the lights to go out, so good night.

Love,
John

LETTER 45

Postmarked Feb. 1
Monday nite

Dear Folks,

It won't be long now. Then your son won't be a college boy Marine much longer. There was a list up today of the boys who are leaving for sure and my name was on it. Right between Hollar's and Kessler's. It's an awful relief to know for sure what the next near future holds for me. But the breaks were bound to come after all the bad deals I've gotten, now if I just don't sluff off and flunk out. It wouldn't be hard to get messed up in physics and flunk, but I don't think that would effect me much as they consider other things along with subjects. And I happen to know that I have a pretty high rating as far as military bearing and drilling are concerned. They keep mighty close tab on us around here.

You asked me about Hollar being a sergeant. It's pretty nice although it's quite a bother, and doesn't mean much after leaving here. He got it mainly because he's big and rough.

Well, I guess Dorothy will be thirteen tomorrow. So, "Happy Birthday" Dorothy, and I wish I were there to spank you good and hard. So math is hard, eh Dorothy? Guess you're just like your brother. I've sure had to study my heart out to make good marks in it up here. But it's not so important for girls to learn the stuff. It's lucky Jerry gets along so well in it. He's the one who should be an engineer. I'd better close now.

Love
John

LETTER 46

Postmarked 4th?
Friday nite Feb. 4

Dear Folks,

Three weeks left to go, but I'll be a nervous wreck before it's done. I've been a studying fool for the last three weeks and will be for the next three. Then I can relax and forget about books for two months. Guess there won't be much relaxing, but at least I won't be beating my brains out. It's going to be mighty rugged down at P. I. -- getting up at 4:30 A. M., toting a nine pound rifle around, and marching through the sand. We'll be down there at the best time of the year -- spring. It won't be so beastly hot and not too cold either. But Quantico will come during the heat of summer. I don't care though, if I can just get those gold bars on my shoulder as soon as possible. It'll be nice to come home some time with a slick officer's uniform.

Say, is this kid getting tough. We had wrestling this week. I wrestled 4 times and won every time. Pinned three of 'em in about ten seconds, and won the last one on points. He was bigger than me. Next week I have swimming. Boy do I dread that--its awful cold even if it is an indoor pool.

Got back a math test today over Solid Analytical Geom. with an 88. I feel pretty good because that's rough stuff and geometry has always been tougher than algebra for me. Did I tell you I got 88 in surveying test? That saved my life for sure. I should have gotten a 96, but I made mistake in simple multiplication. I've found that it's the little things that bother you in engineering subjects. Kessler is barely passing math because of little mistakes. I've run out of news, so good night.

Love
John

LETTER 47

Postmarked Feb. 6 or 8
Sunday nite

Dear Folks,

Boy, have I had a good weekend. Doris, the little brunette I told you about, took me home for Sunday dinner today, and also supper this evening. They had a wonderful fried chicken dinner. I ate until I could hardly walk. In fact, I ate for 30 minutes after the family finished. But they wouldn't let me stop and I didn't want to. Her folks are awfully nice. They make you feel so much at home and everything. Their house is real nice although they aren't rich or anything. Just people like us. The type of family I want to marry into some day. It's probably a good thing I'm leaving soon, because I might begin to get all kinds of ideas like that.

Don's girl, Barbara[1] was up here this week from Topeka. He's running around like a chicken with his head cut off. I guess they're going to get married just as soon as he gets a commission. If they can hold out that long. I think it's a big mistake, but you sure can't tell him that. Don's brother is back from the South Pacific after a year of action. He's a major with all kinds of decorations. I guess he really made a name for himself down there.

But just wait till they get this kid down there as a combat engineer. I'll really be a whirlwind. Building bridges, blowing up bridges, locating enemy land mines, etc. I'll be the rage of the Marine Corps for sure.[2]

How is Dorothy making out with all her little boy friends? I bet all those little boys in Junior High are crazy about her. I suppose Jerry is still going to all the dances and things. Does he work at Penney's any more?

Well, two more weeks, final week, and I'll be thru with Notre Dame. I can hardly wait. Guess we seniors won't be getting home. Our finals are over on a Friday, and we get leave till Monday morning at 8 o'clock. That's hardly enough time to get home. If my finals were over a couple of days earlier, I might make it. But this way I won't. Anyway, maybe I'll be getting a ten day furlough the first of May.[3] If I get to go straight to Quantico, they'll give me one for sure. Gosh, I hope so. I'll need a little break in there.

Well, it's time to hit the sack, so good night all.

Love
John

P.S. Say, Mother, would you send me one of those pictures of me like the big one I gave Mary Ann. Just one of those in a folder, I mean. Please send it so I'll get it before Saturday. Guess what I am going to do with it?

---

[1]Don and Barbara Hollar were married when he got leave while waiting for his OCS class to begin. They had two girls. LH

[2]John later had the option of being an infantry officer or an engineering one. He and Bill Kessler chose the infantry. Bill and John were the only Cavaliers who saw action. The others chose engineering which delayed their going overseas. Several were still in the States or heading overseas when the war was over. LH

[3]At this time, he was still hoping to get home on leave, but it was not to be. It was the summer of 1945 after he was wounded and in the hospital for three months before he got home for a month's leave. LH

LETTER 48

Postmarked Feb.??
Friday night

Dear Folks,

At last I've found a few minutes in which to relax for awhile. But not for long. This week I've been studying plenty hard--had a math test and surveying test. In math I got a ninety five. We had the surveying test today, so I don't know what I got. But I should have done very well, because I knew everything he asked, if I just didn't make silly mistakes. In engineering, those little foolish errors cause the most trouble.

Tonight I thought I was going to get a little rest, but tomorrow we are having a bunk display of all our clothing. At eleven the captain will be around to inspect. So tonight I'll have to polish up shoes, mend socks, and get the room spic and span. Ho hum. No rest for the wicked, I guess.

Just think, one more week of this routine, then one week of finals. After that I can toss studies aside for a couple of months. That will be a wonderful relief.

I got a letter from Don Jones the other day. He is now in Lexington, Virginia at the Virginia Military Institute. He says it is a fine place and thinks he'll really like it.

Well winter has come back again in Indiana. It started snowing early yesterday and hasn't stopped yet. I'll sure be glad to get down in sunny South Carolina. Boy, do I have a funny final exam schedule. Two tests on Monday, one on Wednesday, and two on Friday. Nothing at all on Tuesday or Thursday. I should be able to get plenty of studying for finals this time.

I suppose I should stop now and get busy on my shoes, so good night. And don't expect to hear from me too much during the next two weeks.

Love
John

LETTER 49

Postmarked Feb. 29, 1944
Tues. Feb 29, 1944

Dear Folks,

I've been awfully slow writing, but I didn't want to until I knew for sure which direction I was going from So. Bend. So my new address will be, "Recruit Depot, Marine Barracks, Parris Island, So. Carolina". And don't forget the Pvt. before my name and U.S.M.C.R. after. Train connections are poor, so we will have a long, dull trip. We leave at 6:30 Wed. evening. Don't know for sure, but we are going via one of two routes. Either we will go through Washington, D.C. with a five hour stop over or through Atlanta, Georgia with a twelve hour trip. Hope it's the latter, because that's where Cecil is, I think. I'm going to look him up if I get a chance and can find him.[1]

Of the 86 boys scheduled to leave only one flunked out, so apparently all the dummies and lazy ones went out last Nov. Of the whole detachment, only 25 guys go to San Diego. And as I expected, I flunked physics myself. It was too hard for the time I had to put in on it. Surveying and math were plenty hard and were more important anyway. I got an 85 in surveying with an 87 as the highest grade in the class. I sure sweat blood for that. In math I only got an 86. Would have had a 90, but was over confident in the final. So I made some silly mistakes, such as forgetting to work two parts of a problem. I just felt like I knew that book from cover to cover. And I really did almost. In mapping I got a 95 and 94 in Literature. Hollar flunked two subjects, but studies aren't everything. They knew he was good officer material, so they are sending him on through. He had an awful close shave though.

Ever since Friday, we have just been laying around doing nothing. They might just as well have sent us on home for a spell. We certainly aren't needed around here. All day we play cards, wash underwear and socks, press trousers and shine shoes. Then in the evening we get liberty, 4:30 to 11:00 P.M. There isn't much to do in that length of time, so I just go down to Doris' house or to a show. I'm enclosing a picture of her in this letter. I have a tinted one just like it in a regular folder made for servicemen to carry around with them. A big one in a frame wouldn't work, so well in boot camp or in Quantico.

They paid us this morning, but it wasn't for a full month, so I only got $20 dollars. That's all right though, because I won't be needing anything in Parris Island. Should be able to save most of my next two pay checks. Then I'll probably need it in Quantico because we get liberty to Washington, D.C. almost every weekend. Say, that ten dollars was sure a happy surprise. It came in mighty handy this week.

Gosh it doesn't seem possible that I have finished 4 years of college. And one year at Notre Dame. I'll probably never go back to school if I can get a regular commission in the Corps. Sure hope I can, although after the war, I might not want to.

Sure wish I could have gotten home this time. This sitting around here made me get almost homesick When you are busy, things like that don't bother you. As soon as we get to P.I. I'll get over it. It doesn't seem possible, but I'll be toting a rifle in less than a week. My days as college boy Marine are past. The tedious and dull part of my officers training is over—now the hard, but interesting part begins. I'm going to like it and I sure hope I get through.

Well, I'd better close now as I have some socks to wash and mend before liberty starts. Also I have to pack my sea bag. I'll drop you a card from Atlanta or Washington D.C.

Love
John

[1] See letter 61 for information about Cecil Casburn. MV

LETTER 50

Postmarked Feb. ??
Tuesday morn

Dear Folks,

The end is getting closer and closer now. But the last few days are the hardest. The time this last four months has flown by mighty fast, and I'm not sorry I had to stay now. Because it will take less time to get a degree after the war. I kind of think now that I will try to get a regular commission and stay in after the war. The Colonel who spoke to us said there would be a pretty good chance to do that as the Marines aren't going to cut down so much. They'll be left to police the world. I know I'd like to be in on that as an officer. That sort of life appeals to me—it always has. Boy, even though I'll have a commission by Fall, I'll still be training for some time after that. It'll probably be a year before I even leave the States.

We've sure had the snow around here lately. It snowed constantly for three days. There's snow all over the place.

Just got back from chow and there's sure a bunch of excited guys around here. Of the 190 boys who are supposed to leave this semester, they are only taking 96 of us. But the announcement was made today that those who are left over will have the opportunity to transfer to the Navy and go to officer's school. They will have commissions in the Navy by July 1st. Also they will see action just as soon as they are made ensigns. An awful lot of them are going to do it, too. I don't know what I'd do if I were in their place.

Well, I've got to get to work, so I'd better close. By the way, I left a pair of summer trouser khakis when I was home. If you can find them, please send them immediately. I'll need them in Parris Island.[1]

Love
John

---

[1] John said he would have made a career of the Marine Corps, but that decision was made for him. Because of his wound he was unfit for duty and the Marine Corps retired him as a second lieutenant in 1946. LH

Note This is John's last letter from Notre Dame. A copy of his academic record at Notre Dame appears on the next page. MV

RECORD OF STUDENT — UNIVERSITY OF NOTRE DAME, NOTRE DAME, INDIANA

Student: Hyderman, John Spencer
College of Engineering
Parent (or Guardian): Eugene B. Hyderman
Home Address: 624 N. Washington, Wellington, Kansas
Major Subject:
Distinction in Graduation:
General Average:
Date of Birth: Oct 2, 1922
Entered: Aug 6, 1940
Degree:
Date:
Has Honorable Dismissal

PREPARATORY WORK

At Wellington H.S.
Wellington, Kansas

Date of Graduation: 1940

ENTRANCE CREDITS

GROUP I (All units required)

	Units Req.	Cr.
English	3	3
History	1	1
Algebra	1	1
Adv. Algebra	½	½
Plane Geometry	1	1
Solid Geometry	½	
Physics		
Language Spanish		2

GROUP II (Two units required)

English	1	1
Latin	2 to 4	
Greek	2 or 3	
German	2 to 4	
French	2 to 4	
Spanish	2 to 4	
History	½ to 2	1½
Trigonometry	½	
Astronomy	½	
Botany	½	
Chemistry	1	
Physiography	½	
Physiology	½	
Zoology	½	
Algebra	½	
Psychology	½	

GROUP III ELECTIVE COURSES (Three units accepted)

Sociology	½
Biology	1
Typewriting	2
Vocations	½
Phy. Education	1
	17

ENTRANCE DEFICIENCIES

Solid Geometry ½
Physics 1

EXPLANATORY NOTES

1) The passing grade is 70%.
2) The semester is the unit of college credit.
3) F.A. — failure on account of absences from class.
4) ...

COURSES IN COLLEGE

FIRST YEAR

Course	Courses Failed	Sem. Hrs.	Grade	Year	Sem. Hrs.	Grade	Year
Relig. 11 & 12 : Commandments, & Sacraments							
English 11 and 12 : Rhetoric and Composition							
Mathematics 13 : Trigonometry							
Mathematics 15 : College Algebra							
Mathematics 16 : Analytic Geometry							
Chemistry :							
Mechanical Engineering 1 : Pattern Shop							
Mechanical Engineering 4 : Metal Processing, I							
Engr. Drawing 11 and 12 : Elements of Drawing, and Intermediate Drawing		2	83	'43			
Phys. Education 11 and 12 : Physical Training		Credit		'43	Credit		'43

SECOND YEAR

Course	Failed	Sem. Hrs.	Grade	Year	Sem. Hrs.	Grade	Year
Religion 21-22 : Apologetics, and Dogma							
Mathematics : Differential Calculus, and Integral Calculus							
Physics 21 and 22 : General Physics	'43 60	5	76	'43			
Biology 21 and 22 : Elementary Hygiene							
Geol. 1 General		3	89	'43			
Engl. 15-16 Readings in Dram Lit. I-II		2	97	'43	2	94	'43
Math 1v-2v Math Anal. I-II		5	93	'43	5	86	'43
Engr. Dr 3v Mapping and Map Reading					3	95	'43
Civil E. Plane Surveying I					2	84	'43

THIRD YEAR

FOURTH YEAR

L. to r. kneeling: W. Abell (St. Louis, MO), Bill Kessler, (Wichita, KA), Verlie Abrams, (MO), Standing, l. to r. Grant Hall (ID), Don Hollar, (Wichita, KA), John Hyndman, KA), Gunnar, Hald, MN).

The Notre Dame Cavaliers

WELTON RALPH ABELL* enlisted in the Marine Corps on October 23, 1942 and was sent to Notre Dame with the first V-12 class on 1 July 1943. He was commissioned a Second Lieutenant in March of 1945 but saw no service in WWII. He was awarded a Journalism Degree from the University of Missouri in 1946. He was a First Lieutenant when called to active duty in 1950 and served in Korea with the 2nd Battalion, 7th Marines. During a heavy enemy counterattack, he suffered a painful shoulder wound at the Battle of Chosin Reservoir, but refused medical attention. He regrouped his depleted company to fight off an attempted encirclement. He led his men up a steep hillside in a blinding snowstorm. For his heroic action, he received the Navy Cross. After the war, he moved to California and worked in advertising. Abell died in 1998 and is buried in Arlington Cemetery.

VERLIE ABRAMS* played football at the University of Missouri. On January 1, 1942, he played in a 2-0 game in the Sugar Bowl against New Mexico. In July 1943, he entered V-12 School at Notre Dame. He received his commission, but did not get overseas in time to see action in the Pacific. After the war he returned to the University of Missouri. Upon graduation, he was employed at Dupont E. I. deNemours and became an expert in the area of work force initiative and job development. He was a successful negotiator for his company. He died in Tennessee on August 21, 2008.

GRANT HALL, after Notre Dame, Grant went to Parris Island, S.C. to boot camp, then Lejuene, N.C. From there to Quantico, Va. where he was commissioned a second lieutenant. On to Camp Pendleton for infantry training, Grant was then transferred to Amphibian tractors[1] at the Boat Basin at Pendleton. Hall was an Amphib instructor for our troops and English officers. Finally, he was sent to Hawaii, then to Maui to join the 5th Amphib Battalion. They were training and about ready to load out for Iwo for maneuvers when the war ended. After school at the University of Idaho, Grant was hired as a County Agriculture Agent in Bonners Ferry. Idaho—from there to Caldwell, Idaho Then to Boise, Idaho.

---

[1] Amphibious Tractors or Amtracs, called Alligators by GIs, were one of only two truly amphibious vehicles of WWII. These vessels were driven by tractor treads at sea and could crawl up onto a beach and land their human cargo dry shod. The other amphibious vehicle was the DUKW or "Duck," a truck driven by a propeller at sea and by wheels on land. MV

GUNNAR HALD* was a native of Minnesota who was called into a V-12 class at Notre Dame University on 1 July 1943 with the rest of the "Cavaliers." He went on to Boot Camp at Parris Island and to Camp LeJeune for infantry training. After serving with the Marine Corps in the Pacific, he returned to Notre Dame where he received a law degree in 1948 and a Master's degree in Science and Education from Notre Dame's Graduate School. He was a realtor in the Dallas-Fort Worth area and taught Real Estate Courses at the University of Texas at Arlington. Gunnar Hald died in 1979.

DON HOLLAR was another fraternity brother who enlisted in 1942 and went to Notre Dame to V-12 school. He went on to Boot Camp at Parris Island with John and on to OCS at Camp Lejeune where he became ill and had to drop out and wait for the next OCS to begin at Quantico. He was in Hawaii when the war ended and was sent to Nagasaki, on the island of Kyushu in Japan, and on to China. He and John finished their geology degrees at Wichita U. in 1947. Don was a successful geologist in Wichita, Kansas. He is retired and still lives there.

BILL KESSLER* was another fraternity brother at Wichita State who enlisted in the Marine V-12 program in 1942. Like John and Bill Busch he was called up in the V-12 "sweep" of July 1943 and sent to Notre Dame and then to boot camp at Parris Island. Like Bill Busch he went on to Quantico to OCS, received his commission as a Second Lieutenant. He was sent overseas in time to participate in the Okinawa operation. After the war, he attended Oklahoma University where he earned a degree in geology. He worked as a geologist in Houston, Texas. Bill Kessler died in 2002.

and

JOHN HYNDMAN

*For more information about Ralph Abell, Verlie Abrams, Gunnar Hald, and Bill Kessler see Appendix IV.

PART I. ENLISTED SERVICE - MARINE TRAINING

UNITED STATES MARINE CORPS RECRUIT DEPOT
Parris Island, South Carolina
3 March - -3 May 1944

INFANTRY SCHOOL
Camp Lejeune, North Carolina
3 May -- 17 July 1944

LETTER 51

Postmarked P. I. Mar. 5, 1944

March 5, 1944

Dear Folks,

It's Sunday afternoon with myself dead tired. Right now is the first time I've had to relax even for a minute. We've been on the go every minute. The food is fair, but we eat it so fast that we never taste it. This is really life in the rough. The drill instructors don't like V-12 boys, so they make things extra tough. They yell at any little thing and you've got to let what they say pass over. If you didn't, life would be plenty miserable around here. So far it's a lot better than school work—though it will probably get harder, we'll get more used to it too.

Yesterday we checked out our rifle, bayonet, field pack, mess kit and cleaning equipment. These rifles are mighty nice, but heavy. Last nite we learned how to take the rifle apart and put it back together. That's called field stripping. Then we cleaned and oiled it. It's pretty complicated, but I can take it apart pretty well now.

We've been up at 5 A.M., eating at six and sometimes at seven. In the meantime before 8 o'clock, our beds have to be made (no wrinkles), floors swept and mopped (with elbow grease), and rifles taken apart to wipe off the oil that we put on the night before. So everything is done on the run and pretty much in the dark. After morning chow,[2] we have an hour of calisthenics which is going to be the toughest thing. They really put us through it.

This morning we spent two hours practicing the manual of arms. They made us slap those blame guns until out hands were purple. I was really tired when we got through. Wednesday we are having a big review, so I dread tomorrow and Tuesday. We'll throw those rifles around till we drop.

But I still like it better than Notre Dame and they'll have to make it plenty bad before I change my opinion. Got to stop now as we get physical exams pretty quick.

Love
John

---

[1] John's drill sergeant was named Ellison. John said he was from Georgia and didn't like Yankees. The Sergeants were extra tough on OCS candidates. He called him John Hindman (short i) all during boot camp. John ran into him after boot camp and to his surprise the sergeant called him by the correct pronunciation. LH

[2] Chow is food or a meal. The term is still heard, but it was universally used among servicemen of WWII. Among the many variations were to chow down = to eat, chow hound, the man always first in line who tried to eat as much as possible, etc. MV

LETTER 52

Postmarked March 12, 1944
Saturday nite

Dear Folks,

Well, I've been here a little better than a week now and am still alive. It's not too bad at all—at least not yet. I'm getting quite a sunburn, my face and neck will be black as a nigger's[1] before long. Also my hands are getting tough and hard. When we do the manual of arms with the rifle, we have to slap it pretty hard. My hands were awful sore for a couple of days, but they are getting tough now. The toughest thing here is the calisthenics every morning. They are plenty tough, but I can tell the difference they are making in me already, especially in my stomach muscles. We started out running ½ mile after calisthenics, now they've increased it to ¾ miles. It will get more and more as time goes by.

They give us all kinds of inspections every day. Our locker box has to be in perfect order with clothes put in it in just the right way. Bunks must be made up G.I.[2] and perfect with no wrinkles. The floors must be swept and mopped every morning before 8 A.M. Also any other time during the day they decide we should. Then there's the rifle which is as much trouble to clean as a two story house. It takes 45 minutes in the evening and 15 minutes in the morning. At nite we clean them and oil them up good. Then in the morning we wipe off the oil. Each time it has to be taken clear apart. At first it seemed awfully complicated to strip down, but now it has become second nature. And you just can't get the durn thing clean enough to satisfy the Drill Instructors. But then you can't do anything to suit them.

This morning we had to make up a field Transport Pack which is composed of a knapsack, haversack and long blanket roll (2 Blankets). The haversack is filled with: poncho, 1 pr. shorts, 1 t-shirt, 1 pr. socks, mess kit, toilet articles, 1 army C ration and 1 army choc. D ration. The knapsack is filled with 1 pr. field shoes, 1 pr. trousers, 2 shirts, 2 T-shirts, 2 shorts, 2 pr. socks. Then the blanket roll around that. It's pretty hard to put together and is plenty heavy. We had to put them on, then go out and march doing the manual of arms. I thought those straps would cut right thru me.

It started to rain this afternoon and hasn't stopped yet. The weather here is miserable, going from hot to cold. One night it got cold and we almost froze to death. We've had a fire ever since. The food isn't so tasty, but there's quite a bit of it. We can go back for seconds if we want. Personally, I kind of like this life. Heard today from our lieutenant that there isn't much chance of going straight to Quantico. But it's really better because the training at New River will be plenty good for me.

So you think Doris looks older than me, huh? Well she's almost 2 years younger than me. Now don't get excited when I tell you this but she's a Catholic.[3] But don't let it worry you.[3] I'm not married yet.

---

[1] The use of "nigger" was not politically incorrect at the time. LH

[1] G.I. =Government Issue. The abbreviation came to be used in a variety of ways. All US servicemen came to be know as "G.Is." The G.I. Bill at the end of the war was funded to give veterans a chance to complete their education. The "G.I.s" was diarrhea not too common in continental training camps, but a real complaint in overseas assignments. MV

[3] John's family were Protestants from Northern Ireland and marrying a Catholic was frowned on to say the least. LH

Well, I've got to close now as it's almost time for lights out. From now on I can write more often. They've been keeping us pretty busy after evening chow this last week.

Oh yes. You can send me some food if you want. Please some Milky Way candy bars if you can get them. They won't let us buy any candy around here. Also send cookies.

Well, goodnight all.

Love

John

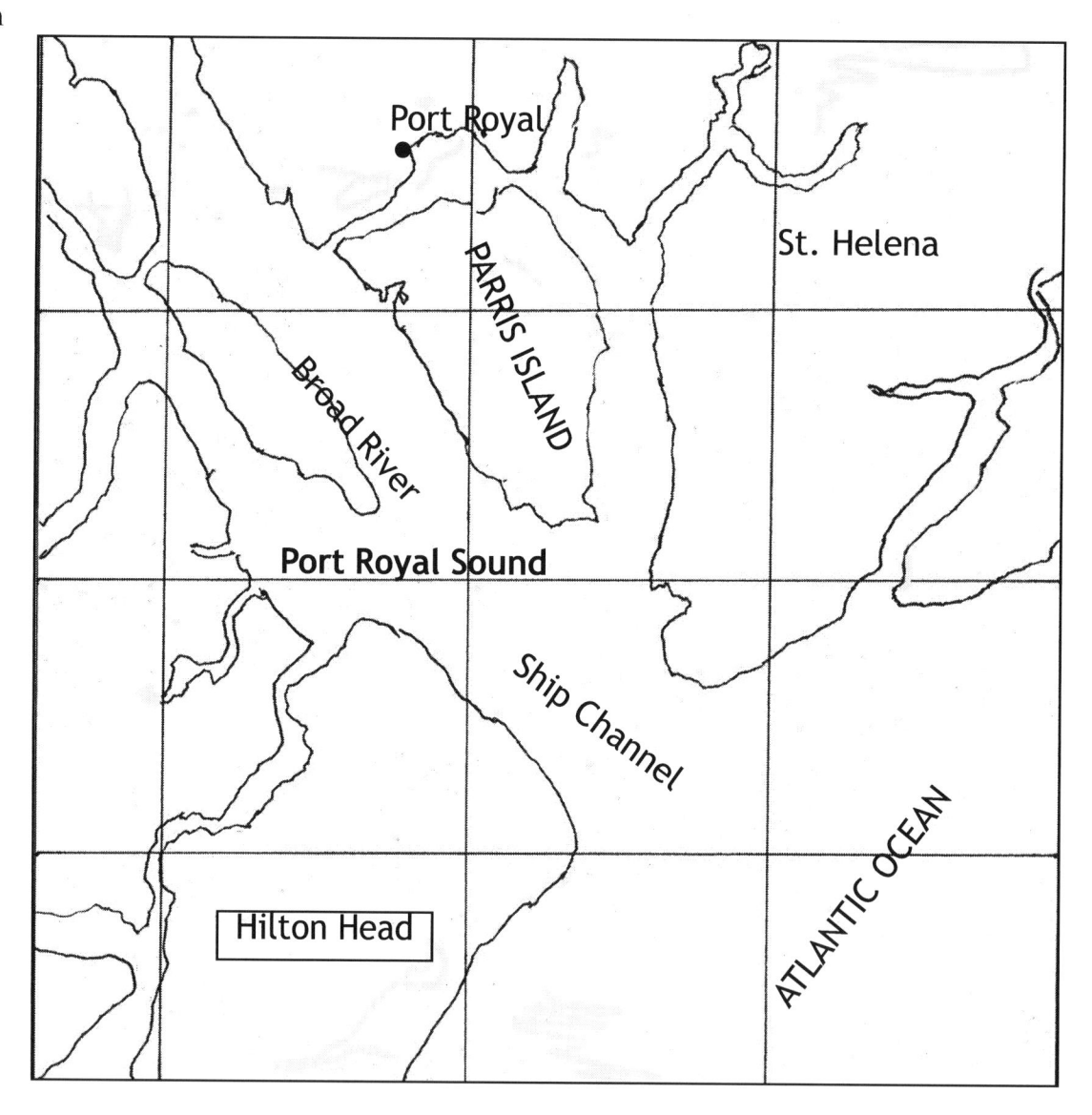

Parris Island and Port Royal Sound.
Parris Island is one of the sea islands of South Carolina. This is tidal country with many salt water creeks and rivers. The tidal range is about six feet. The islands are surrounded by thousands of acres of salt water marsh. John arrived for boot camp at the little town of Yemasee about fifteen miles north of Port Royal via the Atlantic Coast Line Railroad. MV

LETTER 53

Postmarked Mar. 12, 1944
Sunday noon

Dear Folks,

I wrote you a letter last nite, but I got Mother's letter this morning, so I thought I'd write a short note and answer some of your questions.

As for John Murray,[1] I've never seen him and it will probably be a miracle if I do. There are about 1600 V-12's here altogether along with jillions of regular recruits. I would like to see him, but doubt if I will. I might in New River or Quantico.

Bedbugs haven't bothered me although some of the boys have bites on their hands and feet. Don't know for sure whether they are bedbugs or not.

As far as seeing the ocean,[2] I still haven't anything on you. I haven't seen it either. Parris Island is a big place and we came on it from the back side. It's bordered on one side by the ocean and swamp on the other. All this county around here is very poor with very little growing and lot of nigger shacks standing around.

We went thru Atlanta at night and only stopped 15 minutes, so I couldn't have seen the Casburns anyway.

Lights go out here at about 9:45, so we get enough sleep, although morning comes awfully fast. They practically shaved my head—it's really funny looking. You'd die laughing if you saw it.

Why they don't like the V-12's, I don't know unless it's just jealousy. Also some of the college boys are a little cocky and have poor attitudes.

Well, it's almost time to fall out for noon chow, so I'd better close now.

Love
John

---

[1] John mentions him on March 12, 1944, September 29, 1944, and January 6, 1945. John Murray lived in Wellington until the third grade and then moved to Wichita where he went to East High. He and John were fraternity brothers at Wichita University. John said Murray went to V-12 school at S. W. Louisiana (Lafayette) and was commissioned at Quantico. Murray was at Pearl Harbor when the war ended. After the war he became a lawyer and now lives in Houston, Texas. MV

[2] John had no chance to see the Atlantic Ocean which was perhaps seven miles down the sea channel leading out of Port Royal Sound to the ocean. (See Sketch map on preceding page.) MV

LETTER 54

Postmarked Mar. 14
Tues evening
Dear Folks,

Well, I'm finishing up my 12th day at good old Parris Island. So far it has been a dud—not nearly so bad as all the stories I've heard. But can see where it would be hard on someone coming in straight from civilian life. The first few days are the hardest, then you get adjusted. We've sure got a poor platoon. About half are boys from Michigan and they can't march or handle rifles worth a darn. That ruins the whole outfit. Wish they hadn't split up the Notre Dame boys because we could really have a good outfit.

The sun is getting plenty hot and my face is brown as a nigger's.

Tomorrow we are having a big parade. Hope our platoon doesn't mess things up. It will be a pretty big affair, I guess-- Dress greens and everything. Also starting tomorrow we get instructions in boxing. There are so many guys I don't see how they can get much across to us. Glad I've already had some at Notre Dame.

Friday morning we are going on a long march. Don't know for sure just how far. Probably too long, that's for sure. Exactly two weeks from today, we'll go out to the rifle range. That's the place I'm anxious to go. We can do something with these guns besides throw them around from one shoulder to the other.

Well, I'd better close now as I have to do my washing (that's what I hate) and oil my rifle and bayonet.

Love
John

Three Boots. John, Unknown, and Don Hollar.
Note the Quonset huts in the background. Named after Quonset Rhode Island, these structures were widely used in WWII and remain in use today.

LETTER 55

Postmarked Mar. 17, 1944
Thursday nite
Dear Folks,

Well tomorrow I will have been in Parris Island 2 weeks, although the first week didn't count as far as training time is concerned (they were the toughest by far). We get 48 training days, not counting Sundays. The way we have it figured out, the end should come on May 3rd. I'll sure be glad to see that time come, although I don't mind it so much. Right now I think boot camp is a snap. But I'm knocking on wood. There's sure a lot more studying to do then I ever imagined. We get all kinds of lectures on which we have to take notes for tests. There's a million parts on the rifle to know—also history of the corps, camp sanitation, field sanitation, first aid, map reading, naval law (court martials, etc.), extended order drill, guard duty, scouting and patrolling, and functioning of the rifle. And I guess there is more to come. The regular recruits don't get so much of that stuff, that's just given to officer candidates. It's not hard to learn, but there's an awful lot and you've got to have it on the tip of your tongue, because at inspections they ask you all kinds of questions and raise heck if you can't answer 'em right.

Yesterday we had a regimental parade, dress greens, that lasted three hours. Boy, was I tired and hot when that was over. Got a fresh sunburn on top of my tan. Saturday we are going on a big march—don't know for sure how long, but probably plenty long. We'll probably be plenty ready for bed that night.

It's about time for taps now, so I'll have to close. There really isn't a lot to write about around here, but I'll try to keep you posted as well as I can.

Love
John

Private John Hyndman, Parris Island Boot Camp.

LETTER 56

Postmarked March 26, 1944
Monday nite
Dear Folks,

Whew, have I been on the go for the last couple of days. Yesterday was Sunday and I wanted to write a bunch of letters, but didn't have a chance. Our platoon drew guard duty, so I had to walk a post twice. Three hours once and 2 hrs. the other time. Then I had to spend the rest of the time getting everything cleaned up for the Colonel's inspection. Had to lay out all our "782" equipment, which is rifle, bayonet, haversack, knapsack, poncho, mess kit, canteen, first aid kit and cartridge belt. We stood at attention while an officer came thru, inspected the equipment, and asked us questions. In the afternoon we had to take a written exam over everything we've had lectures on before—some things we haven't. It wasn't so bad though, in fact, I think I got almost 100% right. After chow tonight we had a "field day". Had to take everything out of the hut, then get down on our hands and knees and scrub the deck with a brush. The same one we use to scrub clothes--and how I hate to wash clothes!

Now I'll try to answer your questions: New River[1] is in the eastern part of North Carolina, but not on the coast. It is about 100 sq. miles and is divided into two parts. Camp Lejeune, the nice part and Tent City, the part that isn't so nice. That's where I'll be. No town within 70 miles. And you ask me if I ever get liberty around here. Definitely not. In fact, we can't even leave our own little company area except when the instructors march us someplace. Saw one outdoor movie and went to the P.X. once for pogie bait.[2] By the way, will sure be glad when I got a box from you all. Still I haven't seen John Murray. Jackie Cooper was in the Navy at Notre Dame, and he flunked out. Went to Great Lakes. My rifle is a Garrand. Its real name is the U.S. Rifle, Cal. 30, M1, commonly called M1. The army uses the same thing. It's a pretty fine weapon, costs about $80. It will fire as far as 5,200 yards and is effective at 600 yards—that's as far as you can see well enough to hit what you are aiming at. It weighs about 9 pounds, is 41 inches long, and has thousand of nooks and crannies to catch dirt.

Maybe I didn't but I could swear that I wrote to Paul and Olive about the cookies. Got to stop now and clean my beloved rifle. They say that if a Marine works 23 1/2 hrs in a day, he'll put in the other ½ on his rifle.

Love
John

---

[1] New River is a tidal waterway leading to the town of Jacksonville (a city of 65,000 tody). Camp Lejeune was NE of the river, the area John calls Tent City is southwest, Cherry Point Marine Air Station is a few miles north on the Neuse River. MV

[1] Pogie bait is the name used by Sailors and Marines for candy, chewing gum, cookies, etc. LH

PACK HAPPY?—Pvt. Hewitt H. White stands by patiently while Pvt. John Hyndman adjusts his pack. Both are members of Platoon 117 12th Battalion.—Photo by Shivers.

Newpaper of the Recruitment Depot at Parris Island.

LETTER 57

Postmarked March 27
Sunday morn
Dear Folks,

Here it is, 8:00 A.M. and I've been up 3 1/2 hrs already. Worked like a slave too. This is some life. I'm not kidding a bit. But I like it a lot better than Notre Dame, although I'll be glad to finish boot training and get a little closer to a commission.

I've been kind of slow on my letter writing this week, but they've had us on the go all the time. No rest for the wicked they say and I must have been awful wicked in my day.

Heard from Don Jones (See Appendix V.) yesterday. He's been taken out of school and is somewhere in Pennsylvania now. He doesn't know for sure what's going to happen to him now. But he says the Air Corps is closed up tighter than a drum. Boy, did that guy get a raw deal from the Army. He says he'll be lucky to even get a corporal's rating now.

It sure is a cloudy and foggy day down here. Looks like it would rain any minute. Last week it rained almost every other day. To get paid one day we stood in line in a downpour for two hours. I learned to hate this country[1] down here right then. It's good for nothing except a training camp and it's not so hot for that. Hope N. Carolina is a little bit better than this, although we'll get there right when it starts getting hot. There is a pretty good chance that I might get to go straight to Quantico if I'm lucky and get the breaks. An awful lot depends on the breaks in getting to be an officer. It's too much that way, in fact. But it can't be helped I guess.

Wednesday morning we pack all our stuff in our sea bags and move out to the rifle range. That's going to be a lot nicer than what we are doing now. Did I ever tell you that Don Hollar and I have bunks next to each other? We've been pretty lucky that way so far. Better close now. Kessler[2] lives 2 huts down the row.

Love
John

---

[1] Most trainees whether Army, Navy, or Marines hated the Camps or Training Centers where they went to Basic Training or Boot Camp. Most were located away from cities. Many were in the south where the climate was warmer, but many were in swamp land, the Sand Hills of the Piedmont, almost never in well-populated land. A city kid sent to basic training in a camp in Louisiana thought he had been sent to hell while coping with 90° heat, insects, harsh training, rain, and even the occasional cold weather. Neither Parris Island nor Camp Lejeune were resorts with good weather and pleasant surroundings. Quantico in Northern Virginia and San Diego were about as good training centers as a Marine could hope for. MV

[2] Because most men in WWII were assigned alphabetically to billets, John and Don lived in the same tent. MV

LETTER 58

Postmarked March 28, 1944
Tuesday afternoon
Dear Folks,

I've got about 30 minutes, so I guess I'd better drop you a line. Received the candy bars Sunday afternoon and they tasted mighty good too. Of course they didn't last very long with 23 hungry guys in my hut. I would have liked to have eaten them all myself, but they just don't do things that way. Yesterday, I got a huge box of cookies, candy, oranges and nuts from Doris. It almost knocked me off my feet, because she'd never said anything about sending a package and I had never hinted or anything. Anyhow, it was plenty good and awful nice of her. She writes everyday, too, and sometimes twice a day. No, I've never heard anything more from Boydine. I don't even know whether she's still alive or not and care less.

Well, we should move out to the range tomorrow, but there's a chance we may have to wait until Saturday. They postponed the march we are to go on today until a later date. As far as I'm concerned, they can just forget about it, because those packs get awful heavy. Last nite the sergeant had a mad on and took us to the mess hall to work like he did last week. Now rumor has it that we are going over tonight. I don't know his idea in giving us that detail, but I think it's a dumb trick. He's certainly not going to get anything out of these guys by pulling that stuff. He treats us like we were a bunch of Kentucky hill billys and it doesn't work.

We're going over to get our haircut again pretty soon so I'll have to close.

Love
John

Marine with a Rifle - - John Hyndman.

LETTER 59

Postmarked March 30, 1944
Wednesday night
Dear Folks,

I had a big surprise this evening. Just as we were marching into the chow hall a guy came running up calling for private Hyndman. He told me to dress in greens and report to the guard hut. When I got there they told me I had a visitor down at the main station. Couldn't figure out for the life of me who it was, but I ran down there and found Murray Dressback waiting there. He's the guy that married Don Jones' sister, Dorothy. Beechcraft has him doing some kind of work down in this part of the country. It sure seemed good to see someone from home. I got to talk with him for about an hour. Did you know that he and Dorothy have a little girl? I didn't.

Also today, I got a letter from Cecil and Marg. They invited me to Atlanta for some weekend. They don't know what a prison this place is. It's as bad as Alcatraz or Sing Sing. Maybe I'll have time to stop over there when I move to New River. Doubt if I'll get enough furlough to get clear home. The train service in this part of the U.S. is so bad it would take a pretty big leave before I could make it home. I'm scared it will be Christmas before I get a furlough of any kind.

Well, we are having one of this God forsaken island's rainy nights. I've never seen such a wet place in all my life. Tonight we should have moved out to the rifle range, but now they aren't taking us till Saturday. I hate that because I'm getting awful tired of this life. The range should be much more interesting. At least it will be different.

Got to close now and clean my rifle. It's supposed to be a marine's best friend, but right now it's my biggest nuisance.

Love
John

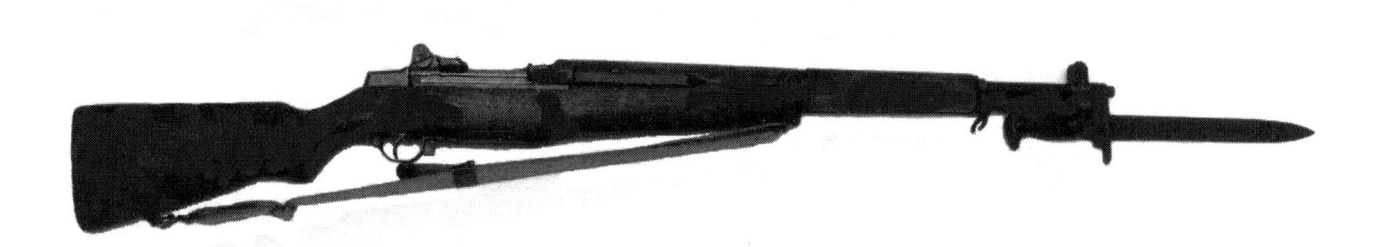

M1 Garand Rifle.

The "rifle" of World War II. Over four million Garands were manufactured during the war. The Marine Corps officially adopted the rifle in 1941. MV

LETTER 60

Postmarked April 1, 1944
Saturday afternoon
Dear Folks,

We're leaving for the rifle range pretty soon. Our sea bags are all packed and ready to be loaded on the truck. Packs are all set and we are waiting on the word to shove off. We have to march out there—it's not so terribly far—farther than I'd ever think of walking in civilian days, but the packs are the biggest the marines have, so we'll all be plenty tired when we get there. But I don't care. I'll be so glad to get away from this. This morning our lieutenant told us that Parris Island has the best rifle instructors of any place in the world. So we should really be able to learn to fire the rifle if we work at it. Hope I can qualify expert, but sharpshooter would be plenty good. To get expert you have to fire a score of 309 out of a possible 342. Sharpshooter is 294. If you qualify expert, you get an extra 5 dollars per month in pay. That wouldn't be bad.

There's one thing I wish you would do for me. Just send a box of those peanut butter cookies. I have an awful craving for them. Pogey bait is a wonderful luxury around here.

Well, I've run out of news now so I'll stop. I'll write soon and let you know what my new environment is like.

Love
John

Bayonet Practice.

LETTER 61

No envelope
April 2, 1944

Dear Cecil and Marguerite,[1]

Please excuse the pencil, but I'm all out of ink. It's kind of unhandy keeping ink around here anyway. We live out of a sea bag and if the lid should come loose, my clothes would all be blue.

I received your letters several days ago and was very glad to hear from you. Your invitation to come to Atlanta is appreciated, but I have about as much chance getting off this God-forsaken island as I have almost as a life termer has of getting out of Sing Sing. We might as well have a ball and chain on our ankles for all the freedom they give out here. There's a chance I might get a few days the first of May after finishing boot camp. That's not too sure, but if it is possible I'd like to come see you then.

Coming down here, I was in Atlanta about the same day as you were in Wellington. The scuttlebutt on the train was that we were to have a 12 hour lay over in Atlanta, so I planned to see you then, but as it turned out we stopped ten minutes. No chance at all to look you up anyway.

Well, Marine boot training is quite the life. It's not as tough as I've always heard, but it's not easy, either. They rout us out of bed anywhere from 4:30 till 5:30, usually much closer to 4:30. From then till ten at nite we are likely to be doing any of a thousand things. The first few days are the worst, then you are used to it. Boot camp lasts 8 weeks—3 weeks of drilling with rifles, 3 weeks firing on the rifle range and 2 weeks of bayonet training, judo and getting ready to leave. I'm out at the rifle range now. Haven't been here long, but I think I'll like it much better than the first period.

No matter how uncomfortable and tiresome things get, I'll still like it better than Notre Dame. I was never so glad to leave a place in my life. When I first got my orders to go to Notre Dame I was thrilled, but after a week there, my opinion of the school changed. All it had was a football team. It was a tough place too. I feel plenty lucky to have passed some of those engineering subjects I took.

As soon as I finish here I'll be shipped to New River. For how long, I don't know. From there I go to Quantico for regular O.C.S. I hope I can go thru it all, but wouldn't be surprised if I didn't. An awful lot of boys flunk out in the Marines. You've got to keep on the ball every minute and get the breaks too.

Thanks again for the invitation, but its just impossible for me to make it.

Yours sincerely,
John

---

[1] Cecil and Maguerite Casburn were John's cousins.. Mabel Casburn (Cecil's mother) was a sister of John's dad. Cecil was a school teacher and administrator in Kansas before and after the war. LH

[2] Sing Sing and Alcatraz were the two most famous prisons in the US in the '30s and "40s. Sing Sing on the Hudson River and Alcatraz in San Francisco Bay. "Sent up the river" was a common expression then for being sent to jail. MV

LETTER 62

Postmarked April 17
Tuesday nite

Dear Folks,

I've been awfully bad about writing lately, but I think you all understand how it is. Thought we'd have more free time out here, but it hasn't turned out that way. We've been on the go more than ever. There's something to do every minute from early morning till taps. Most of it is very interesting though, especially since we really started firing the rifle. For awhile we did nothing but learn fundamentals which was plenty dull. And hard too, because I had a tough time getting into the shooting positions. My legs were awfully stiff at first, but I'm pretty limber now. You'd be surprised at the way you can learn to bend those legs around and sit on them. My bad knee has given me no trouble at all. (John had knee surgery for a football injury a year or so before joining the Marines.)

On Saturday we fired the M1 for the first time at 200 yds., six shots. First we fired three shots in order to determine how to adjust the sights to hit the bulls eye. My coach then set mine to hit the bulls eye. All three went right in the bull. That made me feel pretty good. The rifle kicks pretty hard, but not as bad as I expected. Monday, we fired at 300 yards. Again we had to take three to find where to set the sights. Each man must do this at every distance, because each individual will have a different true zero for his sights at each range. Today I took six shots at 500 yds. That's really a long ways, but I got 4 bulls eyes. If I work hard I believe I can fire a pretty high score on record day. Hope so anyway because it means quite a bit. Also we've been firing a .22 cal. rifle quite a bit. It's pretty good practice for trigger squeeze and aiming practice. We fired for a record today in that. I got 244 out of a possible 250 pts. All you had to have was 226 to be rated expert. But we won't get any medals or anything for that. The score on our big rifle is what counts.

Sometime this week we will fire a sub-machine gun and the carbine. The latter is something like a rifle, only smaller. It is what lieutenants usually carry.

The food out on the range is rotten. The living quarters are worse than those at the main base. 72 men live in one big wooden barracks. Hollar bunks right above me. The rifle range is a detachment in itself and is located 2 or 3 miles from the main station. We move back there the last couple of weeks on P.I. There is only ten days left on the range. And I'm going to hate to leave it despite the food, because the last weeks at the other base are going to be tough. I'll be glad when it's all over, although I don't expect to get a furlough. Probably we'll just climb right on the train and go up the coast to New River. There we'll work a little harder than we have here. But at least the day will be ours after 4:30 or 5 o'clock And we'll be treated like real marines.

Well, I've got to shower before taps so must close. The cookies were delicious. Send more please.

The M1 .30 Cal. Carbine.
This carbine was produced in larger numbers than any other small arms weapon in World War II. The weapon was powerful yet light and handy. The Carbine was used by infantrymen as well as support troops. As John mentions in this letter, they were issued to lieutenants. John has a carbine like this strapped across his back in the photo of him on the beach at Iwo Jima. See page 170. MV

LETTER 63

Postmarked April 16, 1944
Sunday morn.

Dear Folks,

I'm practically an Arab now. We have been moved from the regular barracks into tents right out in the desert, practically. Sand is everywhere. We sleep on folding cots just like one we used to have at home. And I'm too big for one.[1] So I have to spend half the nite trying to get comfortable. Glad there'll just be a week of this as we'll leave the rifle range next Saturday. We fire for record Friday morning. Hope to get a good score, but probably won't. A lot depends on the weather and breaks. There is five dollars per month extra pay if I fire expert and three dollars for sharpshooter. But you have to be pretty good to get that high. The time sure flies by out here. Although we are busy doing something every minute, I like it a lot. I kind of dread the last two weeks back at the main base. It will be plenty of hard work. Forced marches as well as bayonet drill and judo instruction. Then I'll be all through with Paradise Island. Whether I'll get a furlough or not, I don't know. Personally I rather doubt it. They'll probably ship us straight to New River. We might get 2 or 3 days—enough time to run up to Atlanta to see Cecil and family. There's a boy living in my tent who went to Georgia Tech and who knows who Cecil is. But I doubt if Cecil knows him.

So Dorothy has found the girl for me to marry, huh? Guess I'll have to rush right home to see what she's like. But if she's a school teacher, I don't know. Anyone who wants to spend their life in school has something wrong with them.

How is Jerry and all his gal friends making out? Is he still the social butterfly he used to be? In things like that he is way ahead of his big brother. Especially now. I wouldn't know how to act around a girl, or any civilian for that matter. And I'm scared to death to get out of here and eat with civilized people. My table manners are nil. I eat so fast that no one else would have a chance. Eating beans out of a tin tray with a time limit is not a breeder of refined individuals. But they tell me that at Quantico we eat off plates. That will be the life. To tell the truth, I'll be surprised if I ever get to Quantico, and more surprised if I ever get a commission. That's no joke. It's going to be awfully hard to get through. They've got a good deal more candidates than they need. So it looks like a lot of good boys might lose out.

Received the box of cookies the other day and they were plenty good. It only took two hours to finish them off. The boys were crazy about them. Don't worry, I got my share. Send some more if you get a chance. I sure like 'em.

Love
John

.

---

[1] John was 6' 2 1/2" tall. LH

LETTER 64

Postmarked April 22
April 21, 1944

Dear Folks,

Your son is a happy boy, to say the least. We shot for record this morning and the kid came out with an expert's rating. In case you didn't know it that's the best there is (ahem!). We started out at 7:30 this morning on the 500 yard line. It was still too dark as it was very cloudy, but they still made us begin. So I laid down and squeezed off my 8 rounds,[1] scoring 36 out of possible 40 pts. That's considered pretty good, but nothing sensational. Then we moved to the 200 yd. line where we shot 12 rounds slow fire—6 rounds standing, 4 rounds sitting and 4 rounds kneeling. My standing was poor, kneeling pretty good and sitting was perfect (all bulls eyes). Following all that came the rapid fire sitting and kneeling at 200 (16 rounds each in 60 seconds). The target is much bigger there, but it is still pretty tough. I did OK there. Then last of all came rapid fire in prone position at 300 yds. I needed 70 pts. out of a possible 80 at that range to get expert. The pressure was really on because that has always been the jinx. So many guys have lost out because of that. But I lucked out. 75 points and totaled up a score of 310 pts. out of possible 340 gives you an expert's rating. Hollar has been shooting like a professional all the time, then today something happened and he didn't get expert. He got sharpshooter, which is next in line. Don't know what the trouble was. Guess he just didn't get the breaks. He probably tried too hard. This shooting is a lazy man's game in some ways. When you shoot, you've got to be perfectly relaxed, hold your breath, line up the sights and squeeze the trigger. It's different than other sports in that too much competitive spirit ruins you. Any slight nervousness is likely to ruin your score. That's why so many good shots slip on record day. Kessler fired a score of 311, beating me one pt. On preliminary day I scored a 310 also. I was afraid I'd tie up today and lose out on expert, but I managed to score exactly the same thing, which is unusual. I'm no hot shot, but at least I'm consistent.

Well, we go back to the main base tomorrow for 2 weeks. We ship out on the 5th of May. 2 weeks from today. At least that's the schedule now. The sooner that day gets here, the happier I'll be for the DI's will make next week plenty rough.

I'll stop now as we have to fall out in ten minutes.

Love
John

---

[1] The magazine of the M1 held eight rounds. MV

LETTER 65

Postmarked Apr. 26, 1944
Sunday night

Dear Folks,

We're having a lot of excitement on P.I. tonight. They let us go to the show and right in the middle of it an announcement was made for everyone to rush back to their barracks and lock themselves in. A big storm is coming in from the sea with a 70 mile per hr. wind. We are sitting around now waiting for it to come. I'll be disappointed now if it turns out to be a false alarm. But I'm sure glad we're out of those tents at the rifle range. We moved out last nite and came back to the main base. So it won't be long now till I'm out of this hole.

Monday nite

I had to douse the lights last nite, so I couldn't finish. The storm turned out to be a flop. It struck about midnight, but there wasn't much to it. Our hut didn't blow away or anything. I was expecting something big.

Here it is only eight o'clock and I'm in the sack. But I'm plenty tired as we had a busy day. Almost all day long we worked on bayonet drill. It's not so awfully hard, but it's tiresome and boring as heck. And I guess we'll be doing that steady for the next 2 or 3 days. On Thursday, we have to run the bayonet course for qualification. Then I don't know what comes after that. Judo instruction and some guard duty, I guess. Wish I knew for sure when we do leave here. All kinds of rumors are floating around, but we've never been told for sure. The most substantial gossip is that we shove off on the 5th. Then I also heard that we are due to arrive in New River on the 5th. So I don't know what to think. Two or three days one way or the other won't make any difference anyway. And I'm positive there's no chance for a furlough. I also know that the boys who go straight to Quantico will be sent by age. That leaves me out, but I don't mind because a few weeks in New River will be good for me.

By the way, will you get Don Jones' address for me? I've lost it and I owe him a letter.

Must close now and write a couple more letters before I fall asleep.

Love
John

P.S. The big box of cookies came today. They are certainly delicious. "Moon Mullins" one of the boys in our hut says they are "gorgeous." I think he's eaten ten already.

LETTER 66

Postmarked April 26 and addressed to Dorothy Hyndman
Wednesday noon

Dear Dorothy,

I received both your letters this morning and since I have a little time now, I'll answer. Say, you are really taking an interest in my love life, aren't you? You make that girl out to be a regular queen. I can't imagine a school teacher being such a beauty though. None of those I ever had were like that. Guess I'll have to come right home and see her for myself. But I think you want me to marry her so that she'll be in the family and you can get good grades.

We are supposed to have a big parade this afternoon in honor of Gen. Moses who is retiring as Commanding Officer of Parris Island. But it is raining now so we may have to stay inside all afternoon. A little sack time today would feel awful good. This place is getting mighty monotonous and tiresome. I'll be glad when we leave, but I don't know for sure when that will be. All I know is that it will be sometime between next Tuesday and Friday. Hope I get a furlough, but I don't think there's a chance in the world.

Did Johnny Allyn ever come through Wellington? When in the world did he get married anyway. Have you been having much rain in Kansas? It rains all the time down here. Every time it gets a little cloudy, you can bet your bottom dollar it will rain. And I'm getting so I love rain because it means a rest period.

Well, short stuff, there's no news, so I'll have to quit for now.
Be good now.

Love,
Johnny

LETTER 67

Postmarked April 30
Sunday afternoon

Dear Folks,

I'm lying out in the sun this afternoon trying to get the rest of my body as brown as my face and hands. The way I am now, I look like a typical boy fresh from the country. It sure feels good to lie out here and take things easy. I have all my washing done, but I've got to iron a couple of shirts and neckties, so I'll be all ready to shove off when we get the word. Be glad when I get to New River, so I can have my laundry done up right again.

Received several letters from Wellington this morning. Guess the flood delayed the mail a little.

You asked me how I'd take it if I should happen to flunk out of Officers' Training. Well, I wonder myself how I would take it. It's really not much of a disgrace as it's so tough to get thru and so much seems to depend on the breaks, but no doubt it would bother me quite a bit for a spell. That's mainly because so may of the guys I know have made the grade in one branch of the service or another. And I'd hate to think they were any better than me. It wouldn't bother me very long, though.

In our platoon of 71 men, 15 made expert. That's a much larger percentage than most platoons. The highest score was 317. The guy that scored that had had experience in target shooting before. My past experience of shooting rabbits with a .22 didn't help much. It probably did more harm than good as I learned bad habits that way.

I still don't know for sure when we leave. We're scheduled for Friday, but that's likely to change. I hope not as I'm raring to go. Wish I was getting ten days, but I'm afraid that's out. But you can't ever tell—I might pop up at home one day soon. Now I'm dreaming.

Will close now and take little snooze.

Love
John

LETTER 68

Postmarked May 3. 1944
Wednesday morning

Dear Folks,

Boot camp is now officially completed. I thought this coming Friday was the day, but I guess yesterday was. So now we are considered casual—that is, we are here with nothing to do and no orders of any kind. Why they don't give us furloughs, I don't know, but it seems they aren't. This morning the Quantico list was read off and they took 15 boys from our platoon. It was entirely on age, as it looks like I'll be in New River quite a spell. Boy, the guys in our platoon were a bunch of queer ducks. They are the type you can't imagine as officers. I'll be surprised if three guys out of that group get thru.

Oh well, New River isn't going to be so bad. Knock off work at 4:30 p.m. with the rest of the day to ourselves. And liberty every other weekend to go someplace—I don't know where. I guess Raleigh, North Carolina is about the best place to go. And we can make it to New York on a 72 hour leave. Got a letter from Joanne Wallace yesterday—she is going to be in North Carolina the last of June. It's been a long time since I've seen her. Don't even remember what she looks like for sure.

We've got to be in another big parade this afternoon. If it wasn't for that we could lay around this afternoon and sleep in the sun. But now, I'll have to jump in khakis and march around for 2 or 3 hours.

Don't know whether I've told you or not, but I qualified expert with the bayonet. Well, I think I'll lie down for awhile before getting ready for the parade.

Love
John

LETTER 69

Post marked May 6
May 5, 1944

Dear Folks,

Well, the Corps has done it to me again. First they send me to Notre Dame, second they put me in engineering, third, they keep me at N.D. an extra four months; and now, they've extended my stay on this lovable island from today till the sixteenth. They're too crowded in New River or some durn thing. Not only are they keeping me here, but I get some more training—extra curricular activities you might say. And to add insult to injury, I get no furlough of any shape or form. That's nothing but kicking a man when he's down. Can you tell me why the devil they couldn't let us go for a few days? The Quantico boys get ten days and what do they have that we haven't got, except a little age. Why didn't you two get married a little sooner It would have made things a lot nicer for me. Right now no matter how I figure, I can't see how I'll be home before next February or March.[1] That's no joke—it's going to take a long time. Even after I get my commission, I have to go to Reserve Officers training before getting a furlough. Boy, I didn't realize what I was getting into when I went on that diet to pass the physical exam in Kansas City. And I used to think it took a long time to get a commission in the air corps. Oh well, when I do get thru, Ill have something worth having. So I'll just bear with the Corps as they should know what they're doing. Then when I'm an officer, maybe I can take over and get things organized a little better for the outfit. Ho hum!

Seeing as how I have less time than I need to hit the sack before lights out, maybe I'd better close. So, until I have more pleasant news—

Love
John

---

[1] By February 19th, he was landing on Iwo. LH

LETTER 70

Postmarked May ??
Last letter addressed 390888, Plt. 117
Recruit Depot, MB Parris Island, S.C.
Wednesday morning

Dear Mother,

Happy Mother's Day! I'm afraid this will get there a little late, but I will wish it to you. I wanted to buy you something, but there is no chance to get anything decent on this island. But maybe there will be at New River. Surprisingly enough we leave tomorrow—my sea bag is all packed and everything. I suppose you noticed on the envelope that your son has been promoted. As of today I am a Private First Class. Now I make $54 dollars per month plus $5 for shooting expert, making a total of $59. I'm really in the money now. All morning we've been sewing chevrons on shirts and coats. They can't call me a boot any longer.

I also heard some other good news—if it's true! We are supposed to get a 72 hour pass right after arriving at New River. That's not very much, but it's enough to go to Washington, D.C. or some big town I've never been to before. In fact, I could go to New York, but it wouldn't be much time there. Too much time and expense on the train. I might go to Atlanta, but I think I'd rather go someplace where the boys go. Oh well, it'll probably blow up anyway.

Tell Dorothy I got the candy and will write her soon. It was awful good. If I get time, I'll write her this afternoon.

Please send me Don Jones' address as soon as I write you from New River. I've lost it and owe him a letter. I'll write as soon as I get to New River.

Love
John

LETTER 71

Postmarked May ??, 1944 and addressed to Dorothy Hyndman
Wednesday afternoon

Dear Dot,

How's my little blonde sister anyway? Are all the little boys still crazy about you—I bet they are. Your fudge came the other day and it was awfully good. So were the candy bars. I liked them a lot. You should do that again sometime while I'm in New River. I have to get up at two o'clock tomorrow morning, eat breakfast at three, and shove off at four. Hope I can get some sleep on the train because it's a pretty long ride up to New River. We won't get there until evening probably. Boy, I'll sure be glad to say goodbye to Parris Island—almost as glad as I was to leave Notre Dame. Don't believe I'm as sick of this place as I was N.D.

I wish I could come home and see you folks now, but the marines won't let me. Looks like I'll have to be contented with 3 days—and I might not get that. Hope so though!

Have you heard anything about Don Jones? He hasn't gone overseas or anything like that has he? Remind Mother to get his address for me and send it to New River.

It sure is hot down here now. I'm glad I came down at this time of the year. Any later and it would be unbearably hot and any earlier it would have been too cold. So I've been pretty lucky although I'm afraid things will be slightly miserable at New River.

Well, Dorothy, it's about time to go to chow, so I must close. I am enclosing some negatives—have the folks get several prints made of each one and send part to me.

Love
Johnny

INFANTRY TRAINING, CAMP LEJEUNE

On 5 May 1944, the V-12s, newly graduated from boot camp, rode the train from Parris Island up to Camp Lejeune, base of the Fleet Marine Force (FMF) Training Command. The Camp is located on the New River near Jacksonville, North Carolina. About sixteen-hundred strong, they were designated as Officer Candidate Applicants (OCA), formed into platoons and companies and immediately assigned an arduous training regimen while they waited to be transferred to Officer Candidate Course at Quantico, Virginia. For two and a half months, the OCAs were intensively drilled in small-unit tactics for fire teams, squads and platoons. They made innumerable training and conditioning (field trips) with full field-transport packs, underwent infantry weapons training and classroom instruction and spent hours in marches, small-unit tactics and map and compass exercises. Many exercises were at night and field problems lasted three or four days.

The Camp ran a sixteen-hour-a day, six days a week schedule, with Sundays clear for checking out the skimpy liberty opportunities in the overcrowded nearby towns or staying on base writing letters, squaring away gear, and recovering from Saturday night liberty, such as it was. The Officer Candidate Applicants were housed at Hadnot Point, their main side base, which after the tents and Quonset huts of Parris Island struck them as a lovely installation of large red brick and white-concrete buildings set in spacious green lawns and many trees.

After nearly two and a half months, the OCSs were assembled on 12 July and were informed that because of heavy casualties and expansion of the Corps, 430 of them were to be formed into a Special Officer Candidate (SCOS) which would be convened the following Monday, 17 July, at Camp Lejeune. They were told that the Corps had lost about 450 officers, mostly lieutenants,[1] in the Marianas that summer. Actually the losses were greater than that.

Nevertheless, most who were chosen for the SOCS were "overjoyed," no more waiting to go to Quantico and get into the war.

---

[1] t is universally acknowledged that the platoon commander has most dangerous job in the infantry. In extensive campaigns, the casualty rate for Second Lieutenants is often 700. 800. even 900 percent. Lieutenants are wounded or killed, replacements are wounded or killed multiple times for a single platoon. In addition, as the war dragged on, men in US amphibious operations faced more and more stubborn Japanese defenders who seldom surrendered. Saipan had been taken, but Tinian and Guam were scheduled in July and August, 1944. Iwo and Okinawa and Japan were in the future. The Marine Corps was also expanding with the Fifth Division being formed in Camp Pendleton in July of 1944. Manpower planning for a Sixth Division was underway.MV

LETTER 72

Postmarked May 29, 1944
Addressed Co, D Plt.3 C and. Det. Inf. Bn
Sunday May 28th

Dear Folks,

Well, here I am back at the main base, alive and well after a week in the rough. That was quite an experience—plenty tough. We marched the 15 miles back in two hours, compared to 3 ½ hours going out. They gave us no halts for rest and we carried empty canteens. Whether you realize it or not, that is a very fast and hard march. I think we set some sort of record for that distance.

I received your letter with the questionnaire while on bivouac and then lost it. So I can't answer them very well. Don and I are in the same platoon as we are almost the same age and our names begin with "H". But Kessler got in an entirely different company as he is 22 already. His outfit will go to Quantico after about seven weeks while we have to wait about 15. Hollar and I were in that company for half a day while the dividing line was a birth date of Nov. 1, 1922. Those born before that got in that outfit, while those born after were put in the company I'm in now. But they, unfortunately, changed the date to Oct. 1, so Don and I were shoved into the cradle roll as we call it. We're really on the borderline. If enough guys flunk out or transfer to the air corps, I might get to go to Quantico when Kessler does. Hope so.

It's raining here for the first time since I've been here. Glad it waited till we got back from bivouac because that would have really been messy. You know, it's going to be even easier to flunk out here than I thought. Another company that went out on bivouac when we did, kicked out three guys who couldn't stand up under the physical strain. They ran the obstacle course on the last day of bivouac and the poor guys couldn't finish. This is much rougher than I ever imagined it could be—physically I mean. The tests aren't so bad. We have map reading next week. That should be easy as I have had so much of it. More boys flunk out of OCS on that than anything else.

You said you hoped I was mistaken about it being so long before I could get home. Well, to be real frank, don't even count on seeing me next spring. Lately they haven't even been giving out furloughs after finishing up at Quantico. The marines just don't believe in that sort of thing. But you can't ever tell, I might be lucky. I've learned though, never to count too much on anything in this outfit. They disappoint you too often.

Must close now
    Love
    John

P.S. I can get plenty of candy now, but you could sure send some cookies. They would be most welcome.

LETTER 73

Pfc John Hyndman. Co, D Plt.3 Cand. Det. Inf. Bn
Camp Lejeune, N.C.
Postmarked June 10, 1944
Dated June 9

Dear Folks,

Just got back from another week of bivouac. It was pretty easy this time except that it rained one day, which made things pretty miserable. We spent most of the week doing next to nothing. On Wednesday we made three landings on the beach with tracer bullets shooting over our heads and dynamite exploding all around. Quite a thrill, especially at night. I got a little sea sick the first time out on the water in the landing boat.[1] The ocean was choppy and we rode around in circles for a long time. I began to wonder if I was going to be able to hold down my dinner.

An LCVP or Higgins Boat Headed for the Beach at Iwo Jima.
This landing craft could carry 36 infantrymen. It could embark and land a Jeep or Weasel. It ferried thousands of tons of supplies to invasion beaches and evacuated thousands of wounded.

[1] Almost certainly an LCVP (Landing Craft Vehicle/Personnel,) commonly called a Higgins Boat after its designer, Andrew Higgins. Thousands of these boats were built which landed hundreds of thousands of service men on beaches around the world from Guadalcanal to North Africa, from Normandy to Okinawa. MV

How far am I from the coast? Fifteen miles. We bivouac about half a mile from the ocean.

Guess I'd better try to answer your questionnaire. Do I go to church? Yes, we have a nice church here for all Protestants. A different Chaplain speaks each Sunday. They are very good, too. Last Sunday I went to the Catholic church with Doris. It was the first time I had ever been in one. It was very interesting—they sure go through a lot of ritual.

There are lots of Notre Dame boys here. Four from Wichita, counting myself. Hollar, Kessler, Busch and I. Kessler is in another company while the rest of us are in the cradle roll.

Yes, I read the Bible you sent me.[1] Not so much now as I did while at Notre Dame. Around here I do well to get in bed before lights go out. Back at school[2] several of us used to get together every nite and read it to each other.

No, I can't let my hair grow. I'll have to keep it under two inches for the rest of my training as an officer candidate. Speaking of being an officer candidate—please don't count too much on my getting those bars. No joke, they simply don't need officers any more and they're flunking them out right and left at Quantico. So much depends on sheer luck and the breaks. I'm just going to do my best and take things as they come. If I don't make it, I just won't make it and that's all there is to it.

So Jerry wants to join the merchant marine and get rich,[3] uh.

Navy Air Corps is by far the best deal. The infantry hasn't got it. Life in a foxhole hasn't got it. The Air Corps[4] is no more dangerous than anything else, and they live a good life even in combat. I'm sorry I didn't get in that outfit a long time ago—I mean it.

New River is about 50 miles north of Wilmington, N.C, which can be found on most any map. That's the closest town of any size. It's something like Hutchinson in size.

I'll see what I can do to make up a list of Marine "lingo" for Jerry. Got to stop now.

Love
John

[1] John talks about the Bible in many of his letters. His mother was his example through the years. She taught Bible classes in the public schools in Wellington, Kansas for many years, until the Supreme Court declared it unconstitutional. She also conducted the four-year Menninger Bible Course to several groups in her home. LH

[2] Tells about the Cavaliers and Bible study. The Cavaliers were the seven men in the picture at Notre Dame. Verlie Abrams, Grant Hall, Don Hollar, Gunnar Hald, W. R. Abell, Bill Kessler, and John. See the Notre Dame section for photo and biographies. LH

[3] During the war, it was a common misconception that the Merchant Marine was a good berth in which to make money. The pay was good (compared to that of a Pfc. or S1c) but merchant seaman had to join the union, sign up and wait for a ship. Not to mention the hazard, especially in the Atlantic of sub attacks. In 1946. John's brother Jerry (Gerald H.) joined the Navy. In 1948, he was appointed to the Naval Academy and graduated in 1952 and elected to be commissioned in the U. S. Marine Corps. He saw combat in Korea, twice in Viet Nam, and Lebanon. He retired as a full colonel in 1978. MV LH

[4] John is right that all the services held their own hazards, but it always depended on what assignment a man drew. The US Army Air Corps in the European Theater had one of the highest casualty rates of all the services. Of course he couldn't have known in detail about casualty rates at the time he was writing. Incidentally, the Merchant Marine had the highest casualty rate of any service. Mariners received no benefits for their service. MV

LETTER 74

Postmarked June 19, 1944
19 June 1944
And to my Favorite Aunt and Grandmother,[1]

I am forced to admit, Aunt Dott, that your letter received today, boosted my ego considerably. My usual conceited nature will undoubtedly become positively unbearable to my bunk mates. If I had known my picture was to bring about so much swooning and confusion to Remington Arms Company, Inc.—said company housing 3,000 (mostly feminine) employees in its Administration Bldg.—and possibly holding back the work output of a vital defense plant—I would have sent dozens! Ahem.

Seriously, thanks a lot for the very nice build up. As for sending a picture in uniform, I'll see what I can do. But it's going to be very difficult. In this God-forsaken camp there is no place to have a picture taken. So I'll have to go to Wilmington, N.C. to get the job done. It will be several weeks before I will be able to get there because we are beginning a new program in which weekend liberty is almost forgotten. As soon as I do get a chance to leave the base, I'll try to get my picture taken in my snappy private's uniform. Maybe someday I'll be able to have one taken in officer's clothes. That's the day I dream of—but I'm scared it's just a dream. The Marine corps seems to have about all the officers they need, so in O.C.S. they're flunking out everybody and his brother. Some time ago I thought I'd be in Quantico by now, but because of the fact that the folks waited so long to get married, I have to put in some time here. I wouldn't mind it so much, but they are working us to death. I have calluses on my feet 3 inches thick and millions of blisters. But this new program I spoke of is the pay off. They have cut out so much physical work and are giving us all class work.. We go to class from 7:30 a.m. till 8:00 p.m. Then they give us till ten o'clock to clean rifles and study. Nice of 'em! In class we get all kinds of military rules and regulations, tactics, etc. Even math. I think they want us to be mental giants instead of fighters. I am slated to go to O.C.S. on August 16th and should get my commission on Nov. 16. If I get thru! That's sure a long time!

I'm sorry to hear that your family has been having so much trouble lately. Everything happens at once doesn't it? It sure works that way in the Marine Corps. And plenty happens, too.

Well, I could write more, but just haven't time. Must clean my beloved rifle before lights out. You may have heard how the Marines love their guns. That's a terrible lie. It's twice as much trouble as it's worth and I hate mine. I must close.

Love
John

---

[1] To John's aunt, Dorothy Murphy Wheeler and his grandmother, Edna Cobb (Bonnie). Bob Murphy, Dott's son had been in the hospital. LH

LETTER 75

Postmarked June 26, 1944
June 23, 1944
Dear Folks.

Here it is Saturday nite and I'm sitting in the barracks writing letters. But there's nothing else to do. Now that we have class till five on Saturdays, there's little time to go off base. So tonight I went to the show at 6 o'clock and just got back. It's too hot to do much anyway. I doubt if the temperature is any higher than in Kansas, but it makes you sweat so much more. I sweat 24 hours a day. In the mornings I wake up soaked. I even work up a sweat taking a shower.

Boy, today was sure a mess. We got up and worked like dogs getting the barracks all slicked up for inspection. Also had to clean rifles and get into Khaki. You have to get a millions things done in no time at all around this place. That's the thing I hate worst of all—rushing around all the time. I took 4 tests in 1 ½ hours yesterday. We had exams on math, the M-1 rifle, the carbine, and on rules of land warfare. The first three were easy enough, but the last one was a stinker. They pulled it by surprise and I expect that about 90% flunked it. The tests are "fill in the blank" type and you either know it or you don't. I have a better than 90 average so far, so it won't hurt anything if I did flunk that one. This afternoon we had a long lecture on combat principles, both offensive and defensive. The captain who lectured spent two years in the South Pacific, so he had some good stories. All of our officers here have seen combat. Most them were wounded or sent back with malaria. My captain enlisted in the same deal I did in March of "42. But he was a senior that year, so went to Quantico and straight overseas. Just got back about three months ago. If I had been a senior then instead of a sophomore, I would be a captain now with combat behind me. He'll spend the rest of the war training men. And will probably reach a major's rank. If I do get my commission, I'll never get any higher than a 2nd Lt. But of course if the war would end, I'd gladly sacrifice any promotions.

Well, I thought our little ventures in the woods would stop with the new program, but they're not. We're pulling out Monday morning for another week with the ground for a bed, the sky for a ceiling and bugs for playmates. But I don't mind it so much. It's a wonderful break to get out of classes for awhile. Another good thing is that we get off at noon the Saturday after bivouac. So Kessler, Hollar and I are going to Wilmington for a last get together. Kessler is going to Quantico July 6 and Hollar and I have to wait till August 16th. He'll be half thru when we get there. The training there is only twelve weeks instead of sixteen like I thought. About the eleventh week I'll probably get the boot and will be put in some replacement battalion. The reason I think I might get screened is that they've been flunking about 50% of the boys lately. And they'll give you the boot for the least little thing.

Better close for now.
Love
John

LETTER 76

Postmarked June 28, 1944
Tuesday morning
Dear Folks,

I am now a member of the "Junior Firefighters of America". We were supposed to have gone out on bivouac Monday, but a forest fire[1] blazed up in the near vicinity, so we were called out Sunday evening to fight it. I worked from 4 til midnight that nite and also last night. Probably we will go out again today. There wasn't much fire where we were stationed last nite, so some of us built a smudge fire in the ditch and went to sleep. But Sunday we really had to work. Once the smoke got so bad that we had to lie down on the ground to breathe. We had been trying to keep it from jumping across a road into some more woods, but weren't successful. So there we were with fire on both sides and smoke rolling over us. What a mess. There's hardly any woodland left around here that hasn't been burned out. It's spread out so much that there are fires in three counties around here. They have 5,000 Marines, soldiers and coast guardsmen fighting it. But everything is so disorganized that they aren't getting much done.

Remember that I told you I thought I'd flunked a test? Well, I passed it. Guess I'm just pretty smart, because I knew next to nothing about what he lectured about—just need common sense, that's all. Ahem!

Say when are Mother's and Dorothy's pictures coming? I'm anxious to see them. Also I would greatly appreciate some cookies or something like that. They'd taste mighty good!

This has been a mighty short letter, but I haven't done anything except fight fires at night and sleep all day.

Love
John

---

[1] The coastal plain of the Carolinas is heavily forested, primarily with pine trees. In nearly any season, but especially in drought years, forest fires break out in the dry litter of pine needles and cones that collect on the forest floor. The Marines at Lejeune were a handy source of fire fighters. MV

LETTER 77

Postmarked July 13
July 12, 1944
Dear Folks,

The pictures[1] came today and I think they are wonderful. Everybody here raves about my good looking family. And they wonder how you ever got a black sheep like me. I do too!

I'm sorry I haven't written more, but this schedule we're on doesn't leave time to get a drink of water. This going from daylight till long after dark hasn't got it at all. I was getting awfully sick of it until today, then the C.O. gave us some stupendous news. It seems that all this stuff about the Marines not needing officers is a lot of malarkey. In fact, it is so much so that they are going to start an O.C. class here next week. And this kid is going to be in it. They chose 215 boys out of our company of 310 men. So I didn't have to be so hot. In other words, it's no particular feather in my cap, but I'm awfully tickled about it. That means, provided I don't flunk, that I'll be wearing gold bars on October 1. It also means that I won't get stuck in Engineering, which pleases me considerably. So folks, I finally get a break after a year of heart breaks.

So you like my letter to the folks in Independence. You should have seen the one Aunt Dott wrote me. She's a case if there ever was one. I'm the favorite "pin up boy" of Remington Arms and Co. and she really tried to blow me up. They claim they want a picture of me in uniform, so I'll just wait till I get bars, then send her one in officer's clothes.

Well, I must close now, but will write soon.

Love
John

---

[1] The family pictures John talks about were lost at Iwo. After he was wounded, he left the Island with only his dog tags. His watch, pictures, uniforms were never found. LH

PART II. OFFICER TRAINING & SERVICE

SECOND LIEUTENANT JOHN HYNDMAN

CAMP PENDLETON, OCEANSIDE, CALIFORNIA
October 1944--November 1944

MADGE HYNDMAN'S LETTERS HOME
LOS ANGELES AND SAN CLEMENTE, CALIFORNIA
November 1942

SPECIAL OFFICER CANDIDATES' SCHOOL

CAMP LEJEUNE, N.C.
July 1944 – October 1944

REVIEW

James R. Dickenson, *We Few: The Marine Corps 400 in the War against Japan*. Naval Institute Press, Annapolis, D, 2001.

"Desperate for junior officers to meet the wartime demands of its rapid expansion and to replace mounting casualties in its Pacific Battles, the .U.S.. Marine Corps convened a Special Officer Candidate School (SCOS) at Camp Lejeune in 1944. This special class was to augment the regular Officer Candidate School at Quantico, which was operating at full capacity. The young 0 had been enlisted in the V-12 officers procurement program and called to active duty from colleges and universities across the country. Destined to fight in some of the bloodiest battles of the war, then answer the call to arms again in Korea, the Marines of this special class, who called themselves the "SOCS 400,' served in the Minuteman tradition established at Lexington and Concord nearly two centuries earlier. Their compelling story is told for the first time by a former Marine and reporter for some of the nation's best news organizations. He chronicles their experiences from induction through training and combat to the lives they later led. Eliminating some of the traditional training of young Marine officers, this special OCS curriculum concentrated on infantry tactics and weapons, and ninety percent of the class wound up as platoon leaders on Iwo and Okinawa. Forty-eight of them were killed. 168 wounded, for a casualty rate of some 58 percent. For their heroic actions they earned a host of decorations, including five Navy Crosses. Eight more were wounded in Korea and one more earned a Navy Cross. Many believe they had the highest casualty and decoration rates of any Marine OCS class in World War II. This book focuses on ten men representing all six Marine divisions and nearly every section of the country and all types of colleges and universities. The story's appeal bridges professional and general interest".

About the Author

James R. Dickenson, a freelance writer living in metropolitan Washington, was a reporter, editor and columnist for the Washington Post, United Press International and other news organizations. He served as an officer in the Marine Corps from 1954 to 1958.

LETTER 78

No envelope
17 July, "44
Dear Folks,

I am now in officer's training as of this morning. Just got back from a speech by the Commanding General of Camp Lejeune. There wasn't much to it, just a little pep talk to the future officers of the Marine Corps. He told us how much better the corps is than any other service in this country, or any other country. That's the truth, too. And Marine officers are the best trained officers in the world.

Since we moved to another barracks, they gave us the rest of the morning to get squared away. As I did that work last night, the morning is my own. Probably the last free time I'll have in ten weeks. They're going to work the pants off us, but we've got a real goal to work for. Before we were just marking time and had almost forgotten about a commission. Now it's a lot different. From now on we work from 7:30 a.m. to 8:50 p.m. Yesterday, we were issued 17 Marine Corps manuals on every subject you could imagine and some more besides. We'll only have an hour each evening to study and clean rifles. So I'll be paying strict attention in class. Much more so than I ever did in college.

As far as I'm concerned, this is the most wonderful break of my life. But it was time something happened after all the raw deals I've had in this outfit.

I want to tell you again how crazy I am about the pictures. They are going to be with me every place I go from now on. And no doubt I'll be seeing a lot of places in the near future. There's one thing I want to warn you about—don't expect much mail from me for ten weeks. I'll do my best to write one letter a week, and sometimes more. As if I'd been doing much better lately.

Love
John

P.S. Please note the new return address on the envelope.

DEDICATED TO THOSE MEN OF THE SPECIAL OFFICER CANDIDATES' SCHOOL SEPT. 1944 WHO GAVE THEIR LIVES IN THE SERVICE OF THEIR COUNTRY AT IWO JIMA AND OKINAWA

ALLEN, ROBERT WILLIAM	HARRINGTON, CHARLES EDWIN, JR.
ARMIGER, JOHN OLIVER	HARRIS, JAMES DUDLEY
BAKER, WILLIAM LEONARD	HAWKINS, WILLIAM BLAIR
BITTIG, JOHN ARTHUR	HENDERSON, EUGENE
BRUNDAGE, ROBERT PETER	HOLMES, ROBERT DUNCAN
CABRALL, FRANCIS PAUL, JR.	HUTCHCROFT, LESTER EARL
COHEN, ERWIN ROBERT	JONES, DUNBAR
COOK, THOMAS CLAYTON	KALISH, NORBERT
CRANE, DUNCAN McLAREN	LAMPORT, HARRY BOWMAN, JR.
DAHL, JOHN MANLY	LEACH, EDMUND LYONS
DAVIS, DICK LEON	LOUVIERE, CLARENCE JUSTIN, JR.
DeMANGE, EWING ANTOINE	LOWELL, HARVEY WILLIAM
DIEFFENDERFER, JAMES HERBERT	MASON, QUINTIN
DUNNING, CHARLES WILLIAM	McCREARY, KENNETH GRANT
ECKERT, JOHN ANDREW III	MILLER, LLOYD LYNN
EHRISMAN, RICHARD DEAN	MUELLER, DONALD EDWARD
EVANGELIST, NICHOLAS CHARLES	MUIR, WILLIAM MATTHEW
FALCON, LAWLESS CONSTANT	MUNROE, RICHARD POUNDSTONE
FANSLER, JACK WILLARD	MURPHY, DEAN GILROY
FISHER, WILLIAM PARR	PACE, SIDNEY BRANSFORD
FUSSELL, MILTON HOWARD III	RAY, STANLEY
GAILLARD, EDWARD McGRADY, JR.	SAPERSTEIN, SAMUEL
GARCIA, ALBERTO	TODD, GEORGE KENNETH
GINSBURG, DANIEL	WOODWORTH, HENRY DRESSES, JR.

Plaque Displayed at the Rifle Range Theater at Camp Lejeune.
From the Marine Corps Gazette, October 1990.

LETTER 79

Postmarked July 24, 1944
Sunday July 23
Dear Folks,

Only 9 more weeks to go! Ha! Hope I live thru it all. No joke, this is the worst thing I've gone thru yet, by far. Classes eleven hrs. per day, 6 days a week. There is absolutely no time, except Sundays, to relax for a minute. The rushing around is enough to make anyone a nervous wreck, without having sergeants and officers going around taking down names of anyone who even looks like he might do something wrong. Our consolation is that they also write it down if you do something good. Rifles must be spotless and khakis perfectly pressed, and hair neatly trimmed at all times. We have to get a haircut at least once a week. And the only time there is to get a haircut is during chow time. So we have to miss a meal to have our haircut. But it's all worth it if I can just get through. I won't be too much surprised if I flunk out. But I think I'll make it as I know darn well that I'm officer material. If I can make them realize that, I'll get through all right and I'd be a good officer in the corps. Pardon me if I seem to be bragging, but I feel like this is the line of work I was meant for.

Say, what's happened out Kansas way? I've written two other letters telling about this program and I've never received an answer. Personally, I'd like to know what you think of this anyway. I realize I've never written very much, but I've had pretty good excuses, too. Is somebody sick or something? I want to know if they are. Is Jerry still working for the state grain and getting rich? Tell him he'd better send me some of that money. I'll probably need it when it comes time to buy uniforms. They give us $250, but I doubt that'll take care of everything.

Can't think of a single thing more to write about, so I'd better close. Write soon!

Love
John

LETTER 80

Co. D 3rd Plat. Special OCS Schools Reg., T.C. Camp Lejeune, N.C.
Postmarked July 31
July 30, 1944 Sunday
Dear Folks,

Well, two weeks of O.C.S. have gone by and it hasn't gotten me down yet. Fifteen and a half hours per day makes an awful long day, but I guess that's soft compared to what I'll go through when I get overseas. And I don't think that it'll be so very long, either.

We have one more week of all these classes, then we move out to the Rifle Range to fire all the weapons, study tactics, etc. in the field and get more class work too. In two weeks, I have taken 175 pages of notes over 15 different subjects. The tests haven't been so tough either. In fact, I've gotten about 3 perfect papers so far. I got one in the test over the carbine (a weapon similar to the rifle, only smaller, that officers carry in combat) yesterday. Also in a test on offensive combat principles and in defensive combat. They were very easy and anyone should have gotten a hundred.

I had my biggest thrill since I've been in this outfit yesterday. Our platoon was measured for officer's uniforms. We tried on everything and it sure seemed great to have the best looking uniforms in the world. We get them cheaper here than they do at Quantico, and the $250 is going to cover everything we are required to buy with some left over for extra clothes. But after getting a taste of those uniforms, I've got to make it now. I just can't see myself wearing these sloppy enlisted man's clothes the rest of the war. I've been wearing the same 6 khaki shirts and 4 trousers for a year now, and I'm sick of them. The only new things I've had are socks, skivvies,[1] and shoes. I got two new pair of dress shoes the other day which I'm going to wear after I'm commissioned. They're really good shoes and look as good as the more expensive ones the officers buy. Of course, I'll get one pair of the others for more dressy occasions, but that's about all I'll wear them for. We'll also keep all our clothes we've been issued to wear when working, etc.

Received a change of address card from Don Jones the other day. His address is now in care of the postmaster New York, N.Y. So I guess he'll be seeing a little action in Europe. That's a little better than where the Marines invariably go. But after this war is over I expect to tell my grandchildren that I've been in Japan. Maybe the Philippines and China, too. Who knows! And I'll be seeing them as a line officer in charge of a rifle platoon instead of combat engineer. You don't know how thankful I am to have gotten out of that.

Must close now and go to dinner.
Love
John

---

[1] Skivvies = underwear. MV

l to r., Don Hurson, John Hyndman, Orel Irby. Lester "Bill" Hutchcroft, July 4, 1944.
SCOS, Camp Lejeune, NC. This photo appears in Dickenson's book.

John Hyndman at SCOS, Camp Lejeune, NC. 1944.

LETTER 81

Postmarked Aug. 7
6 August, 1944

Dear Folks,

Here I am again! Another week has gone by with seven to go. That's not very long compared with the 57 I've already put in, but it'll seem like a long time out here at the rifle range. We moved out last night, on our own time. The schedule's too full for them to do extra things like that on "company time". The barracks haven't been lived in for some time, so they are very filthy. We spent the whole morning on a field day, using bucket after bucket of water on the place. It is now spic and span almost livable—much better than the tents we expected to live in. That's the only consolation about the Range. There's absolutely nothing to do on what little liberty we do get. We are going to work very hard. Much harder then we have ever worked yet. But that's all right. It will make time go faster and the Marines should know by now that they can't dish out any thing I can't take. Anyway, after the next 7 weeks are over, I'll probably wish I still could have them ahead of me, because there's little rest and plenty of responsibility for a second lieutenant. That's OK though. Gold bars are a lot better than a single Pfc stripe. As far as I'm concerned, it would be terrible to be an enlisted man in combat. From my experience in our practical field work during the last three months, a private doesn't really know just what's going on out there. Instructions are passed down the line from the guys who know, and by the time a private hears it all he knows is that the enemy is somewhere and he's got to dig a hole quick like. That's why I want to be an officer, because I'm going to be over there much sooner than I ever imagined. As I expect you've already guessed that's the reason they're running this special O.C.S. We were told we'd be overseas by the first of the year. But now they say most of us will be over by the first of November. That's why I think maybe I'll get a furlough around October 1st. I sure hope so, it seems like a hundred years since I have been home.

Well, Hollar got another tough break. He got sick last week and is in the hospital. If you miss over 2 days around here, you are supposed to be dismissed from the program. Since they need officers so badly, he'll be sent to Quantico and get a commission anyway. But it'll take longer that way. Although he's liable to be better off in the long run.

It looks like I'm not going to vote this time—anyway for the primaries. We sent to our home states for absentee ballots and stuff. But mine got lost in the shuffle. Well, I must close and get some sleep.
Love
John

(My correct address is on the envelope) (It's Co. B instead of D).

On the Rifle Range at Camp Lejeune, NC. 1944.
Left: John Hyndman. Right: Frank Helms.

Lester "Bill" Hutchcroft during V-12 Training in Kalamazoo, Michigan.
Bill was a good friend of John's at SOCS and was commissioned with John. They served together until John was wounded on Iwo Jima. Hutchcroft took over the platoon when John was wounded and was killed in action three days later. Bill's death is a sad example of the casualty rate among second lieutenants leading a platoon in combat on Iwo.

LETTER 82

Postmarked Aug. 14, 1944
Empty envelope
Postmarked Aug. 22, 1944
Sunday afternoon

Dear Folks,

Four down and six to go. Time marches on. Maybe some day I'll actually finish my training and be somebody. This rifle range is really a hole. I've never seen so many mosquitoes in all my life as I have in one week out here. But outside of that it's not too bad. Practically all our work is outdoors and we haven't had any time to ourselves at all. They won't even give us a complete Sunday off. This morning we got up early and went in to the main base for physical examinations. I got thru with flying colors except that I need work done on my teeth. One doctor also told me it was a miracle they ever let me in the V-12 program with my knee operation. He said there was supposed to be a rule at that time to boot out everyone with bum knees. So I'm very fortunate to be here.

There is a strong rumor that we are supposed to go thru 3 week platoon leaders course after being commissioned. And we are supposed to get some time off before that starts. But I don't know whether it will be a regular furlough, or just a few days off. Boy I hope it's a furlough. A guy can't go on forever without a little time to go home and take things easy. But I'm beginning to think the Marine Corps doesn't think that way. I think I'll get a furlough before going overseas though. It's only logical.

Sounds like Mother and Dorothy are enjoying themselves at Tulsa. Wish I were there with them. I remember when I spent two weeks down there drawing pictures. Guess I just about drew myself out because I've never drawn since. Does Aunt Kitt paint as much as ever? Tell Jerry he'd better quit trying to make so much money and take things easy while he can. There's no percentage in working one's self to death when so young. He's got a whole lifetime to work and save money. Must close now and do some work so I can go to the show. And I'm going if it's the last thing I ever do.
Love
John

---

[1] Aunt Kitt is Mae Allyn Schupbach. She was a well-known artist and teacher in Tulsa, Oklahoma. She was John's grandmother's younger sister. John inherited a number of her oil and watercolor paintings. LH

LETTER 83

Postmarked Aug. 29
26 August, 1944
Dear Folks,

Six down and four to go! Another weekend has rolled around. They come pretty fast, but they can't come too fast for me. It will sure seem wonderful to have the pressure off after having it on you constantly for over a year. And it's really on in this place. I'm not kidding just a little bit. Everybody is nervous and tense and jumpy all the time. It's a wonder there hasn't been a million fights in the barracks at night. Guys yell at each other and gripe and complain all the time. No matter what you are doing around here, there is always someone watching with pad and pencil ready to mark you if you do a poor job. Of course, if you do something well, they may mark that too. But it's a lot easier to get a bad mark than a good one. They booted out quite a bunch of boys this week for various reasons—military bearing, attitude, grades, etc. One guy was kicked out for cheating on an exam. It was kind of sad last nite watching those guys pack their sea bags to leave. They felt bad and none of us knew what to say to them, so we just sat around and looked funny. Some of them aren't so bad off as they are going to Quantico later for another chance. But some are just going to join regular outfits and go overseas soon. It wouldn't be so bad if they'd just flunk out the guys who were no good, but it seems like they drop the good ones and leave the bad ones in. Of well, such is life!

Got a card from Hollar today. He's home on a fifteen day furlough and according to the card he was married to Barbara today. I suppose he'll be too settled down for the rest of us boys now.

Just got back from my usual Saturday nite show. It stunk, but now days I get just as excited over a show as I used to over a trip to Colorado or something. And to make matters worse, the regular personnel at the rifle range are holding a dance tonight which we aren't allowed to go to, so we stood outside and looked in. What a terrible feeling. They even had some civilians inside which makes officer candidates one notch lower than a civilian. I can hear the music now and it sure makes me homesick.. It has been many a month since I've been to a dance. I've probably forgotten how to dance by now.

I sure can't think of anything to write about anymore. Nothing ever happens. I just live from day to day thru the same old dull routine. But, as you told me about Notre Dame, "Even this will pass away." So I refuse to get too dejected about any thing.

Well, I'll close for now and hit the good old sack. I intend to spend most of tomorrow in the sack.

Love
John

LETTER 84

Postmarked Sept. 15, 1944
Thursday Sept. 14

Dear Folks,

Seeing as how I didn't write this week-end, I thought I'd better write you a line during study hour this morning. Last week all my old Notre Dame buddies came up to Lejeune from P. I.[1] So I took liberty, the first time since the first week in July, and went in to the main base to see them. It was sure good to see them all after 6 ½ months. None of them have changed a bit. This military life can't seem to change any of the boys in this program. They're still a bunch of college kids in uniform. Combat might change 'em, but right now everyone is still the same. Bull sessions at nite are exactly like they used to be. Although we've had a whale of a lot of training, you seldom hear anyone talk military in a bull session. The only difference is that now we talk about what we did last year or what comes after the war. Before the subject was what happened last nite or what is going to happen tomorrow. Now we know nothing happened yesterday and tomorrow will be the same thing over again. It's a very dull life to say the least. Right now everyone is a bit nervous and worried because the screening board meets in a couple of days. No matter how well they've done, everybody can think of a least one incident that might cause him to go up before the board. Rumors are going around that only a few will get the boot, but no one knows. We were told definitely, that half the outfit will not stay here to go through the originally planned 3 week platoon leaders course. But we don't know where that half will go and what they will do. It makes very little difference to me where I go just so I get a furlough before too long. They did tell us to cancel any plans for graduation guests because so many of us wouldn't have a chance to see them. So apparently the half that doesn't stay will ship out graduation day or the day after. If I should move then, I don't know how I'll carry my gear. Of course, I've got a sea bag to take all my enlisted man's clothing, blankets, etc. But now I've got a million field manuals and note books to take care of as well as my new uniforms. There are regular bags that officers can buy, but we have absolutely no opportunity to do so. There's nothing out here at the range and we don't get off early enough Saturday to buy anything back at main base. You all may have to send me a couple of borrowed suitcases till I can get something.

Thurs. afternoon

Here I am in another study hour. This has been about the easiest day in the program. And since there are only 2 more exams left the need for study isn't too urgent. Since we didn't take our rifles out in the field today, mine is clean, so I'll have time to study tonite. We have an exam on landing operations tomorrow and one on the rifle company next week. Tomorrow will be plenty rough though. All day we have field exercises on rifle company tactics with an exam following at 4:30. Then tomorrow nite we make a night attack, so I won't be getting much sleep. Saturday, we make landings all day and I'll be plenty wet and tired when liberty begins. To top all that off I'm planning to go to Wilmington with Hollar, Gunnar Hald and Ralph Abell[1] (boys just up from P. I.) so I'll probably go through the next week half asleep. Do you realize that there are only 10

---

[1] Don Hollar, Gunnar Hald, and Ralph Abell were three of the Cavaliers from Notre Dame. LH

training days left. They end on Tuesday the 26th. That's a couple more days than I expected, but still not bad. If I can I'll call you after getting the bars. If I don't call I'll wire and let you know I made it., I won't be sure of it until the gold shines on my shoulders.

Hollar, the married man, is going to Quantico Monday. He is plenty happy and is feeling fine. Well, I'd better close for now.
Love
John

John Hyndman at SCOS, Camp Lejeune, N.C.
The photo on the right was in Lester Hutchcroft's possesions that his sister had. She sent me a copy last year. Lester wrote Kansas on the top of the photo and John Hyndman below.

LETTER 85

Postmarked Sept. 21
Wednesday nite
Dear Folks,

I've got time for a short note, so I'd better write now. Went on liberty again last week, so didn't write. This week end I'll be out on a four day maneuver, so there'll be no chance to write then. Yesterday morn we went out with full packs on a field problem that lasted until this evening. It was plenty tough and to make it worse I had to carry a Browning Automatic Rifle which weighs 20 lbs. as compared to the 9 pounds of my regular rifle. Then when we got back we had to take an exam on the Rifle Company Tactics. It n wasn't hard though and it was our last test. It's sure a good feeling to have finished all those tests. And we sure had a lot of them. I got an 89 on the rifle platoon tactics exam which was the hardest test I've ever taken, except physics. That grade was among the highest ones, so I'm satisfied.

Remember that three week training I told you were going to have. Well, tonight they gave us blanks to fill out showing whether we wanted to go to Camp Pendleton, Calif. for that training or stay here. I marked Pendleton. First, because I might get traveling time and a leave on the way out there. Second because I want a change. Third, because the trip out there will be a rest between training periods even if I don't get a leave. And I'll come just as near getting a furlough after the training as I would here. Fourth, because I'd rather pick up my platoon out there than in Tent City here. Fifth, I'd rather have liberty in San Francisco and L. A. than in Wilmington, N.C. Sixth, I've always wanted to see California. As for reasons to stay here, I can't think of a one to save me.

Well, Bill Kessler is a lieutenant now. He received his commission the 12th of September. Hollar is in Quantico now, but is just getting started. He's got five months ahead of him there.

I received a letter from Daddy tonite in which he mentioned my discharge papers. Don't know for sure, but I don't believe we'll be discharged before receiving our commissions. For several months I believe the Marines have been just promoting the boys to 2nd lieutenant. I don't know for sure what the idea is except it is easier to break the boys who don't do the job right. But we've never been told anything definite, so that may be all wet.

So Jerry got knocked around a bit in football scrimmage? Well, he hasn't seen anything. I'll never forget the days when I first went out and Bill Benson and some of those boys worked on me. Many was the time I thought I was going to die and wished I could.

Monday, the screening board met and called in all the doubtfuls. They sort of dropped the axe a little harder than everyone expected. I don't know for sure how many, but they screened quite a few. Thank the Lord this kid got by that. Guess I'm almost a cinch now unless I get in trouble or something. Of course you never know for sure until the bars are on your shoulders. But I don't expect to lose out now.

It's time to close now. I'll write as soon as we come back from the 4 day maneuver.
Love
John

LETTER 86

Postmarked Sept. 29
Wednesday afternoon
Dear Folks,

Seeing as how I'll be a lieutenant in a few days, I thought I'd write my last letter as a PFC. It's really hard to believe that after fifteen months actual training and 2 ½ years enlistment that I'm finally getting what I started after. I'm forced to admit that eleven weeks ago, before O.C.S., I had almost completely forgotten and given up. Then I was just sort of marking time and expecting word any day that all men awaiting O.C.S. here at Lejeune would be sent to guard duty. But suddenly the big break came--about my first one in the Marine Corps. The reflection from the gold bars began to blind me again. Now all the training days have passed and we are spending the last few days in the middle of a long mess of red tape and the nights at picture shows. This few days of leisure are so nice that I almost wish there were a few more.

This morning we went in to the main base and picked up uniforms. Boy are they nice! and everything fits well, too. You can't tell me clothes don't make the man. The queerest gook here looks like a king.

Friday nite I have to be all packed and ready to shove off for California immediately after being commissioned Saturday. And best of all, if something doesn't happen, I'll stop by home for 2, 3 or possibly four days—depending on train connections.[1] Then I may get a regular leave after finishing Reserve Officer's Training School at Camp Pendleton. If I do get to stop by home on the way out, expect me anytime next week. We have until the 9th of October to get to California. The Marine Corps figures 5 days from coast to coast, so I should have four days according to that.

I received a letter from Daddy today and had one yesterday from Mother. I am glad to hear Jerry got to play in the game. That's a lot better than I did. If I remember right, I think I had been out about two years before getting in a first team game. Of course you can tell him that doesn't make him better than me. It's just that I had tougher competition! Ahem!

I just took time out to stencil my name—Lt. J.S. Hyndman-on a large trunk[2] that was issued to us today for $11.60. They had a stencil all made out with Lt. on the front, the first indication that my goal has been reached[2].

Well, it's time to go to chow, so will close for now.
Your loving son and future general!
John

P. S. Oh yes, I saw John Murray a couple of times. He's thinner than he used to be, I believe. Received a card from Hollar in Quantico. They're keeping him busy.

[1] Still thinking of leave, but it was not to be for almost another year. LH

[2] The footlocker was stored in California with John's winter uniforms when he went to Iwo. It was returned to him in 1948. Both our sons took it to college and it is in our storage room and in use after 60+ years. (Navy and Marines would call this trunk a "sea chest." or footlocker. LH

TELEGRAM

Dated Sept 30, 1944
Camp Lejeune

I HAVE BEEN AN OFFICER SINCE 10 O'CLOCK THIS MORNIING. I'LL SEND NEW ADDRESS. JOHN

Note: I can't explain the gap in letters from the time John left OCS and arrived at Camp Pendleton in California. The excerpt from Dickenson's book, *We Few* with his account of the trip agrees with John's account of the trip as he told it to me over the years.

Lois Hyndman

THE TRAIN TO PENDLETON

After graduation from OCS, half the graduating class of 372 were loaded aboard a train a little more than twenty four hours after their commissioning ceremony. They were bound for Camp Pendleton, California, the Marines' major West Coast base, where they would stage to the Pacific. The other half of the class stayed at Lejeune where they were given the Reserve Officer Course (ROC) for new second lieutenants and went to Pendleton later in smaller groups.

Their cross-country Treks were classic wartime troop-train movements, lasting five to seven days depending on how often they were sidetracked for higher priority traffic. The trip gave most of the new officers their first real look at the huge, enormously diverse nation they were putting their lives on the line for.

They awoke the last morning of their trek, with the train crawling down the coast south from Los Angeles in the dark fog typical of Southern California at that time of year. By 9 A. M., when they arrived at the small station at San Onofre at the north end of Camp Pendleton, the sun had burned the fog off. The sparkling blue Pacific was on their right, the Pendleton's hills were on their left. After a long delay, trucks arrived to take them to Camp San Onofre, a primitive facility informally known as "Tent Camp 2," Here they would undergo ROC.

```
WESTERN UNION

CLASS OF SERVICE                                    1201    SYMBOLS
This is a full-rate                                         DL = Day Letter
Telegram or Cable-                                          NL = Night Letter
gram unless its de-                                         LC = Deferred Cable
ferred character is in-                                     NLT = Cable Night Letter
dicated by a suitable                                       Ship Radiogram
symbol above or pre-
ceding the address.
      A. N. WILLIAMS    NEWCOMB CARLTON    J. C. WILLEVER
      PRESIDENT         CHAIRMAN OF THE BOARD  FIRST VICE-PRESIDENT

The filing time shown in the date line on telegrams and day letters is STANDARD TIME at point of origin. Time of receipt is STANDARD TIME at point of destination.

WZK26 NL PD=LOSANGELES CALIF OCT 7

MR AND MRS G B HYNDMAN=

    624 NORTH WASHINGTON

AM IN LOS ANGELES FOR THE WEEKEND NEW ADDRESS IS HQ INF
SCH BN TENT CAMP #2 TCCP OCEANSIDE CALIFORNIA LOVE=

    JOHN.

    826A


HQ INF SCH BN #2 TCCP.

    THE COMPANY WILL APPRECIATE SUGGESTIONS FROM ITS PATRONS CONCERNING ITS SERVICE
```

John's Telegram from LA Announcing his Arrival in California.

During the war, telegrams were usually used for important messages. Telephone lines were often unavailable and over loaded.

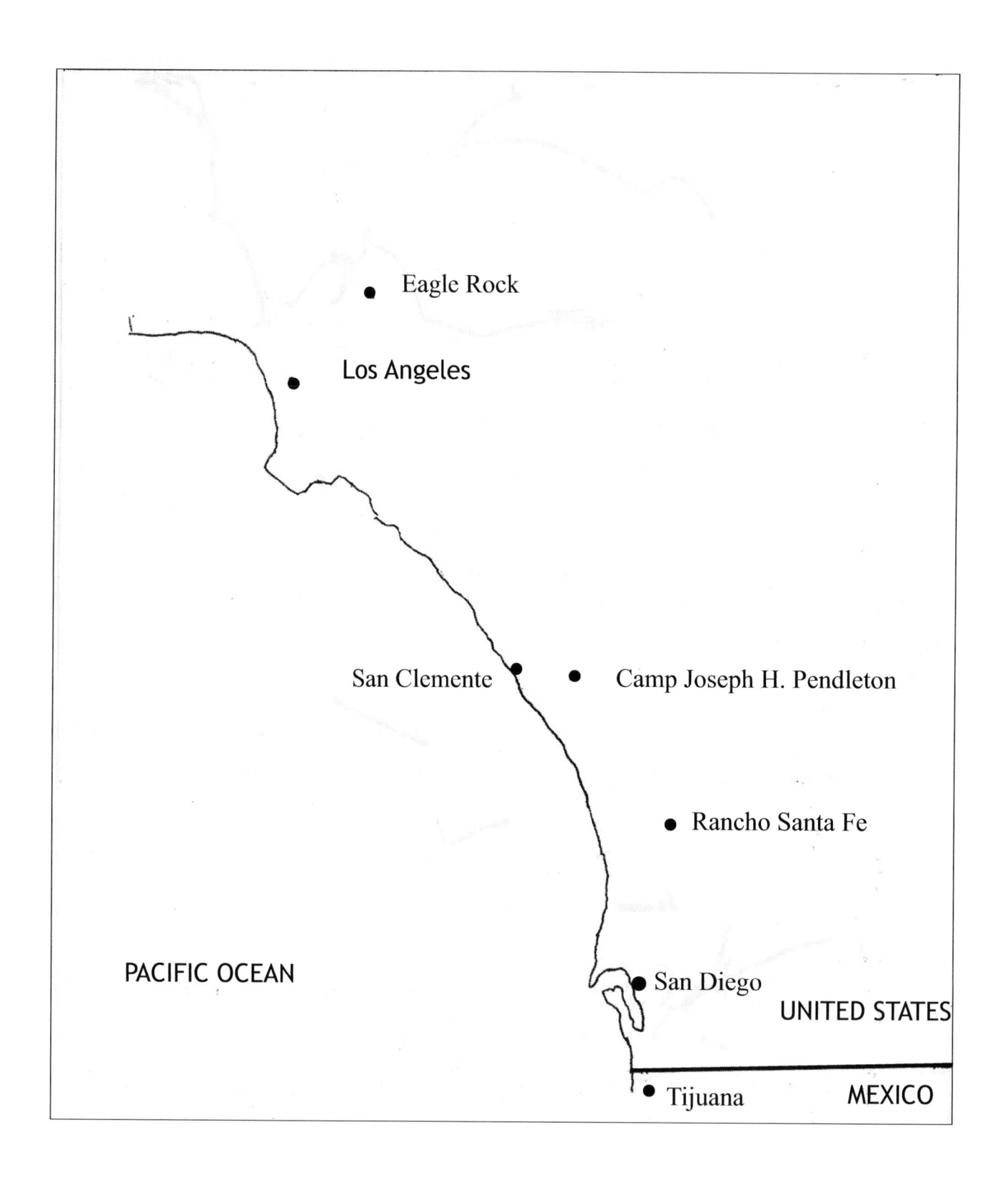

Eagle Rock was where Perce Allyn and his family lived when John and Madge Hyndman visited them in 1944.

Rancho Santa Fe was the convalescent hospital where John recuperated in 1945.

LETTER 87

Postmarked Oct. 21, 1944
Lt. John S. Hyndman U.S.M.C.R.
Special R.O.C. , Inf. Sch. Bn.
Tent Camp #2, T.C.C.P.
Oceanside, California
Friday Oct. 20

Dear Folks,

Just finished my second week in California and began my 22nd year of life.[1] I'm sure getting to be an old man, but I don't feel much different than I did when I joined the Marine Corps. It's been a long time since Hollar and I went to Kansas City to enlist. But it seems longer than that since I was home—almost a year now. Remember that I told you it might be a year before coming home again. Well, the year has gone by now—wonder if I'll be in Kansas in a week. If I'm going to get a leave it will be around the 28th which is a week from tomorrow.[2] While in Los Angeles tomorrow I'm going to get all the information on planes I can. Then if I get a leave, I'll have all kinds of priorities as it will be a pre-overseas leave. Also I'm going to meet Perce and spend the weekend with them. I'll have to spend the while time there as I am flat broke. As we changed bases immediately upon being commissioned, there has been a mix up on our pay. As usual the Marine Corps is fouled up.[3] If the Army is more fouled up than this outfit, I feel sorry for any one in the Army.

My gosh, I can't think of anything to say--------------------

Now I have something to talk about. The boys in my tent just brought me a box full of pogey bait and a fruit cake with a candle in it. Plenty nice, huh? I'm sure living with a swell bunch of boys!! One is Dunbar Jones[4] who is from Wichita. I played high school football against him. There is W.P. Johnson from Texas who is the son of Parks Johnson, the big shot on the Vox Pop Radio Program. There is "Candy" Johnson, also from Texas and H. L. Johnson[5] from Illinois. They said to tell you they'd be my parents for today.

Well, it's about bedtime (8 o'clock) so I'll close.
Love

John

[1]October 20 was John's birthday. LH
[2]No leave. LH
[3]All G.I.s thought the service was fouled up. Two famous acronyms from WWI Illustrate their belief that things would usually go wrong: SNAFU = Situation Normal All Fouled up and FUBAR= Fouled Up Beyond All Recognition. MV
[3]KIA on Iwo. LH
[5]All survived Iwo, but were wounded. LH

LETTER 88

Postmarked Nov. 24
In wrong envelope written about Oct. 24 or so
Wednesday evening

Dear Folks,

Well, here I am in Tent Camp #2 as usual, with 3 days left of R.O.C., wondering what I'll be doing about Monday. True to form, the corps is keeping us all in the dark as to what the future holds for us. Never let anyone plan for the future—that's their motto. As a result of all this "nothing" rumors are flying like mad about the area. Everything from going overseas Monday to furloughs starting then. The latter would be great, and if true that the boys who stayed at New River are now on a ten day leave. But whether or not that has any bearing on our future, I don't know. I don't think the General in charge of this camp knows either. After 16 months service in this outfit, I expect the worst. If I didn't take that attitude I'd lose my mind from disappointment!

I spent a very nice week-end with Uncle Perce[1] and family. The food was wonderful and they drove me all over Los Angeles (where they got the gas, I don't know).[2] Little Jerre is a pretty big boy now, but not as big as our Jerry. Johnny is still at Ann Arbor[3] and Jimmy[4] is in Newfoundland. Mother, they are crazy to have you out here. Do you think you could? It would be wonderful trip for you. In case I pick up a platoon here at Pendleton and am going to be here for awhile I think you should come out. By the first of the week, I'll know what is going to happen and will let you know. Then you can start making plans to come out.

Did you send that package with the cake in it? I've never gotten it if you did.

Well, things around here are about the same—no work, no warm water, and no lights. No more news either, so will close
Love
John

---

[1] John Perce Allyn (Uncle Perce was John's grandmother Bonnie's younger brother who lived in L. A.) John Allyn, his oldest son was John's age. He became an expert in the Japanese language and after the war was a professor at UCLA when he retired. His book, The 47 Ronin Story is the main source for studies of this era in Japanese history. Madge Hyndman tells more about the family as she stayed with them during her trip to California to see John before he went overseas. LH

[2] Gas rationing was tight and the Allyns must have used up valuable coupons to show John around California. MV

[3] Attending the University of Michigan. LH

[3] Jimmy Allyn was a cryptographer (coded and decoded messages) in the Army Air Corps at Gander, Newfoundland. Flying B-24s and B-17s to Europe was vital toward enabling the Air Corps to carry out bombing missions over Germany. Casualties to our bombers were heavy. Even unloaded and with extra gasoline aboard, these planes could not reach Europe from most Air Bases in the United States, The answer was to build a huge airport at Gander, Newfoundland from which our bombers could fly safely to Britain. LH and MV

The Forty-Seven Ronin Story
"...among men, the samurai."

Here at last is an entertaining account in English of the historical mass seppuku (disembowelment) of the forty-seven ronin, or masterless samurai, shortly after the turn of the 18th century in the feudal Tokugawa days of old Japan.

The forty-seven ronin were ordered to commit seppuku for their vindictive slaying of a corrupt court official whom they held ultimately responsible for bringing about the death of their master, Lord Asano. Asano was the brash young daimyo from the country whose ignorance of and unfamiliarity with the changing ways of the Edo court led not only to his own seppuku but also the complete ruin and dissemination of his family and clan.

Though based on an actual incident, many details have been lost to history, and, as a result, several versions of the forty-seven ronin story have been told. But the fact remains that they were given the death penalty for their deed, which, at the time, so embodied the Japanese's ideals of the noble samurai's devotion to his lord that the forty seven ronin were enshrined at Sengaku Temple beside their beloved master, Thus came to a dramatic close the final chapter of what has been acclaimed the most famous vendetta in the annals of Japan.

Sengaku-ji is only a short ride by bus or electric train from the bustling center of Tokyo but inside the temple grounds it is surprisingly easy to go back in spirit to feudal times. The scent of antiquity hangs over Sengaku-ji, as well as the odor of the incense burning before the graves in what has become a national shrine.

Review of the Forty Seven Ronin Story.

John Allyn is a film and music editor in the motion picture and television industries and also a writer/director of industrial films in the aerospace field.

Mr. Allyn attended the Army Specialized Training Program at Stanford University in 1944, majoring in the Japanese language, and also attended the Army Intensive Japanese Language School at the University of Michigan in 1945, receiving a B.A. degree from the latter. During the first four years of the U.S. occupation of Japan, he worked as Pictorial Censor of the Civil Censorship Detachment of G1, SCA, in Osaka and Tokyo. After his return to the United States he entered UCLA in Los Angeles from where he received his master's degree in Theater Arts in 1951.

He is currently working toward a Ph.D degree in Theater History at UCLA, specializing in the modern Japanese theater. In addition to The Forty-seven Ronin Story, Mr. Allyn is now preparing "The History of Modern Theater in Japan." He was born in Los Angeles where he now lives with his wife

LETTER 89

Postmarked Nov. 2
Lt. John S Hyndman
15-Q-1
Camp Pendleton, California
Wednesday Nov. 1

Dear Folks,

Just a short letter to let you know the kid is still alive and kicking. Haven't done a thing so far this week but get paid, buy a couple of flannel shirts, and get my haircut. The rest of my time has been spent in the lovely sack. As far as that goes, most of my time will be free, just be available, until shortly before shipping out. Myself and another guy have been appointed boat loading officers for our replacement draft. We'll have a lot to do later on, but right now there's practically nothing for us. I think the job will be a pretty good one. We will have to make a couple of trips to San Diego to contact the transport quartermaster and the Captain of our boat to make arrangements to load all the gear and men. The job will probably be a headache—glad it's only temporary so that I can pick up my platoon soon as I get overseas.

Well, I hope Mother will decide to come on out here. Tomorrow or the next day I'm going to send a money order for $50. That should help on the trip out here. Be sure and make reservations for a Pullman so you won't be a wreck when you get out here.

I guess Wellington has another pretty good football team. But no doubt they aren't as good as our old team in '39. That was the best in Wellington's history without any question. How much does Jerry weigh now? And what position does he play? Tell my little pin-up girl Dorothy hello and give her a big kiss for me.

Can't think of another word, so will sign off for now.
Love
John

LETTER 90

Postmarked Nov. 10, 1944
Friday, Nov. 10

Dear Daddy, Jerry and Dot,

I've got time for a short line before I start packing and getting some details taken care of so I can get in to see Mother early this afternoon. It looks as though Mother got out here in the nick of time because I think we'll be going aboard ship the first of the week. Yesterday we were ordered to have locker boxes and bedding rolls packed by Saturday morning for trucks to take to the boat. And that means it won't be long now.

Mother arrived in Los Angeles Wednesday afternoon and spent the night at Perce's. Then they brought her down to San Clemente yesterday where I had found a place for her to stay. San Clemente[1] is a small town near here—she's in the hotel there which is pretty nice. Spanish style as all the buildings in town are. I can get a bus in to see her each day.

She sure looks wonderful and she feels fine. It was lucky that she got a pullman on the train. That made the trip a pleasant one and it didn't wear her out. She thinks California is a wonderful place and will probably want you all to move out here.

Before leaving I'm going to get two months pay in advance and give $150 to Mother. The rest I'll take with me. Then I'll arrange to have $100 a month sent home because I won't need much over there. You can do with that what ever you want. It'll help pay back all the money you spent on me for so long.

Well, I've got to get to work now so I'll close.
Love
John

---

[1] Oceanside, CA is the town closest to Camp Pendleton. Most of the towns close to major military bases attracted all kinds of sleazy activities that preyed on the military. John made a good choice in taking his mother to San Clemente, not far away but at that time a quiet little California town. MV

MOTHER'S LETTER 1

Postmarked Nov. 10
From John's mother in CA
Thursday A.M. at Perce's

Dear family--

Well here I am in "Sunny California but it is surely snappy in the mornings and evenings. Had a wonderful trip, but were 5 hrs. late, getting in sometime between 3 or four instead of 10:30 A.M. I got a lower berth at 7 o'clock and was comfortable the whole time no headache at all, thank goodness and the bromide. There was a nice bunch of people on the train and everyone friendly so had a good time and the hours just flew. We sat in the lounge part of the time for a change. Glad I had my sandwiches for you had to wait hours to eat and didn't open at all at noon. Had dinner in the diner at 8 o'clock Tuesday night. Had porter fill my bottles once, but forgot to tell him no sugar, so couldn't drink it.

Perce met me and John had called twice before he got me at 8 o'clock last night. He seems so anxious to see me and has a room at the hotel for me. Perce and Inez are driving me down this afternoon. John gets off at 4 o'clock and we will meet him then. He thinks he will leave right away, so I am thankful you hurried me up.

Perce and Inez think John has a wonderful spirit and says he wants to re-enlist after the war.

We got no election news[1] at all-no papers on the train. Got off Wed. Morning and bought one. Too bad! But as Mr. Corbin says it won't make much difference.

Well, yesterday was my birthday and they gave me a lovely present and had a big cake and candles and a lovely dinner.

I keep looking at my watch, add two hours and wonder what you are doing. I'm awfully anxious to hear from home. I sent cards at Belem, I think-one to you all and one to Bonnie.

The towns are all connected so passed thru Pasadena and Hollywood but didn't even know which was which.

Dorothy girl- -I hope you are getting along fine- -write to me. I love you!

Jerry boy- -be good. Jerre Allyn is a big boy, but not as big as you. He is out for football and is exactly your age and 11th grade.

Daddy- -everything would be perfect if you were with me. It's going to be awfully hard to say good bye to John.

Goodbye till next time
All my love

---

[1] FDR ran for his fourth term in 1944. Election day is the first Tuesday in November. John's family were staunch Republicans, therefore the "too bad" remark. John's father was elected County Treasurer on the GOP ticket several times and was appointed Postmaster of Wellington, KS by Dwight Eisenhower. LH

MOTHER'S LETTER 2

Letter written by John's mother from California, Nov. 1944

Dearest Family,

Well first, I've seen John! And is he a swell looking officer! Here's how and when. I wrote you yesterday morning at Perce's. I received Daddy's and Dorothy's letters and I was so surprised to hear so soon and you can't imagine how pleased and happy I was to get them! My little girl is one in a million when it comes to keeping house!

About one o'clock, Perce came and picked up Inez and me and we started on our trip to see John and the Pacific. At Long Beach we rode around Rainbow Dr. and I had my first view of the sea. It was a beautiful sparkling blue. We followed it all the way to San Clemente where John had a room reserved for me at the San Clemente Hotel (where I am now). We met him about four o'clock. Perce and Inez left as soon as John came. I saw him coming two blocks down the street and could tell him that far away. We came up to our room and talked until 7 o'clock. Then we went out for dinner, took a long walk and then came back and John talked until 11:30 and then left. I will see him again this afternoon at four. He is supposed to pack up today. He thinks he will leave about Mon. or Tues., but of course doesn't know. One boat is completely loaded. He is with the 27th draft (just a bunch of men) but will sail with the 24th draft as it's a bigger boat with more staterooms for officers. He said that way he would have no duties and the trip would be a swell pleasure trip. He thinks he will stop at Pearl Harbor first.

He is drawing two months pay in advance, so he won't need any money from us. He is going to send home $100 a month and wants us to use some of it to put us on our feet again after all this expense. He will send home some of his good clothes. About all he will need in the tropics will be khakis.

He never cared about Doris after she came to see him. Ha! He hears from Mary Ann once in a while. She is in school in Ky., but he likes Joanne Wallace and also hears from her once in a while. Judy never wrote to him. He also never wrote her a card, as she said.

John smokes and has for some time but says he never drinks and won't. Here's hoping! I think he is a little heavy as he eats a lot and is not working. He will lose it in the tropics. His hair is getting nice and long and looks nice. He will probably cut it short when he sees action, as it is easier to take care of.

I slept till 9:30 a.m. and then dressed and went out to a 10 o'clock breakfast which will do me until evening. No picture show here except at night. John said Oceanside wasn't a fit place to take me and almost impossible to get a room there. I shopped a little after breakfast. Got some stationery, a newspaper and a couple if magazines. And now I'm back in my room writing, sitting in front of the register with Jimmy's bathrobe to keep me warm. Yesterday and day before were beautiful, but today is misty. The rainy season is about to begin.

John said why didn't they all come? I do wish you had Daddy. Will write more tomorrow. We hope to spend the weekend with Perce. Tell my Jerry boy to write.

2nd Lieutenant John Hyndman, California, 1944.

John Allyn   **John Hyndman**

MOTHER'S LETTER 3

Postmarked Nov.11
Addressed to Miss Dorothy Hyndman

Sat. Morn. 8:10 San Clemente

My dear ones,

I am just waiting to go to breakfast but will write a line first so I can mail it on the way.

John got over here in good time yesterday afternoon. After a visit we had a nice dinner-fried shrimp. Then we went to a movie about a mile away. We got picked up by the same old man coming and going.

John has really been homesick. Some of the boys went home A.W.O.L. They were so disappointed. Said they didn't care if they lost their commissions, but John does care and is very conscientious. I am so proud of him and his attitude.

They are loading part of his stuff today. I am so thankful I came. There are lots of mothers here and all are Marines. He thinks he will go to Pearl Harbor and then to Saipan. They needed officers hurried up this Special O.C.S. and that's the reason for the hurry.

We hope to go to L.A., but don't know till he gets here at noon today he hopes.

Will write more later.
Mother

John Hyndman, California 1944.

MOTHER'S LETTER 4

Postmarked Nov.13, 1944
Los Angeles, Calif.
Monday Morn at Perce's

Dearest Daddy, Jerry and Sukie,

Well, I told John goodbye last night and I managed to do it with a smile, but I thought he was going to break down. It was very hard. He thinks he will sail today or tomorrow, but there are often delays. Anyway most of their stuff is on board so it can't be long now. If possible he will call me today. He didn't want to go, I know, although he has a fine spirit.

I stayed at San Clemente Thurs. evening and all night—all day Friday—had early dinner together and went to a show then visited till nearly midnight. Then Saturday morning he came by for me in a car with five other Marine lieutenants (in Vox Pop's Johnson's car)—we rode the 60 miles into L.A. Perce met us at the Biltmore and we came out in time for lunch. In the afternoon we went down and had John's picture taken. He had his good uniform packed so had to have it taken in khaki and overseas cap. He looked fine, but I did want one in his good uniform and barracks hat. They only wear khaki in the tropics, so he is sending a lot of stuff home in his sea bag. Then Inez had a grand dinner and in the evening we all played games. On Sun. (yesterday) your letter arrived in good time and it was so much fun to have it. All the family went to church and John and I had one last good talk. He told me something very interesting. Said there were 43 boys in his platoon and that they are all given a sheet numbered from 1 to 45 and they were told to rate the boys in order as they thought they should rate. The sergeant and the captain were to do the same. He and Hollar were rated first or second by practically all the boys and then they were averaged in some way and he and Hollar were among the first five as judged by the boys, also the sergeant and also the captain. Wasn't that something? He said he didn't know the Captain even knew him. And we worried!!!

He hasn't changed much but seems older. He romped with kids all afternoon and played football. It was a nice bright day yesterday and we had a lovely drive in the afternoon. I am so glad I came. He was really homesick.

My room at the Hotel was $8 and I only ate two meals a day, so it wasn't so expensive. John took me to one dinner and I took him to a shrimp dinner. I was crazy about it. Inez certainly had a wonderful dinner yesterday.

I don't know when I'll be home, not too far distant a date I think, as I feel kind of homesick after saying good bye to John. Then it is so rainy and cold now too. It is a very poor time to visit Calif.

I surely like Jerre Allyn and he has taken quite a fancy to me. He is so much bigger than I expected and so crazy about football. He wants to drive back next summer in Jimmy's old Model A which is standing in the garage. He keeps wishing our Jerry were here.

Dorothy, Shirley looks just like Sally Garland and is quite plump. She is a regular tom boy and likes to play football, etc., but I like her very much. Little Vera Lee is awfully cute. How are you and Gene coming along? You didn't mention him or Robert either. Nice Nancy wanted you to stay with her. I would if I were you. How do you get along with Pattie? Hope everything's OK Daddy seems to think you are doing fine. How's math?

Must get this in the mail box. Hope I hear today from some of you. Also hope John calls. He gets to censor his own letters.

All my love

Mother

John, Mother, Perce Allyn, Inez Allyn. **John and His Mother**.

John Hyndman and Jerre Allyn.

MOTHER'S LETTER 5

Nov. 17
Thursday night

Dearest Daddy and all,

Well at last I got a letter today. Received one letter Thurs. after I left on Monday and the "Special" on Sunday—the only two letters I've had since leaving home and I've been gone 11 days! Only one letter from Dorothy and not a word from Jerry. In your letter today, you made no mention of ever having heard from me and I've written at least four!

John left Pendleton early Mon. morning and went to San Diego, so I don't suppose he got your letter that day. He called me at 9:30 that evening saying he had written you that day and that he would have to return to the boat that night. I've never heard any more, so I imagine they shipped out that night or on Tues. They gave them 2 months pay in advance, so he said $300 was all he needed. He said he was no gambler[1] that he lost $2 once and got scared and quit. Ha!

Inez and I went over to the City today and had lunch and went thru the big stores. I have two presents for Jerry—one from John and one from me. I have a nice present in my bag for Daddy from John, and I selected one present for Dorothy from John (he had me get it). Will go back to the City once more and finish. I never saw such crowds.

Well I have my reservations for Friday after Thanksgiving -- leave here at 7:30 Friday night and get home Sunday afternoon sometime. I had to take an upper, but they said I might get a lower later and to call everyday and see. So I will be seeing you next Sunday.

We are going to go everywhere this Sat. and Sun. while Perce is home. We're going to see a broadcast Tues. night, will eat Thanksgiving dinner out here and then come home. I'm a little homesick and have been since John left, but they keep begging me to stay and I suppose I'll be sorry if I don't, so I am staying. We're going to drive over to see Dorothy Owens Myers on our way somewhere. I'm also going to see some more of the sea down on the beach. I was so crazy to see the ocean but now it makes me cry.

Well, I'm surely surprised about Frank Garner. Glad Mabel will be there to help you entertain him.

I hope Dorothy doesn't miss her Mother too much. I'll soon be home. I wish I knew what she would like for me to bring her. Is she getting along all right?

Well please write.

Love,
Mother

---

[1] Gambling aboard troop ships was common among officers and enlisted men who had little to do and too much time. Most transports had card sharks and crap shooters eager to take advantage of the naive young GI. MV

MOTHER'S LETTER 6

Postmarked Nov. 20
Addressed to Jerry Hyndman

Sunday night

Dear Daddy, Jerry and Dorothy,

Well the letters have started coming now and my visit will soon be over. Got up yesterday morning with my first headache. Perce laid off to take me around, so I took a lot of pills and started out. First we went downtown and changed my Pullman ticket. Got a lower for Thanksgiving evening, so leave here the 23rd at 7:15 and due home Saturday afternoon at 2:45 -- hope it isn't late. This will give me all day Sunday at home before starting my teaching on Monday. Then we went out through Beverly Hills and saw all the beautiful homes. Stopped at a market and ate a wonderful meal out in the open. Then we went on down to Santa Monica Beach and really got a swell view of the ocean and watched breakers come in and heard the boom of the surf. Saw the fishing boats and the gulls. By that time I was sicker then a dog so we started home and I had to take time out at a filling station to lose my good dinner. Came home and went to bed - -missed a trip to the planetarium that eve. Today -- Sunday -- a wonderful trip to Palm Springs was planned but spent the whole day in bed. Just got to feeling better at supper time. We went to a show Fri. Eve and I sat too close and it hurt my eyes and that's what gave me a headache. I need new glasses.

Have tickets for Orson Welles broadcast Tues. night at 6:30 here -- 8:30 at home. Better listen at same time and know I am there. Columbia B. Co.

Get John's pictures Wednesday -- and leave for home Thurs. Am so thankful I have a reservation.

Well John will soon have been gone a week. He probably left Tuesday. When he called me Mon. night he gave me his address. He also said he had written home so he surely gave it to you. But in case not here it is. I have written twice.

Lt. John S. Hyndman U.S.M.C.R.
27th Replacement Draft
F.M.F. Care Fleet P. O.
San Francisco, California

He is on a boat with the 24th Replacement, so I don't know when he will be with his own outfit or get his mail, but that is what he gave over the phone that last night.

I enjoyed Jerry's letter a lot and read it to all the folks, Jerre Allyn may come to visit us some time this summer.

I'm awfully surprised my little girl has only written to me once, but I know she has been awfully busy. I'll try to make it up to her when I get home, give her a good rest. I hope Gene wasn't mean to her.

These kids around here surely work like troopers, and don't get to do much going either. We played Michigan and Fan tan in the evening. They are the best kids I ever saw and don't hardly fuss at all. They surely move when Perce speaks, but he is kind as can be.

Must go to bed and will soon be seeing you. We'll fix up a box for John the minute I get home. Can send air mail for 6 cents a half ounce to boys over seas.

Much love and kisses
Mother

John in Uncle Perce's Back Yard. Eagle Rock, California, November 1944.

[1]Michigan and Fan tan are card games. Seventy years ago, families entertained themselves playing card games and board games like parchesi and monopoly. MV

MOTHER'S LETTER 7

Postmarked Nov. 21
Tuesday morning

Dearest Family,

I think you can almost be glad you weren't here Sun. night to say good bye to John. It was so very hard. Inez was sick in bed all day yesterday and still is, however, she is better this a.m., so stayed home all day and I listened for a call from John which he had promised if possible. By 9 o'clock I had given up hearing but at 9:30 the phone rang and it was John. He was at San Diego and had been all day. He was on the boat and only got off to call and had to return right away. He gave me his address said he had written home also. Said he felt fine and Helms was with him and W.P. Johnson I believe. I'm wondering if he's gone this a.m.

Perce is coming home at noon and take me over to the station to see about a berth. It should have been done sooner but is so far and I couldn't say too much about going until they were ready to take me. It has rained so much, but is halfway clear today—also quite chilly. Then we will also get proofs of John's pictures. Had to have them taken here in Eagle Rock, don't know how good the man is, but it will be better than nothing. Took a roll of film Sun.—hope they are good.

Hope I hear today from some of you—didn't yesterday. See you before long.

All my love
Mother

Bill Busch, Gene Steinke, and John Hyndman. San Diego, California. Late 1944
Bill and Gene were John's fraternity brothers at Wichita University. Bill was at Notre Dame, Boot Camp, and OCS with John.

THE ALLYNS

The Allyn's lived in Eagle Rock, a suburb of Los Angeles. (John) Perce Allyn was an uncle of John's mother. He was a much younger brother of John's grandmother, and was almost the same age as John's mother even though he was her uncle. Inez Allyn was Perce's wife. Perce's first wife died leaving him with three boys, John, Jerre, and Jimmy. He married Inez who was a widow with two girls and a boy. John Allyn was John Hyndman's age. Jerre was six years younger and Jimmy was 2 years younger.

BILL BUSCH

Bill Busch was in John's OCS class. He returned to college after the war and earned an LLD. He also served in the Korean recall of Marine Reserve Officers with Marine Air as an intelligence officer but once it was learned of his Law degree, he spent the majority of his time on legal service. He ended his tour as a major. He became president of Medico Life Insurance Co. in Omaha, Nebraska. Deceased 2005.

PART III. OVERSEAS DUTY

TERRITORY OF HAWAII

VOYAGE TO COMBAT

IWO JIMA

ARMY HOSPITAL, GUAM & NAVY HOSPITAL, AIEA HEIGHTS, OAHU

Editors Note: The Fifth Division was formed at Camp Pendleton in July of 1944. Like all combat divisions formed after the war began, its complement held a majority of Marines just out of boot camp or from OCS. Mixed in with the untested men was a sprinkling of officers and non-coms who had battle experience. In the Marine Corps, Regiments are referred to by their number. The First Marines comprise the First Regiment. Sometimes different regiments would be assigned to a division. Those unfamiliar with the Marine Corps frequently confuse the Fifth Marines (a regiment) with the Fifth Division. Three new regiments, the 26th, 27th, and 28th were assembled at Pendleton to form the new Fifth Division. In addition to the three infantry regiments, a division included a number of supporting units.

The Fifth Division sailed from San Diego in September 1944 bound for Hilo, Hawaii. From September until January, the Division trained at Camp Tarawa on the Parker Ranch near Kamuela,[1] Hawaii. The land for Camp Tarawa was donated by the Parker family. The Second Marine Division built the camp after they returned from the bloody Tarawa Operation in November 1943. After training for several months in Hawaii, the Second Division sailed in June of 1944 for Saipan to begin the operation that took the Marianas.

Camp Tarawa was built just south of the Kohala Mountains on the edge of the grassy plain that stretched east to the Pacific. To the south and west, in the rain shadow of Mauna Kea, was an arid land where it seldom rained. The 28th regiment used a sand cone to practice taking Mount Suribachi.

Second Lieutenant John Hyndman was assigned to the 27th Replacement Draft. The Replacement Draft left the states later than the Fifth Division and was based at Hilo Naval Air Station, Hawaii about 60 miles from Camp Tarawa by way of the saddle road that crossed the Big Island between the huge volcanoes Mauna Kea and Mauna Loa. John's letters do not mention whether he ever visited Camp Tarawa.

[1]Kamuela is no longer used. Today to locate the site of amp Tarawa on a map of the Big Island, you have to look for the town of Waimea. MV

LETTER 91[1]

Postmarked
27th Replacement Draft FMF
c/o Fleet Post Office[2]
San Francisco, Calif.
Nov. 13, 1944

Dear Folks,

No doubt it will be a long time before you get this letter. But when you do there will be a lot at once. Well, it finally happened and almost too soon. I left Mother in Los Angeles and promised to call the next day, but they didn't give me a chance. Also I got a check for two months pay in advance which I didn't have time to cash and send part home. So I am now carrying the darn thing in my billfold--useless. Hope there is some place to cash it later on. I didn't get a chance to make arrangements to have money sent home each month either. That too, will have to be taken care of later.

It's a good thing Mother came when she did or she would have missed me. But the three days we had together were wonderful. She looked so well and seemed to feel fine. Perce and Inez were very nice to us, too.

Well, I don't believe the voyage will be so bad. Naturally things are crowded, but the bunks are comfortable and the food is good in the officer's mess. Hope it stays that way. That can mean the difference between a pleasant trip and a hectic one. There is a nice recreation room for officers in which there are cokes to drink, a radio, and tables to write letters on. There is also a table in the stateroom, but other are (censored).[3] Six triple deck bunks—I'm the top one. Right up against the ceiling.

Nothing more to tell now, but will write again tomorrow.

Love
Lt. John S. Hyndman

---

[1] John's first letter after he learned he was shipping out. Hutchcroft's letter says they sailed on 14 November. Because he was unsure when his family would get the letter, John most probably wrote aboard the *USS Callan* but before they sailed. MV

[2] All GIs overseas had their mail addressed to either a Fleet Post Office (for sailors and marines) or an APO for soldiers. MV

[3] Once aboard ship, letters had to be censored. This was one of the duties of officers, who censored the mail of their unit. If officers had their mail censored, it was by other officers in their unit. MV

LETTER 92

Postmarked Nov. 19, 1944
Lt. John S. Hyndman USMCR
27th replacement Draft, FMF
c/o F.P.O.
San Francisco, Calif.

Nov. 15, 1944
Dear Folks,

It's a nice day out, the sea is calm and I'm not seasick, yet. It's really surprising because we did quite a bit of rolling around yesterday. I started to get a little sick while on watch yesterday, but when I was relieved to go eat dinner the feeling went away. The best thing to do is eat every meal and spend the rest of the time in the sack, which I do. I sleep fine during the night, and in the morning, but for some reason I roll and toss all afternoon long. After all the sleep I've missed in the last 22 years, it looks like I could sleep thru 24 hrs. a day instead of only 18.

No doubt right now Mother is having a fine time in Los Angeles and thereabouts. Hope she doesn't decide to stay and leave the rest of the family stranded in Kansas. Wish I could be stranded there myself. Some day I'll come back to Wellington and never leave the place again.

I'm anxious to know how the pictures I had taken in Eagle Rock turned out. Also the snapshots. Please send them as soon as possible.

The food isn't quite as good as the first meal indicated, but it's still much better than I expected. It's nothing like I've heard it is sometimes although the enlisted men's chow may not be so good—I don't know.[1]

If you hear anything from Don Jones, let me know. Also get his address and send it to me as I've lost it again. Every time I move something gets lost it seems.

I haven't any airmail stamps now, but as soon as I can get ahold of some I'll start sending all my mail by air.

That's all for now, but I'll write again tomorrow.

---

[1] Aboard troopships, enlisted men usually ate only two times a day. Galleys and mess halls simply could not serve three a day to several thousand troops. MV

LETTER 93

Thurs. Nov. 16

Dear Folks,

Just a short note to let you know everything is going fine. Things are a little rough today and I've been on the verge of sea sickness all afternoon. Almost, but not quite. As long as I keep a full stomach and spend most of the time in the sack everything will be all right.

I am reading the book "For Whom the Bell Tolls", which is a very good book. Also I learned a new card game called "Casino." Daddy probably knows it. I trimmed Hutchcroft while he was teaching me this afternoon and again tonight. I beat him in double solitaire, too—guess I'm a natural card shark. Tomorrow the officer in charge will probably break open our sealed orders then we should know where we are going and what we will do.

Will write again tomorrow, but there sure isn't anything to write about.

Love

John

LETTER 94

Dated Saturday Nov. 18

Dear Folks,

Well, here it is Saturday nite—liberty nite—and I'm still out in the middle of the ocean someplace. It has been plenty rough the last couple of days. Yesterday it was so bad I couldn't sit up at the table long enough to write you without getting sick, So I just stayed in the sack. Only got out of it long enough to eat and stand a four hour watch down below. There are sure a lot of sick boys on this ship—and no wonder with this weather. It's been clear, but very windy and consequently the Pacific is plenty rough.

A whole paragraph censored out.[1]

Outside of that everything is OK except when the rolling ship almost tosses me out of bed at nite.

Can't think of another word, so will close again.

Love
John

---

[1] I remember John saying they sailed along the coast of California to San Francisco and that this was the roughest part of the trip. I think that this must have been what was censored out. The *Callan's* records show they sailed November 16 from San Francisco. The seas outward bound from San Francisco in November would usually be much rougher than the course from San Diego to Hawaii. LH and MV

From the biography of the *USS General R. E. Callan*, AP139. MV

She embarked over 2,600 fighting men at San Diego and after touching San Francisco 13 November, got underway from that port three days later for Kahului (Maui) Harbor, Hawaii, where she debarked the troops and returned to San Francisco 2 December with over 250 homeward-bound veterans.

LETTER 95

Postmarked November 24
27th Replacement Draft
c/o FPO
San Francisco, Calif.

Nov. 22

Dear Folks,

Just another short line to let you know we're still afloat. But not for very much longer. I think we'll be going ashore pretty soon now. The sooner the better because I'm getting a little tired of this tub. The weather has been good lately and it's been pretty smooth sailing.

Yesterday I wrote a letter to the Allyn family, thanking them for everything. I've been wondering how long you stayed with them. Or did you get homesick and start home? Don't forget to send me some of those snapshots we took that last Sunday and one of the good pictures. Be sure and include photos of all the folks and not just those of me.

I don't think it will be very long before you start getting my mail as it will be mailed soon. Most of it is via air mail.

Love
John

LETTER 96

Postmarked November 24
27th Replacement Draft
C/O FPO
San Francisco, Calif.
Nov. 24, 1944

Dear Folks.

Well, after a long boat ride, I'm finally on good old solid earth again.[1] It sure feels good to step on the ground again--even though it was on the wrong side of the ocean. The island we are on now is very beautiful. Everything is green as it rains almost every night.

(Several sentences censored out.)

But we will only be here a few days as the division we'll join is on another island in this same group. And they say it is a more beautiful place than this, which is saying a lot. I know it's a bigger place.

Living conditions are better here than they were in tent camp back at Pendleton. At least, we have floors on the tents. And electric lights. Would you like lots of short letters or a few long ones? None of which can tell very much,

Love
John

Editor's Note: John did not write letters that explained his landing on Maui, his time on Maui, or much about his duties. His friend Lester Hutchcroft was with John on the ship and in Hawaii and he details the trip in his letter from Iwo. After the operation began, censorship was relaxed and the Marines could write home about where they had been and about how they had traveled to Iwo. The first half of Hutchcroft's letter tells about his (and John's) time in Hawaii, first on Maui and then on the Big Island, Hawaii. Part I of his letter follows:

---

[1] Landed on Maui, at Kahului. The Fourth Marine Division was training on that island. The Fourth and Fifth Marine Divisions practiced landings on Maui on the beaches of Ma'alaea Bay on the leeward side of the island. MV

[2] The Fifth Division had sailed from San Diego in September 1944 and was training at Camp Tarawa. MV

LESTER HUTCHCROFT'S LETTER, PART I

Dear Folks,

I hope this letter will be a little better than the note I sent you the other day. I received word that we could send a letter out about five minutes before the letters were taken up. I was in a hurry to get the letter off and a little excited, I guess, so the result was that so called letter you have probably received by now.

Right now there is a lull in our work so I will attempt to give you a travel log and information about yours truly. I may have to mail this letter in several envelopes so to get any sense from it be sure to read the first-first.

I will start with the last few days in Calif. We received word we were going over and didn't know how soon. Finally word came through that 49 of us were to be transported with the 24th replacement Draft. We were all Lt.'s without our troops. We boarded ship-the *U.S.S. Callan*[1] Nov. 14 and sailed for the Hawaiian Islands. We landed Thanksgiving Day at Kahaula, Maui. Maui is one of the smaller islands of the H. Gp. The 24th Replacement Draft we were with joined the fourth division stationed at Maui. We were to go on to the island of Hawaii to join the fifth division but there was no transportation at that time so we unloaded at Maui and were billeted with the fourth division. That is why we were on the wrong island. We were there for twelve days before getting transportation.

The island of Maui is the most beautiful island of the H. Gp. The people are very friendly and very much American in their ways. Their main crops are pineapple and sugar cane which creates a very picturesque scene. There are two small mountains on the island which also present beauty.

For the twelve days we were there our duties consisted of sleeping late each morning, possibly playing a little out door basketball, eating and then taking liberty starting in the afternoon and ending each night at ten o'clock. There is a ten o'clock curfew on all the islands. As usual the Marine camp was located back in the hills so we had to hitchhike when ever we went any place. I would name the different towns and placed we went to except my spelling handicaps me.

Each night of the twelve we were on Maui, Bill Johnson and myself would go to town for supper and order the largest steak on the menu. We would start out with a banana split, then our steak, and then a banana split again. Always leave stuffed to the gills. Each night we would think it to be our last one because we expected to leave each day.

Finally transportation was provided for us on board a Merchant Marine ship. We had to sleep out in the open on the deck but it was way of getting to our destination.

We arrived then in Hilo, Hawaii the first day part of Dec. Instead of joining the 5th division at their camp in Hawaii, we were stationed at the Naval Air Station which is just outside of Hilo. Here we received our troops and were placed into what is known as the 6th shore party co. I may be snowing you a little so will try to explain as I go along.

---

[1] The *USS General R. E. Callan*, AP-139 was a fleet transport. Her official biography gives her dimensions as dp. 17,250, l. 522' 10." b. 71" 6," s. 16.5 k. cpl. 449; a, 4 5." (Displacement 17, 250 tons, length 522 feet, 10 inches, beam 71 feet. 6 inches, speed 16.5 knots, complement 449, armament, 4 5 inch 38s.) MV

The duties of a shore party co. include loading and unloading ships as they pull up on the shore or beach. It is our business to get supplies ashore and up to the front lines for the assault troops. It is not a job that receives a lot of glory but it is one of the most important jobs of any operation. If it were not for the various shore parties ammunition, food, fuel, water, medical supplies, all other supplies that are so essential in winning battles, would be unable to be landed.

(I will have to find some ink before continuing this letter).

Guess I am still at Hilo aren't I?

Our time at Hilo--the Naval Air Station-was spent in training for our work with the shore party co. Actually it consists mostly of a lot of hard work. One of those jobs that requires little brain work and a lot of muscle.

At the same time we are with the "S.P. CO." we are subject to being used to replace men in the 28th Marine Regiment of the 5th Marine Division. You have probably heard or read about the 28th Marines and the 5th Div. in this operation.

A little explanation may be helpful here also. There are three Regiments in each Div. The 5th Div. is made up by the 27th Marines, the 26th Marines and the 28th Marines, each being a Regiment, but referred to as just the Marines.

We spent quite a little time at Hilo and had a pretty good time. Hilo is the second largest city of the H.Gp. Hilo is pronounced-"he'low". Honolulu is the largest city of the group.

While at Hilo we took a trip up into the mountains and saw a volcano and seven different craters. The steam comes out of large cracks in the ground and is scalding hot.[2]

(The second part of Hutchcroft's letter is reproduced in the Iwo Section.)

---

[1]Camp Tarawa. The camp was named for the bloody battle of Tarawa. The camp was built on land donated by the Parker Ranch, which occupied much of the northern area of the Big Island. When the 2nd Division left for the invasion of Saipan in June 1944. the camp was unoccupied until the 5th Division arrived in September 1944 to begin training for the invasion of Iwo Jima. Camp Tarawa is about sixty miles from Hilo by the Saddle Road that runs over the ridge between the giant volcanos, Mauna Loa and Mauna Kea .MV

[2]They visited what now is Volcanos National Park. The craters around Kiluea were quiescent at this time. Mauna Loa erupted during the early part of the war and lava threatened the city of Hilo. John mentions this trip in letter 100. MV

LETTER 97

Received Dec. 7, 1944
No postmark
27th Replacement Draft, FM
c/o F.P.O. San Francisco, Calif.
Nov. 27, 1944---Monday

Dear Folks,

After so long a time I finally got my check for $500 cashed. I got it on the morning we shipped out and didn't get a chance to cash it. So I carried it in my billfold all the way across. I am sending you a money order for $350. The rest I will keep because there may be a delay before I get any pay over here. Although there really isn't much to spend money on.

It's been raining again around here. They claim it rains every night here at camp and I'm ready to believe it. Guess that's because it is so high.

I met a guy from our outfit the other day from Louisville, Kentucky who met Mary Ann while he was home one time. I gave him her address so that his wife can look her up.

Have Don's folks heard anything more from him? I hope he's all right. Don't forget to send me his address as I lost it moving.

Love
John

LETTER 98

Postmarked Dec. 2, 1944
Received Dec. 7 '44

Dec. 1, 1944

Dear Folks,

How's everything on the home front? Just as good as ever I suppose. Football season is over, so I suppose Jerry doesn't have anything to do now. Or is he out for basketball? Our mail hasn't caught up with us yet, but it should pretty soon now. I'm expecting a huge stack, too. Enough to spend half a day reading. You should have received some of my mail now, because it doesn't take the air mail letters long to get to the states. I got off the money orders the other day, air mail and registered, so it shouldn't be long before you get them.

I went to another dance last night and had a pretty good time. The music wasn't bad at all. What a life I'm leading right now! Sleep all morning and go on liberty in the afternoon. When I do start to work it will probably kill me.

We eat pretty well around here   Much better than I expected. We don't have to pay for it like we did in the states, either.

Bill Kessler finished R.O.C. in Quantico the 27th, and is probably home now on furlough. The lucky dog. Maybe he'll be down and look you folks up. Hollar still has a couple of weeks before getting his commission, then there'll still be 10 weeks of R.O.C. so he's got a long road ahead yet. But I imagine he's plenty satisfied with everything.

Has Bill Romig ever been home yet? He's sure been gone a long time now!. I must close now and get some sleep.

Love
John

LETTER 99[1]

Postmarked Dec. 8, 1944
Dec. 7, 1944

Dear Folks,

Remember what happened three years ago today? That's what caused me to be here now instead of at home where I should be. The day the Japs attacked Pearl Harbor I was at the fraternity house at W.U. I remember all we boys sat around on the floor and listened to the radio. We all expected to be fighting in a few weeks. It has been three years now and I haven't seen any action yet. But it won't be very long now, I can tell you for sure. Don't know where it will be for sure—but it will be a big operation, I think—very big.

I finally left the island I was on and joined our regular draft, which was on an island nearby. The draft is being kept intact as the division we joined is full. We will remain replacements until there are casualties and we are needed. Right now our draft is attached to an engineer battalion and we are to work with them in bringing all supplies from the boats to the beach and on to the supply dumps. It is a nasty job which replacements usually draw at the beginning of an operation. I, with another officer as my executive officer am in charge of 56 men which make up the supply dump squad. There are seven eight man squads. That makes a squad for each of the six dumps with a floating squad. The dumps are: ammunition dump, medical supplies. miscellaneous, water rations and fuel. Other outfits will bring the gear up to the dump and my men will unload it and put it in the dump. Myself and the other officers will have to supervise their work on all the dumps, so you can imagine (how) busy we'll be. It is a rotten job to draw and I don't like it a bit, but I guess I can't expect any thing else on a late replacement. If we had come out a month sooner we would have been dissolved into the division, but now I'll have to wait until the operation starts and take over troops I haven't trained with. Then after that operation, I'll have my own men to work for the next one.

I just finished censoring my men's mail. What a chore that is!! So many of them write the most terrible messes. It can't be read really at all. Some of then try to be so clever in telling where they are, but I cut it out without blinking an eye. It's amazing how terribly some people spell.

Today I received my first letter. It was from Jerry and Dorothy, written Nov. 29. It was a wonderful feeling after waiting a month.

Love
John

---

[1] From Hilo, Hawaii. LH

LETTER 100

Postmarked Dec. 12
Received Dec. 17

Dec. 10, 1944
Dear Folks,

Well, I've had about eight letters from you all now, so my morale is up again. I'm glad to know everything is fine at home and that Mother enjoyed herself in California after I left. The last letter I had from her was written the day she left for home. And I got one today from Daddy telling of Don Jones' feat. I always felt he'd do a good job. It seems his type always does.

By the way, the letter Mother sent enclosing the proofs of my picture had no proofs in it. Either she forgot to put them in or someone took them out. I'm sure the last happened because the letter was unsealed when it got to me. So I guess you'll have to send me one of the real pictures. You really shouldn't do that though because we might pull out of here. Then it might never catch up with me.

Things around here are going fine so far. I had an interesting experience today. An officer who has been here awhile got a truck and took some of us on a sight seeing tour up in the mountains. I saw a very famous crater[1] which I studied in first year Geology. We took sandwiches and cokes along and spent the whole day. I began to feel like a tourist instead of a marine over here on business.

Yesterday I inspected my men's rifles and had to chuckle to myself as they stood there at attention and scared like I used to be. They are a bunch of good boys though and I'll get along with them fine. I was censoring their mail tonight and one of them told his mother, quote, "We sure have two good lieutenants, and they'll treat us nice if we treat them nice." I had to laugh because I figure he thought one of us might censor it, so he said it all for our benefit.

Well, I'd better close and clean my carbine before bedtime. I'm pretty tired tonight because I had to take out a working party until midnight last nite.

Love
John

---

[1] Kiluea Crater on the slopes of Mauna Loa is one of the largest active craters in the world. MV.

LETTER 101

Postmarked Dec. 16
Received Dec. 19

December 15, 1944
Dear Folks,

Just a line to let you know everything is going fine with me. However I'm very busy for a change. But can't complain as I had such a long vacation. When I'm not out with the engineers learning the details of my work in the next operation, I'm here lecturing (got that) to my boys on what I've learned. Also I drill them, hold rifle inspections, give calisthenics, supervise working parties, listen to personal troubles, give advice, and censor mail at nite. The latter is a never ending job and is getting more boring every day. So if you ever hear the song, "2nd lieutenants will win the war", you can believe it's true. But I enjoy it, although I would like to be working with my own rifle platoon. I'll probably never see these boys again after the first few days of the operation.

I received another letter from you all today. They've been coming pretty regular now. I'm wondering if much of my mail is getting through. Especially the money order for $350. It would be terrible if you didn't get that. The letter was registered and all that. So you no doubt have it by now.

The two proofs of the pictures I had taken in Eagle Rock came today. They are better than I expected. You had both of them made, didn't you? I also received the snapshots taken at Perce's. I wrote then a letter, but they've never answered. Also I wrote Bonnie and Aunt Dott, but I don't know Mabel's address. Have my Christmas cards arrived yet?

My old flame, Joanne Wallace, has written several times since I've been over. The fact that I'm across (and probably because I'm a Lt.) seems to have made her sit up and take notice. She is now going to the U. of Maryland which is a pretty nice school.

I'm sorry to hear Aunt Mabel has diabetes, but glad to hear Aunt Dott's little Bobby is better. What's this about some girl Aunt Dott knows writing me. I've never heard from her yet.

Must close now and sleep while I can

Love
John

LETTER 102

Postmarked Dec. 18, 1944
Dec. 17, 1944

Dear Folks,

Well, how is everything at home by now? I suppose you are busy getting ready for Christmas and everything. My how I wish I could be there! Maybe I will be next year—wouldn't that be wonderful if I could. As today is Sunday, I received no mail, but am looking forward to some tomorrow. The Daily News with the story about Don[1] arrived yesterday. It's really rare that the engineers get any glory, so he must have really deserved the honors.

Tomorrow morning we are taking the men out on a hike and overnight bivouac. It's only going to be seven miles, which will be like a stroll compared to some marches I've been on. However the spot we are going to isn't a very good place, so we'll probably spend a miserable night. But as long as it's just one night I don't mind.

I'm glad to hear the money orders arrived safely. The reason I had so much was because they gave me 3 months advance pay instead of the 2 I asked for. Yesterday I drew $100 bucks which I will send most of home. By the time I get back I should have a pretty nice pile saved up. But you folks go ahead and use all of it you want and don't worry about paying it back. I have written letters to Aunt Dott and Bonnie, Kitt and Nelson and the Allyn's. I don't know Aunt Mabel's address for sure so I haven't written her. Is she still in Holland Hall?

I saw a good movie this afternoon, "Song of Russia" with Robert Taylor. Also I had a huge porterhouse steak for 90 cents which would have cost at least two dollars in Los Angeles. I'm glad to hear Wellington has a good basketball team. Pete Buzzard always predicted when those boys were in grade school and junior high, good teams for the future. Maybe they'll win the Valley championship for the first time in history.

Must close now and get ready for the hike tomorrow.

Love
John

P.S. You can tell the Red Cross that my serial number is 041901 instead of 390888.

---

[1] See Appendix V.

DON JONES

Don Jones got an engineering degree but went back and started over in music. He taught at Emporia College where he met Russ. They married after she graduated. Don's son Bryan is an engineer in Alberquerque, New Mexico. His daughter Sarah is at St. Olaf's in Wisconsin. Russ now is married to the ex-president of Grinnell College where Don was teaching when he died of cancer in 1969.

Don's sister Cletis was married to an Army Colonel who was killed. She died of a brain tumor (I saw her once in Wellington, Kansas) and left four children. They were raised by Kenneth Jones her brother who still lives in Wellington. Don's brother-in-law was Murray Dresbach who lives in Washington State. He married Dorothy Jones. She died of cancer some time ago.

Don's feats mentioned in John's letter[1] include the Silver star for devising a way to blow up the Maginot line and building the Remagen Bridge. Don served in the engineers in Italy and he was wounded later in Europe. Murray Dresbach worked in Savannah for Boeing. John saw John Murray a couple of times on OCS.

---

[1] In November 1944, Don was a combat engineer in Patton's Army besieging the fortress of Metz in northern France.

LETTER 103

Postmarked Dec. 26, 1944

Dec. 21, 1944
Dear Folks,

As per usual, I just finished censoring mail. That is getting more monotonous every day. Guess I'm going to have to start working the boys a little harder-- they're finding entirely too much time to write letters. And I drilled them almost the whole morning, too. I've been teaching them a lot of this fancy boogie-woogie drill lately. They get a big bang out of that. This afternoon I organized a softball team and challenged some of the other outfits around here. So tomorrow morning we are going out to practice—"Coach" Hyndman, how about that! It's a good way to keep up morale while waiting around to move out on an operation.

I saw a very good movie last nite, "The Eve of St. Mark". A war story about the boys who were drafted for the year's service, then were sent overseas and caught in the war from the beginning. If you ever get a chance, be sure and see it.

Four more days till Christmas—not very long. In fact, it doesn't seem possible. I'll be thinking of you all every minute and hope to be with you for the next one. Received a letter from Dr. Wallace with a list of all the boys from our church who are in the service. I see where Bill Romig is a corporal now. Wonder where he is. Think I'll write him at home then his Dad can forward it.

I got the Daily News with the story about Don Jones. Looks like the Germans are getting mean over there now—hope they're using all they've got in an all out last stab.[1]

Haven't heard from you folks for several days. Suppose I'll be getting a bunch of mail all at once. Everything is sort of fouled up around here—I'm wondering if you are getting my letters.

Well, I have several more letters to write, so must close for now.

Love
John

---

[1] The Battle of the Bulge, December 16-25, 1945, was the Germans last major counterattack against the American Army. MV

LETTER 104

Postmarked Dec. 27
Received Jan. 1, 1944
December 25, 1944

Dear Folks,

Just finished censoring mail, so now can write you all a few lines. Well, another Christmas is slipping by—and here I am in the middle of the Pacific. I thought of you all day and hope you had a nice Christmas. But I know you did because the Hyndman family always does. Did Kitt and Nelson make it to Kansas? I wrote them a letter, but doubt if it has arrived yet.

Christmas here was pretty quiet. Yesterday I went into town and had a couple of steaks. Also saw "Madame Curie" which was good. Came back in the evening, censored a never ending stack of letters, and sang Christmas Carols with the boys in my hut. At least that part was like home—remember our little programs on Christmas Eve? Today we had a big Turkey dinner with all the trimmings—really fine. Then this afternoon some entertainers came out and put on a show for the boys. Hula dancers and all that stuff.

You can tell Marjorie[1,] there is an army rest camp up on a mountain here. Also I can tell you that you have my location figured out right. Do you ever listen to Tokyo Rose—she knows where we are, too. How about that!

You asked about Helms[2] he is here in the same outfit—even to the company. Vox Pop Johnson is here too, but in a different company. Your letters have been coming in pretty well. Some get here in about a week, then once in awhile I receive one written back in November. So Bill Romig is still overseas. He's certainly putting in a long stretch. You know he joined up with the Reserves. And he went over right away. I doubt very much if he's on Leyte, unless he's an artillery man. I believe they are the only marines in on that operation.

I expect to be aboard ship soon, so there will be a necessary lull in mail from me. It will be quite a long time I imagine so don't get anxious if you don't hear for a month or so.

Must close now as this is my last sheet of stationery.

Love
John

[2]Majorie Champeny was John's mother's friend. She was married to an Army colonel and had been stationed in Hawaii, so she knew the area John had described. LH

[2]Frank Helms landed with John and survived Iwo. LH

LETTER 105

Postmarked Dec. 27
Received Jan. 1, 1945
Dec. 26, 1944

Dear Folks,

I bought some new stationery, so thought I'd try it out on a short note to you. The paper isn't bad, but it doesn't fit the envelopes. However this is the best I could get under the circumstances. I wrote a letter to you last night, so there isn't much to write about. All my men have been going out on working parties off and on, so I haven't had too much to do with them for a couple of days. The whole outfit is working now, parties going out on eight hour shifts, 24 hours per day. From that I imagine you can figure what we are about to do.

Have the Jones' heard anything more from Don. Also can you get Bill Romig's address for me—I'd like to write him. I got a letter today from Bonnie. Sounds like they are really having their troubles. I also received a letter from Mother, written the 1st of October and sent to me as a Pfc. It was written right after you got my wire saying I was commissioned. Sure took a long time for it to catch up with me. Must close now.

Love
John

LETTER 106

Postmarked Dec. 31, 1944
Rec'd. Jan. 4, 1945
Dec. 30, 1944

Dear Folks,

I will start this letter now, but will have to finish later on. Got to see that my men got some gear they are short. Just like a housewife, a second lieutenant's work is never finished. While writing the above four sentences I was interrupted three times by men coming to see me about something or other. I'll be glad when we get aboard ship and get away from all this confusion of preparing to leave. And is it hot around here! I sweat constantly—in the middle of winter too.

We've been awfully busy lately. The boys have been going out on working parties every other eight hour stretch. Officers go out too, but not quite that often. I'm glad of that, because I've decided that it takes more out of you to supervise than to actually work. That's really true.

How is everything at home by now with Christmas past for another year? Hope you all had a nice one. I sure thought of you and wished I were there. Socks up and everything. Has the basketball team lost any games yet?

I am going to the show tonight if I can get away in time. Don't know what it is, but anything will be OK Even if I've seen it before. There's something about a picture that takes your mind off everything.

No time to write any more so good bye for now.

Love
John

LETTER 107

Postmarked Jan. 2, 1945
Received Jan. 8, 1945
January 1, 1945

Dear Folks,

As you can see by the stationery, I received the first package from you all. The fruit cake is gone, the caramels too, the Vienna sausages are open beside me, I writing on the paper and haven't opened the hard candy, life savers, or shaving soap yet. I am thanking you very much for everything. It was extra good. Aunt Mabel's box arrived the other day. It was nice, too.

Well, did you all see the New Year in last nite? Or do you go for that sort of thing. Personally I hit the sack early although there was no need for it as I haven't done a thing all day long. Except give one kid a good reading off. I think it was a little too good—he's been going around with his tail between his legs all day. Old soft hearted John feels like patting him on the back and saying, "that's all right, Bobby." But that can't be done. Now I have another boy who is reporting to me tonight to be "read off". What a tough guy I'm getting to be. The tyrant!

Received a letter from Daddy today—Wellington sure is going to town in basketball. First decent team they've had in years.

No more news, so will close.

Love
John

P.S. I keep thinking each letter will be the last for awhile, but now I know I have almost a week yet.

LETTER 108

Postmarked Jan. 6, 1945
Received Jan. 10, 1945
January 4, 1945

Dear Folks,

Your second package arrived here yesterday. I'm thanking you a lot. The razor is a good one and I sure needed it. Also the gumdrops and Vienna sausages were popular with men in my hut. I have been using the Yardley's shaving cream you sent in the first package. It is very good stuff—even with cold water. Remember the Yardley's hair oil I had one time. What a smell.

Well, time is passing by and I'm still here on the same island. But it certainly won't be long now. In many ways I'll be glad to board ship—the confusion of getting the outfit ready to go is terrific. Almost enough to drive a nervous person nuts. Glad I've got steel nerves. Ha!

Received another letter from you yesterday. You asked me some questions, but I believe all have been answered in letters you hadn't received yet. Glad to hear John Murray got his commission—he's a good man and will make a good officer. It certainly didn't take him long after going to P.I. Of course he spent an extra four months in V-12 school. Hollar is pretty well along in R.O.C. now—received bars December 16. Kessler is stationed at New River, but I don't know just what he is doing there.

I am enclosing a money order for fifty dollars which you can use or add to the pile. Will close now and get some sleep as I am Officer of the Day tomorrow. It is a 24 hour tour of duty with plenty of responsibility. Especially here and now.

Love
John

LETTER 109

Postmarked Jan. 11, 1945

V-mail letter[1]

Dear Folks,

Just got some V-mail stationery, so will try it out. I don't like it very well, but imagine it will come in handy on some occasions. Received a letter today mailed the twenty third. You had just been to the high school Christmas program. So Jerry and Dorothy both sing-guess I'm the black sheep of the family in the music line. Tell Jerry I know just how he feels about going to the Rainbow Dance with the girl who doesn't "send him". It's awfully hard to say no to those girls.

Nobody sews up the holes in my socks now. When they wear out I just throw them away and get more. You asked if I might wind up an engineer--no chance, thank the Lord. Once in the infantry it's hard to get out and I don't want to anyway. All the guys think I'm crazy for wanting the infantry and maybe I am!

I will write Aunt Mabel and thank her for her package. As I told you, only one of your packages has arrived here. The other may not catch me for a long time yet.

Will close now, so keep writing and I'll do my best.

Love
John

---

[1] V-Mail letter forms were provided to our GIs overseas and available to their families back home. They provided a convenient way to write a brief letter. Because John was a better letter writer than most men, he probably found them unsuitable for most of his correspondence. This is the only V-Mail letter John wrote among all 131 of his letters. MV LH

Photographs from Hawaii, November 1944.

Photographs from Hawaii, November 1944.

PART III. OVERSEAS DUTY

VOYAGE TO COMBAT

From Hawaii

to the Beach at Iwo Jima

COMBAT -- D-DAY AND BEYOND

From Hilo to Honolulu

SECTION V EMBARKATION AND MOVEMENT TO OBJECTIVE (Cont'd)

10. On 17 January, 1945, all LST's and APA's rendezvoused at Lahaina Roads, Maui, T.H. All officers and enlisted on LST's #731, #787, #684, and #1033 and the USS MISSOULA embarked aboard the USS DICKENS and sailed for Honolulu, Oahu, T.H. Total on board USS DICKENS - 41 officers, 979 enlisted.

11. Arrived at Honolulu, Oahu, T.H., on 18 January, 1945, 2 enlisted transferred from USS DICKENS to U.S. Naval Hospital at Honolulu. 1 officer debarked from USS DICKENS and embarked aboard LST #758 on 21 January, 1945. 1 officer debarked from USS DICKENS and embarked aboard LST #1033 on 21 January, 1945.

12. 18 January, 1945, to 26 January, 1945, liberty and recreation in Honolulu. Twenty-five percent of troops embarked were granted liberty daily. Twenty-five percent of troops embarked engaged in organized recreation daily. This recreation consisted of swimming and athletic contests at a Naval Recreation Park.

13. All ships sailed from Honolulu, Oahu, T.H., on 27 January, 1945. Total on board USS DICKENS - 39 officers, 890 enlisted; USS TALLADEGA - 1 enlisted; LST #785 - 1 officer; LST #1033 - 1 officer.

14. Troops were briefed daily on the voyage on the coming operation. Arrived at Eniwetok, Marshall Islands on 5 February, 1945.

15. Arrived at Saipan, Marianas Islands, on 11 February, 1945. 1 enlisted transferred from USS DICKENS to U.S. Army General Hospital at Saipan. Officers and enlisted as listed, were transferred from the USS DICKENS to ships as listed:

16. The following number of officers and enlisted embarked aboard LST #1033 on 11 February, 1945, from USS DICKENS.

	Marine Officers	Marine Enlisted	Navy Officers	Navy Enlisted
1stBn., 28th Marines	4	258		5

17. The following number of officers and enlisted embarked aboard LST #449 on 11 February, 1945, from USS DICKENS.

	Marine Officers	Marine Enlisted	Navy Officers	Navy Enlisted
1stBn., 28th Marines	11	239		10

SECTION V EMBARKATION AND MOVEMENT TO OBJECTIVE (Cont'd

A Page from the Action Report of the Iwo Jima Operation.
This page records the movement of the 5th Division while embarking aboard ships in Hawaii until the transport division sailed from Honolulu for Iwo Jima in late January 1945.

LETTER 110

No envelope
Received Jan. 22, 1945

17 January, 1945

Dear Folks

At the present time, censorship regulations for obvious reasons, are very strict, and there is absolutely nothing I can say. Except that I am fine and hope you are the same. We haven't been getting any mail for about two weeks, but should get a huge stack sometime in the future. The chow is good now and I get plenty of sleep. Helms bunks next to me—looks like we'll be pretty much together all the way through.

Have the Jones' heard anything from Don lately. I hope he's all right. The Yanks have been having a tough time over there. Wish I knew what outfit Bill Romig is in. Then I could look him up if I happen to go where he might be.

Tell Jerry and Dorothy to be good and write me sometime. Don't let Jerry get rash and enlist at 17. Make him go to college. Guess that's another year off though. I'll say happy birthday to them both now as I won't get a chance to later. Is Daddy still working on two jobs? I think he should knock that off. Too much is too much.

Well, my mind is a complete blank for something to say—so will close.

All my love,
John

LETTER 111

Postmarked Jan. 21, 1945
Received Jan. 25, 1945
January 19, 1945

Dear Folks,

Here it is 9:30 and I'm not in the sack yet. These late hours will be the death of me yet. But this is war and one must sacrifice for victory.

Yesterday we had our first mail call in some time and I received quite a stack of letters. Even one from Judy Van Deventer. She's teaching school in Gridley, Ks. Just as busy as ever. She didn't say anything about being engaged—wonder if she still is. Also I heard from Don Hollar who is now in R.O.C. at Quantico. He graduated from O.C. sixth in his company. That's pretty good, but he had enough starts at the thing.

So Neal Lauterbach is still farming—I've often thought about him. Tell him hello if you see him again. He and I used to have some big times together back on the farm. And Vernon Edgar[1]—I'm surprised he let the service get him. Thought he was too much of a family man. Guess they're getting everybody now days. Is Bill Romig[2] in the artillery—I believe they are the only marines in the Philippines. No, I'm not in the convoy sighted in that vicinity.

I still have the folder of pictures you folks sent me while at New River. Every once in awhile I get them out and look at them. I have no plans now to keep them out in front of me all the time. Don't forget to send the pictures[3] of Jerry--I can't imagine him almost as tall as me. But he certainly doesn't weigh nearly as much as I do. I'm a good two hundred pounds stripped now. Fat! But I'll lose a lot of it before long.

Well, I'm all out of something to say, so will stop.

Love
John

[1] Neal Lauterbach and Vernon Edgar Stewart were neighbors on the farm near Mayfield. They continued to farm there until their deaths. Neal died in 2000. LH

[2] Bill Romig was a Wellington High friend. He enlisted in the Marines and served with the Third Division, four battle stars and being awarded two Purple Hearts. The Third Division invaded Bougainville, Guam, and Iwo Jima. I recently located him at his cabin in New Mexico, but learned he was moving back to Kansas. LH

[3] Pictures of his family along with everything he took to Iwo were lost except his dog (TAGS) when he was wounded. LH

The Transport Division was led by the *USS Auburn*, AGC 101. Following were four columns of ships, with an interval of 1000 yards between columns and a distance of 600 yards between ships. Colonel Liversedge, CO of the 28th Regiment was aboard the *USS Talledega*, APA 208. John was aboard the *USS Dickens*, APA161.

USS Auburn
AGC 101

USS Thurston AP 77	*USS Talladega* APA 208	*USS Cecil* APA 86	*USS Rutland* APA192
USS Lenawee APA 195	*USS Missoula* APA 211	*USS Deuel* APA 160	*USS Highlands* APA 119
USS Whiteside AKA 90	*USS Lubbock* APA 197	*USS Darke* APA 159	*USS Sandoval* APA 195
USS Yancey AKA 93	***USS Dickens*[1] APA 161**	*USS Hocking* APA 121	*USS Hansford* APA 106
USS Brule APA 66	*USS Stokes* AKA 67	*USS Tolland* AKA 64	*USS Whitley* AKA 91
	USS Nemasket AOG 10	*USS Athene* AKA 22	

The Transport Division Convoying the Fifth Division to Iwo Jima.

Many other vessels of the Iwo Jima invasion force were underway to Saipan. The vessels in the Fourth and Fifth transport divisions were escorted by destroyers and patrol craft as protection against Japanese submarine attack. At this stage of the war, the danger was small, but the vulnerable ships with their irreplaceable fighting men aboard had to be protected. LSTs and LSMs left earlier for Saipan. With a speed of about 10 knots, they could not keep up with the transport divisions. The vessel types are as follows: AGC = Auxiliary Command Ship, AP = Auxiliary Transport, APA = Auxiliary Attack Transport, AKA = Auxiliary Attack Cargo Ship, AOG = Auxiliary Gasoline Tanker. MV

[1] John was aboard this ship.

Enlisted Quarters aboard an Attack Transport.
Fifth Division Marines on the way to invade Iwo Jima, February 1945. Official Marine Photograph.

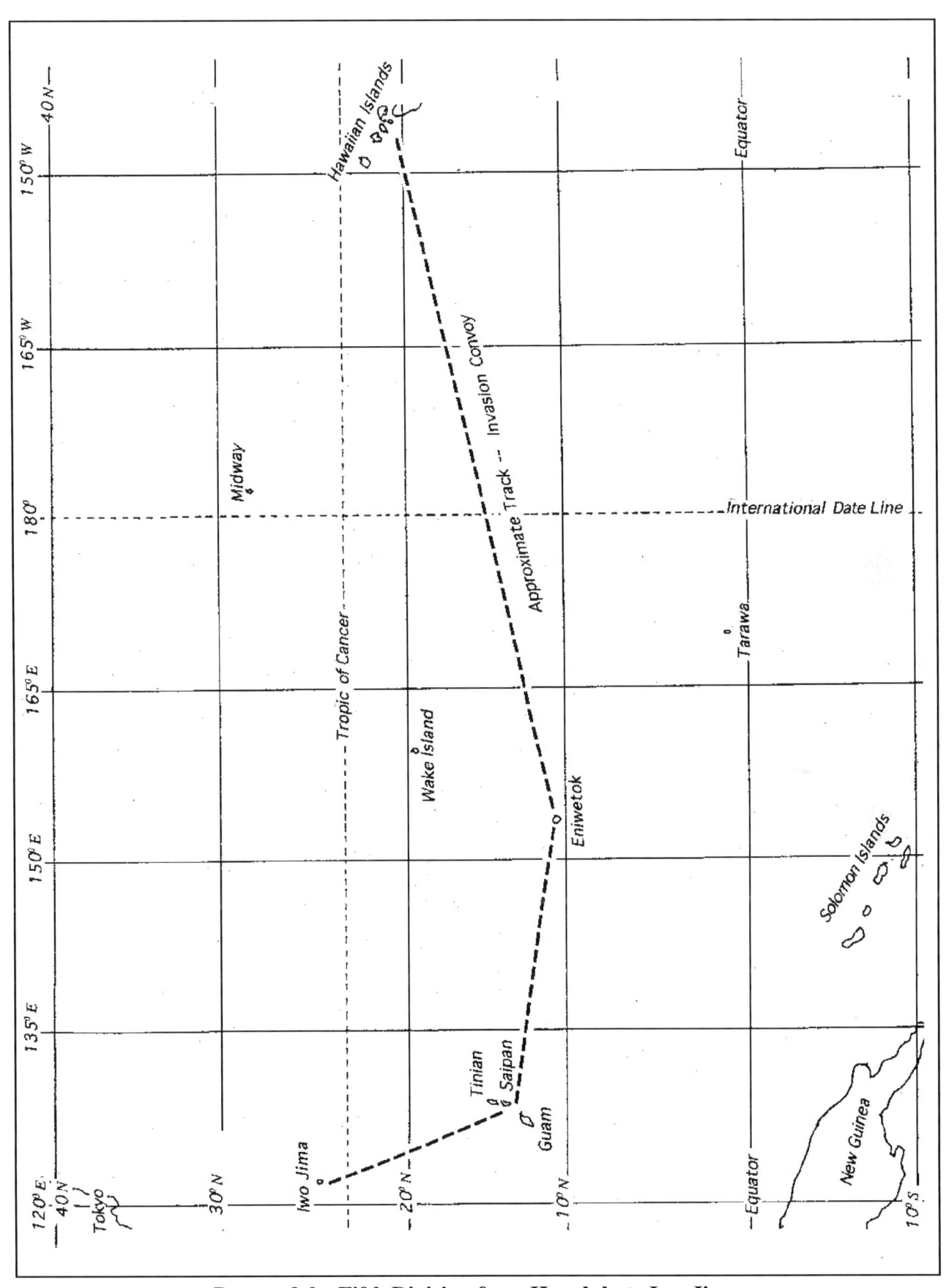

Route of the Fifth Division from Honolulu to Iwo Jima.

LETTER 112

Postmarked Jan. 27, 1945
Received Jan. 31, 1945
January 26, 1945

Dear Folks,

Everything is still fine—I'm well-fed and my morale is high. Have been receiving lots of mail lately from everybody more than I can answer. Got one of the Phi Sig news letters yesterday. The boys are scattered all over the world. There is one Phi Sig left at W.U. What a celebration there will be when we all get back together again. An awful lot of the boys have been wounded, but very few killed. Kendall Bowman,[1] one of my best buddies was killed over Germany. I may have told you that before as it happened almost a year ago. The letter gave a list of the boys who had been home. Bill Kessler was included as was a whole slug of others. The lucky guys.

Did I tell you I ran into one of the Phi Sigs over here. We had a big bull session all one afternoon. Then unfortunately I moved out the next day. He was Bill Brackman,[2] an ensign in the Navy Air Corps. His mother was West's school teacher in elementary school. He pledged Phi Sig my junior year, so he's a couple years younger than me. Being in the Air Corps, he's living the "life of Riley" over here. Has better quarters than I ever had in the states. You asked what I think Jerry should join—army, navy or marines (Air Corps not included). Now I don't see that. The air corps is by far the best deal, even if they do wash out a lot. Everyone that washes out gets good duty. And just because Francis Carr had a tough time is no reason to think Jerry would. And when they wash so many out, it is no disgrace. But I'll bet Jerry[3] would make it. He's athletically inclined and smart in math. That's all it takes. I don't want him going into the other branches and remaining an enlisted man. They live a terrible life overseas—poor living quarters, chow and everything. His chances for a commission in the army, navy or marines would be almost be nil—and I don't see how anyone with intelligence and ambitions could stand being a private. An officer in the air corps leads the best life in the service, especially Navy Air Corps. And if he should flunk out, he'll still be better off than in the line branches. But of course it will be some time before he's seventeen—so just wait and see how things are then.

I received a letter from Bertha Clark[4] the other day. Also heard from Nellie Ann Cowan, the one who came between West and I. Don Jones wrote me a long letter—he seems to be getting along fine although they've had a rugged time. Naturally he didn't mention the incident for which he was praised so much. He gave me Bill Romig's address. Bill is in the 3rd Division. Wish I could tell you which division I'm with—it's a great outfit and you'll be reading a lot about it in the future.

Must write some more letters.

Love
John

---

[1] Kendall Bowman was the older brother of my best friend in junior high. He was lost off the coast of England while flying a Navy plane looking for German submarines. LH
[2] I couldn't locate Bill Brackman. Some of his fraternity brothers told me they though he was still alive. LH
[3] Jerry, John's brother, had just finished his junior year in high school when the war was over. When he graduated, he joined the Navy and was granted an appointment to the U.S. Naval Academy later. He became a Marine officer upon graduation and served in Korea, Vietnam (two tours) and Lebanon. He retired as a full colonel. LH
[4] Bertha Clark was one of John's teachers in Wellington. LH

LETTER 113

Postmarked Feb 18, 1945
Received Feb. 25, 1945

February 3, 1945
Dear Folks,

I have some time tonight, so will drop you a line to let you know I'm OK As we are aboard ship, it will be some time before this is mailed. I can't say how long, but we've been aboard ship for some time—much longer than you would guess from letters you probably have received. We dropped off some mail at one time, but weren't allowed to say we were aboard ship. Now we can say we are moving and that we are on the way to combat. But that's all the details I can give. You'll know for sure when we hit though. The publicity will make Doug MacArthur look sick.

You may be interested to know how I feel about being on a transport going into combat. It's very funny, but I feel no different than I did going from New River to Pendleton. Less excited than when I went from Wichita to Notre Dame. I remember that a long time ago I wondered how I'd feel in this situation and expected it to really be a sensation. It's amazing how quickly and easily people can adjust themselves to new situations. One thing that helps is that they keep us so busy we haven't time to sit around and get nervous. Inspections twice a day plus briefing the men on their job in the operation, getting briefed ourselves and a thousand other things keeps everybody busy as bees. Some of the work seems unnecessary, but I really believe it's a good idea. A lot of people have such vivid imaginations that they'd go nuts if given a chance to think much. You know, it's really amazing how much is known about the place we are going. We know everything except what time of the day the Japs go to the head (bathroom). And they might even find that out before we get there.

Mother I guess I should have explained when I told you I had been Officer of the Day. It's no honor like Times Man of the Year. It is just a job all second lieutenants get frequently at regular intervals. Wherever there is a camp, there is a guard, with sentries posted—and the Officer of the Day is in charge of the guard for a 24 hour stretch. So you had better tell your friends I'm not the famous officer you thought. Ha! Must close and sleep.
Love
John

LETTER 114

Received March 4, 1945
February 14 1945

Dear Folks,

Here it is 1:45 in the morning and I'm writing letters. How about that? I'm in the ship's guard office in frequent capacity as O.D.[1] It's a very boring and tiresome job for sure.—I always dread it.

Well, how are thing at home? Everything is fine here. I'm well fed and get plenty of sleep on this boat. But we won't be aboard much longer. The day we've all been waiting for since coming overseas is rolling around pretty quick like. It seems funny—I thought that by now I'd be all tense and nervous. But I still feel like I might just be moving to a new camp. Guess I'm almost disappointed. Don't suppose I'll get nervous until the nite before D-Day.

Wish I could tell you where we are now anchored. If it weren't for this place I'd still be back in the states—maybe home on furlough.

Helms is still with me—his bunk is next to mine. Johnson is on another boat in the same convoy. There is one guy with me who went to N.D., boot camp, New River, Pendleton and overseas with me. Now he's going to ride in the same Higgins boat with me on D-Day. His name is Granell—I don't think I've mentioned him before. He's from Denver, Colorado and is a good boy.

Hollar should be home on furlough pretty soon. Maybe he'll come down and see you all. I wouldn't be surprised if he did because he's always been pretty good about such things. Much better than I ever was. Of course, now he's got a wife to occupy his time. I think by now Kessler is on his way overseas—or at least out in California waiting to leave.

It seems so funny for me to be over here and both of them still in the States. And I always figured they'd both, especially Kessler, would beat me to the war. Why, I'll be a veteran in a few weeks.

Received a letter from Aunt Dott telling me all about that girl in her office. My how she raves about her. I wonder how her taste compares with mine. She sent me the girl's address saying they both thought it more proper if I would write first. I wrote, but it will be some time before it gets mailed the same with this letter.

Don Jones' mother sent me a valentine with a very nice note in it. I think they are fine people. Several days ago I wrote to her, but it will be quite awhile before she gets it. Don sent me Bill Romig's address, so I wrote him, too. He's with the 3rd Marine Division—a headquarters man in a battalion, so I imagine he's been pretty much rear echelon all along. The 3rd Division hasn't done too much anyway.

Well, I was a little long winded tonight, or rather this morning. So will stop before I get boring.

Love
John

[1] O.D. = Officer of the Day. MV

HUTCHCROFT'S LETTER, PART II

Note: Bill's letter was written from Iwo Jima, dated 28 February. After capturing Suribachi and raising the flag on 23 February, the 28th Regiment was placed in reserve until February 28. This was the first opportunity that the men of the 28th had to write home since they landed. Hutchcroft took advantage of the time and filled in the story of his service from the time he left San Diego.

In January, we boarded ship and prepared to journey farther westward. I put 19 of my 28 men aboard one ship. Two aboard another and seven with me on an A.P.A. ship.[1] We rode to Pearl Harbor this way and then were moved around some more. We finally ended up with men on four separate ships and I on the fifth ship. That was the way we left Pearl Harbor. I guess it couldn't be helped but it certainly complicated things for me.

While in Pearl Harbor we got liberty off the ship and besides seeing Honolulu we got to go swimming at Waikiki Beach.

We sailed from Pearl Harbor to Eniwetok Island where we stopped for fuel and water. Also got mail there and that was where all my back mail caught up with me.

From Eniwetok we went to Saipan. All this time I was aboard L.S.T. 756. At Saipan on Feb.11 I transferred back to the A.P.A. All that I left at Pearl Harbor.

Saipan was our staging area for this operation. Here clothes were issued and all final plans were gone over.

I got ashore one day and located Ben Shutt, Chas. Davis and Lloyd Dean. Old home week!

We left Saipan around Feb. 15th and headed for Iwo Jima and combat.

For three days prior to D-day, Feb. 19, our navy shelled and our air force bombed the island of Iwo Jima until it was thought impossible for any person to remain alive. We knew it was the most heavily fortified island of any we have taken in the Pacific and were prepared for the worst.

The island of Iwo Jima is shaped like a pear with a small mountain approximately 660 ft. high at the small end. This Mt.—known as Surbachi Mt.—was the key position of the island. An observer on top of this Mt. can see what is going on all over the island and therefore who ever controls this Mt. has the outlook of the whole island.

It was the 28th Marines of the fifth division's duty to capture this Mt. They encountered the worst fighting of the Pacific there before the hill was taken. The 27th and 26th Marines were called to assist the 28th Marines.[2]

---

[1] An APA is an attack transport. APAs carried landing craft aboard and could land Marines onto a beach. MV

[2] Bill is in error here. The Fourth Division and the 26th and 27th Regiments had their own objective: the airports. The 28th took Suribachi without any assistance from the other regiments on Iwo. All regiments of the invasion force were faced with a bloody task and all suffered casualties at about the same rate. MV

This operation was one when the navy and air force did not fail the Marines. The navy blasted away day and night and the air force threw all the forces they could muster together in supporting our landing.

Like the landing at Tarawa the Japs let our assault units land and held their fire until the shore parties and supplies began to come in on the sixth wave. Then they really opened up on us. One of my boys worded it like this—"They threw everything at us but the kitchen sink and I don't know why they didn't throw that."

The assault waves that landed on D-day and also D plus one received the heaviest attack. The fifth shore party Co. landed on D-day and the sixth shore party Co., the one I am with, were held in reserve on our ship. John Hyndman and several other of my 2nd Lt. friends were in the 5th S.P. They really received a lot of enemy fire but only one of the Lts., James D. Harris, another Special O.C.S. brother was killed and two other Lts. Wounded.

The nineteen men I had aboard a L.S.M. 266 ship with a corp. in charge landed on the evening of D-day. I had no way of contacting them and didn't have any idea where they were until I landed on D plus days. By the time I got in the 19 men were old veterans of war. They shouldn't have landed until I did but things were a little fouled up.

Our 6th S.P. Co. was on a ship just off the shore about 2 miles watching the war with field glasses. We couldn't go ashore until given orders to by the commander on the shore.

When we finally got ashore on Feb. 21 about 2 p.m. our beach was fairly safe. All we encountered was machine gun fire, a few snipers and very little mortar fire. I was given orders to set up security on the left flank of the beach in case of a counter attack at night. While we were taking those positions we received more machine gun fire and sniper rifle fire. That was when one of my men got hit. It was their, or rather our, first experience of enemy fire and he was frightened so that he didn't dig fast enough. He got hit in the left elbow and left leg. Both flesh wounds so nothing serious.

I finally got my men placed in their positions and kept yelling for them to dig in. I told one kid to dig—rolled over onto my other side to check on the rest of my men to see if they were digging and then looked back to see if the first kid was digging. He was and almost out of sight! I was so busy at the time trying to get my men into safe positions that I didn't have time to get frightened myself—at that time anyway!

Our position today is very secure and safe. This end of the island is secured with the exception of a few Japs in the mountain as yet. There is quite a network of caves in old Suribachi Mt. They even have a six shafted elevator in the heart of it. That is the only way you can get supplies to the top.

We have the first of the three air fields captured and nearly ready for use. In fact, they are supposed to land planes on it today. The fourth Div. is encountering very stiff resistance on the other end and some of the worst fighting is yet to be done.

Supplies are coming across our beach now in full force. We have enough help now that we are able to get our needed rest.

Our chow is very good.[1] I eat with some of my men and cook or at least warm up all our food. They are preparing dinner now.

---

[1] The Beach Parties for the first few days were exposed to enemy fire. In one respect, they were lucky, their food was better than the infantrymen in the front lines who lived on K-Rations for days. MV

Of course, we are living in fox holes now. Mine is well constructed with sand bags.[2] It makes a very good bomb shelter except we haven't any! I am eating and working with my men now more than ever. I find I have a lot of characters in the outfit. We have a lot of fun—as far as fun goes in an operation like this- Most of the men are good workers. In fact they all are when the chips are down.

After this operation is secured we are supposed to go to Guam[2] to rest up before the next campaign. However rumors have it that we are going all the way back to Hilo so we will just wait and see.

As for what I will be put into next I do not know. Since we are a replacement outfit we will probably fill in any vacancy the 5th Marine Div. has which means I should get back into the infantry. I am expecting to hit the islands north of Japan next.[3] Just how far off I am in my predictions I will find out in the near future.

There will soon come a time again when I will be restricted as to what may be said so think nothing of it. Right now I am as safe[5] as if I were back in the States—well anyway almost.

In summing up this operation on Iwo Jima I can truthfully say it has been, and still is in the northern section, the toughest operation the Marines have hit yet. This is not because I am in on it because I didn't even get a good sample compared with the infantry assault troops on the front lines. You will hear and read about the heroes of Iwo Jima and there is no way of expressing the "HELL" that the fellows have been through.

When praise is given out do not forget to include the Medical Corps men, the stretcher bearers, the Doctors and the Chaplains who risk their lives and lose their lives doing some of the hardest work there is to be done. All through this operation as with all operations they were right on the front lines doing better than the best they could do.

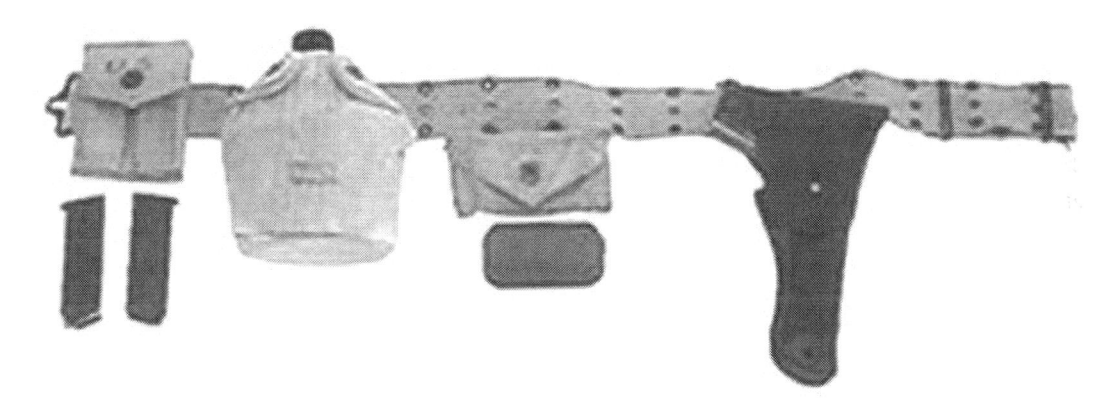

The Web Belt Worn by Infantrymen in World War II.

From the left: ammunition pouch with two magazines, canteen in pouch, first aid kit with bandage and sulfa powder, a .45 automatic in holster. Few men ccarried a .45 on their belt. Other items that could be attached are grenades, compass, possibley a map case. Too much on your belt could be inconvenient or dangerous. MV

[1]Sand bags were used to make the hole safe from cave ins on the beach. Men in the front lines seldom had time or sand bags to fortify their "living quarters." The men at the front were constantly on the attack and seldom lived in the same foxhole more than one day. MV

[2]The Fifth Amphibious Corps was scheduled to be in reserve for the Okinawa operation (1 April), but as Bill notes, the scuttlebutt was right on. The Fifth Division returned to Camp Tarawa on Hawaii. MV

[3]The Division was scheduled to invade Japan on 1 November, but on Kyushu, not in the northern islands. The war ended before the Fifth Division faced more combat. MV

Green Beach. D+2.

Despite the high surf, LSMs and LSTs line up to disgorge all manner of supplies and equipment. The weather is foul and vehicles and smaller landing craft lay swamped in the surf, but the beach party carries on. The tall Marine withe the M-1, 30 Carbine on his back was identified by Lou Hindbaugh, one of John's men. When he showed me the photo and identified John, he said he had marched behind "his lieutenant" too many times not to recognize him in the picture. Official Marine Photograph. LH

On D-Day, sea and weather conditions for landing were good. From the time the Japanese opened fire for the next three or four days, the beach conditions were chaotic. As casualties mounted, evacuation of the wounded became a priority, but at the same time, supplies and fresh troops had to be landed. In the afternoon the weather changed and a heavy surf begun running. For the next two days, the beach parties had all and more than they could handle.

As a member of the beach party, John was in the thick of the acion on Green Beach. The following photos from the National Archives illustrate the landing site, the condition of the beach in the first few days, and the work of the beach parties as the Marines of the Fourth Division, the 26th Regiment and the 27th Regiment pushed toward the airports. The 28th Regiment was supplied by movement of supplies over Green Beach as it closed in on the capture of Mt. Suribachi. MV

Establishing the Beach Head on D-Day.

Iwo Jima Beach. D+3.
Official Marine Photographs.

Iwo Jima Beaches Red 1 and Red 2 (foreground) and Green 1 (background). D+12.
Note the wrecked landing craft and equipment on the beaches and the vehicles scattered in the sand near the southern end of Motoyama Airfield #1.

John's parents received the following two letters from Iwo on March 10 and March 16. They had no more news until John's letter from the hospital in Hawaii arrived on April 6 almost a month after he was wounded. The papers were full of news of Iwo Jima and the terrible casualties. John's father came home with a paper with this picture of a dead Marine on Iwo. His mother met his father at the door with a copy of the same picture and said "I think it is John." John's sister remembers finding his letter in the mailbox after they had given him up for dead and rushed into the house waving the letter. Later the letter postmarked April 10 came from the American Red Cross in Hawaii. Then finally on April 13 or so the telegram from the Marine Corps arrived. LH

LETTER 115

Postmarked Mar. 4
Received Mar. 10

Feb. 28, 1945

Dear Folks,

Well how's everything at home these days? It's pretty rough in the field—have you heard and read the news of the fight on Iwo Jima? And what a place it has been—the worst ever in the Pacific. But the kid came thru in great shape—I did cut my finger with a hunting knife. Ha! There were quite a lot of casualties, but I just lost a few men—all wounded. The officer who was working with me was shot in the leg and evacuated the first day. But thanks to all of our prayers, I'm leading a charmed life and will never be hurt.

Much to our surprise we received a little mail[1] the other day. Got a letter from you with a list of questions I'll try to answer now.

1. You don't need to send me a thing unless it's good Gillette razor blades. All other things are easily available in rest camp—when we get there.

2. When we go back to rest camp, I will be taken out of this draft and put in an Infantry outfit permanently.

3. Yes, I do have the same boys I worked with before—a great bunch.

4. I'll get Helm's mother's address after the operation and send it to you.

5. There's no one else with me that you would know. When back at the other place it took about six days for your letters to reach me. You can't tell now—and I hear we are going back there again.

6. As for the letters I have received I couldn't say right now.

Must close,

Love
John

A World War II Helmet.
John was probably wearing a helmet like this one when he was hit by shrapnel.

[1] Every effort was made to deliver mail to men in combat. Nothing could match it for a morale booster. MV

LETTER 116

Last letter received before wounded

Postmarked Mar. 8, 1945
Received March 16, 1945

March 6, 1945

Dear Folks,

I'm still on Iwo Jima and in good shape. No more am I in the replacement draft, but have been transferred to the infantry outfit you see on my return address. That's the outfit I was attached to while working on the beach. I joined the platoon (1st of B Co.) while on the front lines, but after two days we were relieved and we are now camped back of the lines. And hoping the island will be secured before we have to go back again. It has been a very rugged operation and I hope there are never anymore like it.

Well, I just now received a letter from you enclosing some more pictures of Jerry & Dorothy & Daddy. It was a pretty old letter but was good to get anyway. Yes, I had received pictures before but had forgotten to mention it. I have never received Bill Romig's address from you yet, though. The reason I could never mention the division was because we were replacements and they didn't want it known yet. There are six marine divisions in the Marine Corps and I'm in the 5th. The 3rd, 4th and 5th are on this operation.

Well, there isn't much to say and writing conditions aren't the best so will close.

Love
John

P.S. I have written Aunt Mabel thanking her for the package—and I have not received your third one yet. But should when we get to rest camp.

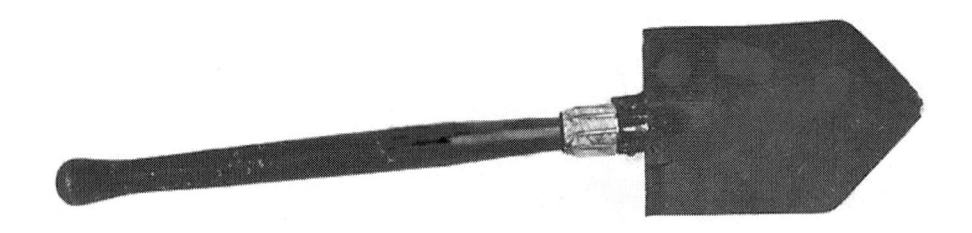

Entrenching Tool.

This little shovel could be folded back and attached to a web belt. Folding it to 90^0 turned it into a pick. Thousands of foxholes were dug by this shovel on Iwo Jima, probably millions by GIs in World War II. In the soft sand of the beaches, it was easy to dig (although the sides of a foxhole often collapsed.) Sandbags were used to reinforce a foxhole. On the northern end of the island, the soil was rocky and foxholes were harder to dig. MV

LETTER 117

Letter to John From his Father
Postmarked Mar. 25, 1945 -- Sunday 3-25-45

Dear John,

Well Iwo is no longer in the headlines and we are anxious to have another letter from you telling us you are all OK and back in a rest camp. From the way things look I really expect the war in Germany to be over by the time you receive this. Don Jones' outfit is with the 9th Army now so I wouldn't be surprised if he is helping them cross the Rhine today.

The first part of this week I turned on the radio down here at Larabees about 11:54 P.M. and tuned in Phil Harris's radio program and shortly after that they said we will now take you to Iwo Jima. In a minute a Sgt. Glen Nelson came on the air and carried on a three way conversation with Phil and his parents in San Francisco. I was sure jealous that you couldn't talk to us.

I am wondering if you ran into Bill Romig on Iwo.[1] Several people here seem to think he was there with the Third Marines. His Father died this week and was buried yesterday. I guess he has suffered a good deal the last few months. He was operated on in a Winfield Hospital and died that evening. I guess he had a cancer.

A boy from Argonia, I think his name was Floyd, was killed on Iwo . He had a brother who was a star athlete at Okla. A.& M. A boy named Dashler who was in High School here with you is with some supply company of the 5th Marines. There is also a Stephenson boy from Wellington who I think is with the Marine Air Corps who was at Iwo Jima.

Don Denny is home on furlough. He was in the Naval battle at Leyte and his ship was sunk and he was the only one of his gun crew to escape. It sure has changed him a lot.

Jerry goes to Wichita this week end to the State contests. He is to be in the chorus,[2] also the double quartet and a 1 act play. Your big brother is getting to be quite a performer. A man downtown told me he would rather hear Jerry sing than any kid he ever knew. Your little sister is also making a name for herself as a singer. She sang a solo at Blue Triangle this week.

Well garden season is here again and I am trying to have a garden[2] along with all my other duties. I have peas, radishes, lettuce and beets up. I also have my potatoes planted and have a swell looking strawberry bed.[3] I heard yesterday where they brought a lot of fresh vegetables and watermelons to Iwo from Saipan and Guam. I hope you got some of the watermelon as I know you would enjoy that. We have had unusual warm weather here the past two weeks and everything is sure green and looks like Spring. I suppose we will have to have another freeze to kill everything.

Love
Daddy

[1] Bill Romig was not at Iwo because he had been injured at that time. LH

[2] John's brother Jerry later was in the US Naval Academy chorus singing bass. His sister, Dorothy, sang at my sister's wedding. She was a bridesmaid at our wedding or she would have done the same for us. LH

[3] His Dad's garden was on a vacant lot and was quite large. He kept his family and friends well supplied every summer. LH

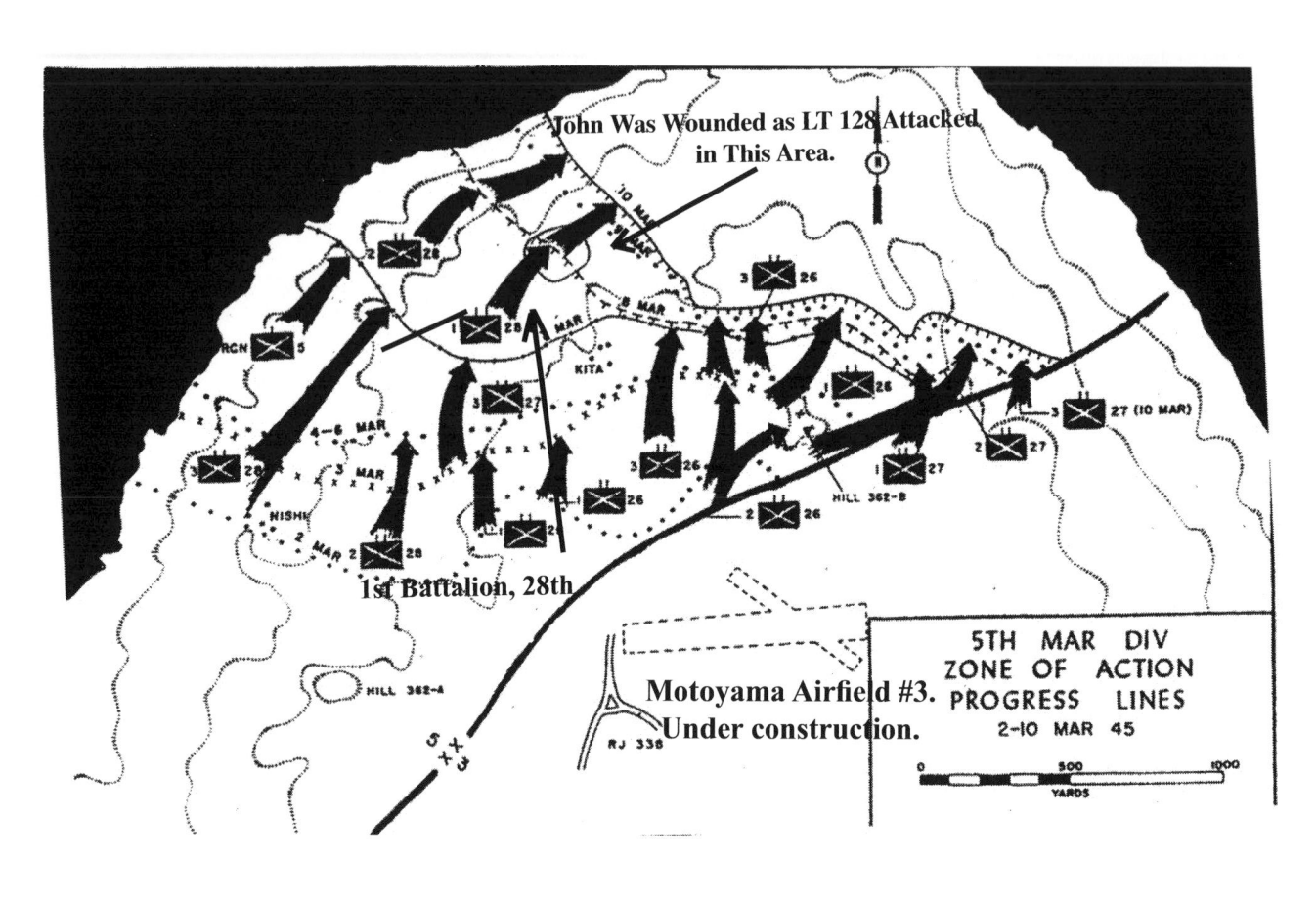

The Rugged Terrain Where the 28th Marines Wiped out the Last of the Japanese Defenders.
Official Marine Photograph.

LETTER 118[1]

This is the first letter his parents received from John after he was wounded.

Postmarked April 3, 1945
Received April 6, 1945

March 31, 1945 (22 days after being wounded).

Dear Folks,

I suppose you've heard by now that I was wounded on Iwo Jima. Got shrapnel across my head—quite a crease—fractured my skull. But I am feeling fine now. I am not stateside, but almost am. Yesterday I received my Purple Heart in bed from Admiral King.[2] He pinned it on my pajamas. What a beauty it is. I will send it home soon, in the box it came in. I feel proud of it, but didn't want the thing very bad. I'll tell you that for sure. Before getting hit in the head—I joined a regular rifle company. Picked up the first platoon—shook hands with my platoon sergeant and five minutes later moved out in an attack. Didn't know a soul in the platoon. That's really doing things the hard way. We stayed on the lines all that day and nite. The next morning we were relieved by another outfit and marched back to the other end of the island. It was only a two mile walk. But after three days on the front, the boys were pretty tired. They had put in an extra day up there. We rested them for a few days (three), and moved back up again. I got hit about the second day up—did a blackout, and the next thing I knew, I was in an army hospital[3] where I spent eight days. The nurses have all been wonderful, except when they shoot me with penicillin, or morphine. I haven't an unstuck place on my body. Everything is sore clear down to my toes. Even my toes hurt. My head aches, too. Oh well, such is life! I haven't heard a word from you folks or anyone else since leaving the little "hell on wheels".

Well, I'm a wounded veteran now—how do you folks feel about it all? Not too badly, I hope. War is hell! Things are tough all over. The sooner I get stateside, the better I'll like it! It may not be too long, either. I have an open wound on my head which they are waiting on to close. Otherwise they'll close it up for me. That's all that's holding me up. Thirty days at home would be good for the soul!

This is quite a hospital.[4] Service is great and we live in luxury. I should have been hit on D-day and saved myself all the grievances of Iwo Jima. In the room with me is a 1st Lt. from Idaho. He was a forward observer for artillery. Spent nine of his eleven days in the front lines. Usually with an assault platoon. He received a terrific thigh wound from a sniper. They operated on him here and he now has two incisions almost a foot long in his leg.

I just received a penicillin shot.[5] Right where I sit. What a pain it was. Almost killed me. They claim that when these things start hurting, the patient is getting well. The Lord only knows I feel well!

---

[1]Letter 118 describes what it meant for a young platoon leader to lead his men on Iwo Jima in the final clean up of the Fifth Division Zone. The men of the Third and Fourth Division had nearly completed their work. Iwo Jima was declared secured on 14 March. Men of the Fifth Divison did not reembark until 26 March. MV

[2]Adniral Ernest King was Chief of Naval Operations, the senior officer in the U. S. Navy. MV

[3]On Guam. LH

[4]In Hawaii. LH

[5]Penicillin was new and only available by injection, usually every four hours, 24 hours a day. LH

March 31, 1945

Dear Folks,

I suppose you've heard by now that I was wounded on Iwo Jima. Got shrapnel across my head - quite a crease - fractured my skull. But am feeling fine now. I am not stateside, but almost am. Yesterday I received my purple heart in bed from Admiral King. He pinned it on my pajamas. What a beauty it is. I will send it home soon, in the box it came in. I feel very proud of it, but didn't want the thing very bad. I'll tell you that for sure. Iwo Jima was quite a place. I stayed there for a good many days. Before getting hit in the head - I joined a regular rifle company. Picked up the first platoon - shook hands with my platoon sergeant and five minutes later moved out in an attack. Didn't know a soul in the platoon. That's really doing things the hard way. We stayed on the line all that day and nite. The next morning we were relieved by another outfit and marched back to the other

The First Page of John's Letter Telling his Parents He Had Been Wounded on Iwo Jima.

The doctor just changed my dressing with two other doctors observing. They asked me all kinds of questions. Such as: "When were you wounded?", "When were you operated on?", "How long were you unconscious?, and Do you have any pain?" I couldn't answer any of them except the last one. The answer there is "No". I can get up now and go to the head—am pretty weak in the knees. Lost a lot of weight and all that sort of thing.[1] As I remember, I had the same trouble two years ago when they operated on my knee. That very knee gives me trouble now when I get out of bed and hobble to the head.

Well, a lot of people got hurt on this operation—especially officers. We are the vulnerable ones. You can't see for heck where they are shooting from. Their pill boxes are wonders to behold. You can sit right on top of one and never see it. They really had the beach covered. Boy, it was murder. For fifteen days I watched guys around me get hit—killed or wounded. Some were terrible. Lost legs, arms, fingers, heads and every other thing that was attached to their bodies. Bullets through the stomach, chest, face, heart, arms, legs, neck, fanny, and all those places combined. The Japs used a bullet like the .22 hollow point that made a small hole going in and a huge one going out. One guy here got hit in the chest and it came out his back injuring his backbone and spinal column. He's paralyzed from the waist down to his toes. Has no control over his urine and bowels. The doctor thought I too, might be paralyzed, as he stuck me with a pin up and down the legs. I could feel it, believe me! I almost lost control of urine, and they threatened me with a title drainage system. Wet the bed too many times, so that they had to change my sheets and pajamas too frequently. Very embarrassing. Now they ask every ten minutes if I need a" duck" (urinal). Of course, I never have to ride the silver saddle anymore. All that duty is done in my trips to the head. Such is life. My roommate suffers on a bedpan each day. What a miserable feeling! I've been on a bedpan once since being confined to the sack. Then they gave me an enema—very unsatisfactory.

My oh my, this sack time is getting tiresome. Can't seem to get comfortable, can't sleep at night, muscles ache and all that sort of thing. Nurse just gave me a sleeping pill, so should be able to sleep tonight. The nurses around here are very nice, except for one very efficient race horse. She's very sharp with the tongue--has been known to very thoroughly read off half dead patients. She has given me the devil a couple of times. I talk right back to the gal. Harass the patients—that's her motto. And that she does! That is everybody but my roommate and myself. He and I stay right on an even keel with her. No harsh words or blows exchanged, no nothing. (SEVERAL SENTENCES WERE CENSORED OUT AT THIS POINT.) for them at all. A very good friend of mine was killed by a mortar burst on D-day. They waited until we hit the beach and then opened up on us. It was mighty hot for a few days. We had to throw our plans to the winds and then go to work. My how we did work! I've never worked like that in all my life. Twenty four hours a day—no sleep. After the bullets stopped whistling around, I began to feel like a slacker. Then as an answer to my desires, I was called up to join a rifle company. Five others went at the same time. Two of them were killed. One other was killed after I was evacuated. I picked up a fifteen man platoon—all that was left of an original 50 man outfit, with machine guns. When we got through that first day I only had twelve left. I had three machine gun squads attached—lost four of those boys, too. All to one well hidden sniper. Snipers were really mean—very accurate, too! They wore Marine uniforms, and if you saw them out front, you thought they were your own men and held fire. We were finally replaced by replacements from the shore parties. Some of my old men joined my platoon. I hated to see that as they were awfully green—didn't know the scoop. A

---

[1] John weighed about 205 when he landed on Iwo. Later in Hawaii, he weighed in at 175 lb.

177

lot of those boys were killed on the lines—more from their own ignorance or stupidity than anything else. Didn't realize there could be snipers behind them as well as in front. Or didn't realize the accuracy with which Japs fire their mortars. Knee mortars are a terrible thing, as well as their 90mm., 150 mm. and 240 mm. mortars. Our largest mortar is the 81mm. mortar. And it doles out a lot of trouble. Can be fired 3200 yards and goes 1960 yds. up in flight. That's where it's fired at a 45 degree angle. At high angles, it can be fired at much shorter range. Two hundred yards to be exact. Our 60 mm. mortars can be fired as close as 100 yds. With a very high angle of fire. It's not so deadly though—doesn't explode with as much force or fragmentation. The latter mortar goes with the company wherever it goes, (the mortar section usually staying with the C. P.[1] Company). The 81's are a battalion outfit, and go with the battalion C.P. Whenever a company wants 81 fire, it calls battalion and usually gets it. Same with artillery fire. Call for it and if they aren't busy firing elsewhere they'll fire for you. That's all there is to it. Oh well, the island was finally secured—it was slow going—about fifty feet per day. The little rock was really an arsenal. The terrain was terrific—for defensive purposes. You couldn't lead a platoon across that country for love or money. Three divisions on line on a space two miles wide at its widest point. No room to maneuver—it was all just straight ahead movement into heavy fire of Nambu's[2] and snipers. .25 caliber bullets don't do too much damage at long ranges. They were good marksmen though, right in the head, neck, chest or stomach every time. I got awfully tired of seeing it happen—you'll never know how I felt about it, that's for sure. Always wondering when I'd get hit, walking around careless as "hell". Finally a mortar fragment creased my cranium. Didn't even know a thing till I was several hundred miles away in a hospital. Now I wonder who took over my platoon. I had a corporal acting as platoon sgt. My only sergeant was hit the day before I was. At least I guess I was hit the next day. One never knows does one?

Well, I've rambled on too long now, so must close up shop. This is almost a book.

All my love
John

Lt. John S. Hyndman

P.S. Please don't worry about me. I am in great shape (Better than ever).

John

P.S. (Jr.) This hospital life is the best yet. Sack time all the time, I love it.

---

[1] C.P = Command Post. MV

[2] Kijiri Nambu was a Japanese career army officer who founded the Nambu Arms Manufacturing Company. His company produced many of the firearms use by the Japanese Army. John is probably referring here to one of the Nambu machine guns. MV

LETTER FROM LOU HINDBAUGH

Des Arc, Mo
Nov.11, 1996

Dear Mrs. Hyndman,
I am writing hoping to find out about my officer in training and landing on Iwo Jima with your last name. We landed on Green beach I on Iwo "D" day morning and was assigned to Beach party ammunition. We were than with the 27th repl. Bn. Lt. Hyndman was immediately taken from us to replace officers in a different who were killed and wounded. Our other officer Lt. James stayed with us but he was wounded on "D" day evening and evacuated. We carried out our duties until no longer needed there and then what was left of us joined D co. 2nd bn. 26 reg. 5th Div. I made it all the way past the third airfield and had about another 200 to 300 yards to be taken when I was severely wounded. I was paralyzed in everything but my right arm when I was wounded, but thankfully I have made a good recovery and have had a decent life and am still fairly healthy and really enjoy life.

While I was in the hospital in Pearl Harbor I still could not move, but two men from our unit who were wounded and recovering came by my bed and visited with me. They were Pvt. Hodge and Pvt. Hitchener. They told me they saw Lt. Hyndman there and he was severely wounded. He was still alive, but not in very good condition. That was the last I heard from then and about the Lt. I hope it was my officer and he recovered and had a good life. He was a wonderful officer and I was proud to have served under his command. Please let me know if he was my officer.

One of the men of our original unit went with him and served as his runner. His name was Icasa (I am not sure of the spelling and he was killed .in action.* I have only been able to locate one other man alive from our original unit. His name was C. Heron and he was from Tenn. I believe Lt. Hyndman was originally from Kansas.

Louis E. Hindbaugh

---

*John told me about losing this particular man. They were in a fox hole shortly after John took over the platoon on March 5, and since be was new, John warned him to keep his head down. He showed John a picture of his family in the Rio Grande Valley of Texas and then raised his head. A Japanese sniper shot him between the eyes. LH

Lou came to visit us in Texas and filled me in with what he remembered of his time with John. We keep in touch. At time of publication, Lou is the only man left from John's outfit. LH

LETTER 118A

Letter from John F. Garner

April 9, 1945

Dear Cousins,

Am just in receipt of your copy of John's letter. Thank God he still lives! It was a newsy letter giving much more detail than most boys write home. No doubt he will soon be home and let us hope, home to stay., I am going to write him direct today. Iwo Jima was the worst battle of this war. No one will ever know except the boys who were in it, how terrible it was.

It does look like the war in Europe is about finished, but I am afraid we have still a long fight ahead in the Pacific—unless the Japs realize there is no hope and are willing to give up to prevent annihilation.[1] Keep a stiff upper lip folks, the worst is over for John and you still have much to be thankful for. It is terrible the suffering he has had to undergo, but just so he gets well. Always let me know what news you have because I am terribly anxious about John always.

Fondest love,
John

---

[1] After our carriers destroyed the power of Japanese Naval Aviation, especially the loss of experienced pilots, at the "Mariana Turkey Shoot," the Japanese turned more and more to a strategy of suicide attacks on our naval forces and fighting to the death in land operations. Kamikaze attacks during the Okinawa operation caused more naval casualties and damage or loss of ships than during any other period of the war except at Pearl Harbor. On Iwo and Okinawa the Japanese casualty rate was over 90% **Killed in Action!** Predicting the future is usually a fool's game, but after the experience with civilian Japanese on Saipan and Okinawa, it seems likely that the invasion of Japan would have been a blood bath for our invading forces, the Japanese army, and most of all the Japanese civilians. The two atomic bombs over Hiroshima and Nagasaki in August 1945 saved men scheduled for Operation Olympic from the worst campaign they could imagine. MV

LETTER FROM THE RED CROSS

American Red Cross

Postmarked April 10, 1945

> U.S. Naval Hospital
> Navy No. 10 (one zero)
> C/o Fleet Post Office
> San Francisco, California

Mr. Eugene Hyndman
524 N. Washington
Wellington, Kansas

Dear Mr. Hyndman:

    We are writing at the request of your son, Lt. John S. Hyndman, to give you news of his condition.

    You have undoubtedly received notice from the combat area of Lt. Hyndman's injury. He sustained a compound fracture of the skull, and was unconscious for a week. You will be happy to hear that he has now improved so much that he can be up and around the ward, where he can visit with friends. His memory has returned for all events except those immediately following his injury. He will, however, have a long convalescence. His transfer to a hospital on the mainland is under consideration.

    You may rest assured that your son is receiving the best possible medical and surgical attention. This is a large naval hospital whose staff members are experts in their respective fields. Nurses and corpsman provide continuous nursing care, and Lt. Hundeman's (their spelling) ward medical officer has him under constant supervision.

    We join you in your relief that your son's injuries were no worse. Please let us know if there is any special service we may offer him.

> Sincerely yours,
>
> (Miss) Antonina Hansell
> Caseworker
> (Mrs.) Ruth H. Horton
> Field Director

LETTER 119

Postmarked April 14, 1945
Received April 18th

This letter was typewritten.

April 12, 1945

Dear Folks,

Received your very welcome letters yesterday addressed to the Hospital address. They got here in very good time. At the present time I am an "up" patient and am able to get up and walk to the movies. They are usually pretty good, so I think I will go pretty soon, and not knowing what is on, but trusting that it is pretty good.

Also yesterday, I received letters from Aunt Dott and Bonnie—they had also heard about it. They both said they were very anxious to hear from me as it had been a long time. Dott asked me to write to Betty again. She had already answered my first letter and was expecting to hear soon. Betty is now on her vacation, so I will write her this afternoon and address it to Aunt Dott's house.

Dott also said that Marilyn was getting ready to go to her first dance with her first date—all duly chaperoned, etc. She claims that Marilyn looks just like me—chuckle, chuckle!

Right now I am enjoying myself as much as possible in the surroundings. But am anxious to get started for the States. My roommate left yesterday for a Navy hospital in the States. Personally, I hope they send me to the one in Hutchinson. My bandage came off this morning, so I took a look at the wound in the mirror.[1] John Quite a little gash I have there—an operation to put a metal plate over it is in order now. That will probably be done in a mainland hospital. Just received another penicillin shot in the arm—I can hardly type now. It aches like mad as soon as they pull the needle out.

There went the fire alarm—the corpsman will be running in the room soon to close the windows and door.

This typewriter is quite the thing—I borrowed it from Keith Wheeler,[2] combat correspondent from the *Chicago Times*. Have you ever read his columns? He was on Iwo Jima and is now a patient here. Almost everyone who was on that island got hit. Colonels, correspondents, corpsmen, observers—everybody! Even doctors. We have one here in this ward who was with the 26th Marines. That's a regiment of the fifth division. I was in the 28th Marines—or have you already received my letter from Iwo Jima. It was written the day before we moved back up on the lines—I got hit two days later.

Aunt Dott tells me that she may have to get married next fall in order to get rid of a guy. How about that!

I received two letters from Bill Kessler who said his sister married Jack Cady, a fraternity brother of mine who is in the Navy. A Lt. (J.G.) who has been overseas for some time. Will be in the States for a good six months. Bill is in New River training boots, just out of boot camp. It's a tough life. But

[1] John said he could see a pulsation in the wound and he nearly fainted. LH

[2] Keith Wheeler mentions this typewriter in his book, *We are the Wounded.* He borrowed it from someone else. LH

now that I've been through an operation, or a part of one, I'm happy. It's pretty discouraging to be injured on your first one, but I'll soon get over it. On the second one, a guy kind of expects to get hit again. And I thought a steel helmet would ward off shrapnel. I can't remember, but my helmet must be a terrible mess. My pack, my billfold, my clothing roll, in fact, all my earthly possessions are still on Iwo Jima. Here I am getting ready to come home and haven't a thing with me. Not even a cent! Oh, well, I can draw some money as soon as I get stateside. Don't know when they are going to ship me out, but it will be any week now. The minute I arrive in California, I will wire you all. I'm hoping they will fly me back, but no doubt I will draw a slow ship. That will take me almost a week to make it. About six days to be , exact.

Yes, I am pretty close to where Marjorie was at the time of the (censored) attack. In fact awfully close. That is, if she was where I think she was. And you know where I think she was!

I have lost track of Frank Helms, so can't give you his mother's address. He joined an outfit after I did. I have no idea where he is or if he is safe. I don't think he knows whether I was wounded or not. Probably thinks I am dead—that's the rumor that was around. Several of my boys are here with the story that they heard I was dead. I guess I was out so cold that anyone who saw me thought I was dead. I know that there was one guy who was unconscious who I would have sworn was dead, but the corpsman working on him said he was alive. I couldn't even feel his pulse. But the corpsman said he was still breathing. The kid I was speaking of was my runner,[1] a new replacement who didn't know the score. He stepped right out on the skyline and got shot. He finally died though. Litter bearers failed to get to him and we found him in the same place next day—dead as a mackerel. I felt very bad about that—but you know how it is. One can't have any feelings in combat or he would go nuts! I have a new roommate, a Navy pilot who was hit off the coast of Japan by flak. He has psycho neurosis or combat fatigue. Sudden noises make him jittery as heck. Shell shock I guess. He's pretty miserable—has to lie on his stomach all the time. Has wounds in back of his legs so that he can't stand to lie on his back. His name is McCarthy and he is from West Springfield, Massachusetts.

Wish I could tell you which hospital I was in before coming to this one, but it is against censorship rules. All I can say is that it was an Army hospital very near Iwo Jima. The exact day that I got hit was the 9th of March. I found that out from my platoon sgt. who was hit on the eighth, one day before me. He is here now, going out on liberty, but I can't go out as long a I have a bandage on my head.

Well, I wrote too much last time, so will close with what I have already written. The letter hasn't been very good I'm sure. Who all did you let read the other letter? It's not that I object, but am curious to know. I am writing this on a Corona Zephyr portable which isn't any too good. I suppose you've noticed that already. I hate writing letters on a typewriter because I can't type as fast as I can think. I received a nice Easter card from West the other day. A lot of your letters have caught up with me since I arrived here in the hospital. The one with a picture of Bertelli[2] in it, also the one Daddy wrote enclosing the account of Wellington winning the Ark Valley championship from Arkansas City. Jerry Waugh sure went to town this year didn't he? Is Harold Rogers[3] the only sophomore on the All-Ark Valley team? How come Jerry didn't go out for basketball? I always thought he was a good

---

[1] The runner's name was Frank Icaza. I am trying to locate some of his family. LH
[2] Angelo Bertelli was the quarterback of the Notre Dame football team in 1943. MV
[3] Harold Rogers later married John's sister. He was an All-American honorable mention basketball player at Oklahoma State. LH

basketball player—a good left hand shot and all that. What is he going out for in track, anyway? Not the high jump I don't think. He never could jump very well—too heavy on his feet. You can tell Jerry I also received his letter telling me how big he is. And that I am sorry I called him chubby before.

It's too late to go to the movie now, so I will wait until evening to go. That will be a long wait for me. The days drag here you know. Right now I must go down to the QM and draw an issue of clothing. Hope they have some good field jackets. Must close.

All my love
John

The following quote from Keith Wheeler's Book. *We Are the Wounded,* tells of the typewriter John used to type this letter.

The following day Lt. Comdr. Kenneth McArdle, once of the San Francisco Examiner *city desk and then Navy public relations officer at Saipan, and Lloyd Tupling of United Press came to see me. They brought a stack of copy paper and carbon, two cans of beer, and a bottle of whiskey, plus Tupling's typewriter. I sat up in bed, curled my leg around the typewriter, and went to work. I didn't feel much like working and my head was full of cobwebs, but it seemed about time to explain to the Chicago* Times *office why no copy was coming from Iwo Jima.*

Mr. Wheeler wrote a wonderful book about his experiences on Iwo and then his experiences after being wounded. Reading it made clear what must have happened to John. From the records we know he was wounded on March 9. His records show he arrived at Hospital #204 (Guam) on 12 March 1945. From talking to Lou Hindbaugh and reading Wheeler's book, I believe he was evacuated from Iwo by the Hospital Ship, *USS Solace.* On 20 March, he told me he was conscious when they flew him from Guam to the Naval Hospital at Aeia Heights, Hawaii. He told the story of his flight from Guam in a plane where the wounded were stacked one above the other. The navy asked him if he could us a "duck" (urinal) on the trip. He indicated he could. However, later on during the trip the man below complained of urine dripping down on him. John said the nurse gave him a dressing down for lying to her. (The brain injury affected his social skills for awhile and he had to relearn some.)

On April 26, he set sail on the *USS Kwajalein,* CVE 98 to San Diego arriving about May 3. John recognized a friend from Wellington aboard ship named Jim Tout. I located him in Austin Texas. This letter tells about the meeting and also his war experiences.

Lois Hyndman

See pages 214-216 for letters from Jim Tout

LETTER 120

Postmarked April 15, 1945
Received April 19, 1945

April 13, 1945

Dear Folks,

Just received another letter from you as well as Harriet Felt. This made the second letter you had written since receiving my "book". I almost had to send it in a box. You said Dotty wanted to know where my wound is—it is just above the hairline on my forehead-right in the middle. I shall be bald right in front so good-bye to the old long, wavy hair.[1] Yes, I can still handle Jerry, although I'm not much heavier than he at the moment. I have lost about 25 to 30 pounds since D-Day. Weighed about 205 then. I got on the scales yesterday and tipped them at 175. Just a mere 30 pounds lighter than before. I was on the beach at the time the flag was raised on "Hot Rocks", but could see it go up. You should have heard everyone cheer! We thought the island had been secured. In fact, when the news came down next day that it would take another week, I couldn't believe it. Incidentally, it took 3 more weeks.[2] I was only on the rock 19 days. But I am surprised you were never notified of my being wounded. My other roommate's wife was notified. That's the guy from Idaho—MacDonald is his name.

So Dorothy had 20 shots of penicillin last summer, huh? I've only had 246. Take that back 247 about 15 minutes ago. Everyone tells me that when they start hurting, you are getting well. Hope so anyway.

You know, it's funny, but I also think my wound was a blessing in disguise. I never knew what hit me—can't even remember a shell exploding in my vicinity. No memories at all. I don't even know what I was doing at the time. That morning early, we moved out in a big push. I was hit about one o'clock in the afternoon, so they tell me. On an empty stomach too—how about that. Guess I didn't eat for several days after that. At the Army Hospital, the corpsman always fed me—I learned to drink coffee there. Drink it three times a day now—black. Was sorry to hear about (censored out) "missing in action." Anybody in that fix on Iwo could be considered dead. You couldn't get lost there.

Yes, I did fly here—only a day and a half. The army hospital was located at the first place you mentioned. That's all I can say about it. I did lose all my personal belongings, including toilet articles. The Red Cross supplied me with a few things, such as they are. The plastic razor isn't worth a hoot. Also need good shaving cream, after shave lotion and powder, toothbrush, paste and ditty bag. Please send a little money if you can. I would certainly appreciate it. Something to buy cigarettes with, you know. There is plenty of good reading

---

[1] The surgeon was able to save enough hair in front of the scar to cover it for many years. The scar became more visible as he grew bald. John had many more shots of penicillin until the wound healed so that a plate could be inserted. He mentions this in later letters.

[2] The flag was raised about 1030 on the morning of February 23, 1945. The island was declared "secured" on March 14 and a ceremony was conducted. The Fifth Marine Division continued cleaning up the north end of the island until March 26.

material here you know, but would love some eats. Cookies, candy, etc. I love that stuff. Maybe I could gain my weight back too. Be sure and send the package first class. It'll get here sooner. Also surer! Hope I'm here long enough to receive it. A hospital anywhere in the States[1] would make me happy, but Hutchinson would be even better.[2] Then you could visit me pretty frequently. I could go to Wichita on liberty, too. That would be pretty good. How about it, is there a ten o'clock curfew there now—I hope not.

Must close and go to sleep
All my love
John

---

[1] GIs in WWII didn't consider Hawaii as a part of the US. The Hawaiian Islands were a territory until statehood in 1959. MV

[2] He was sent to San Diego Naval Hospital as it was the closest hospital that had neurosurgery. LH

LETTER 121[1]

Headquarters U.S. Marine Corps
Washington, DC

13 April, 1945

My Dear Mr. and Mrs. Hyndman,

A brief report has just been received that your son, Second Lieutenant John Spencer Hyndman, USMCR, was wounded in action against the enemy on 9 March, 1945 at Iwo Jima, Volcano Islands.

Your anxiety is realized, and you may be sure that any additional details or information received will be forwarded to you at the earliest possible moment. Please notify this office of any change in your address.

Sincerely yours,

D. Routh
Major, U. S. Marine Corps

---

[1] This is a copy of the telegram John's family finally received from the Marine Corps over a month after he was wounded. LH

LETTER 122

Postmarked April 23, 1945
Addressed to Mrs. W. K. Moore

April 21, 1945

Dear Mary Margaret,[1]

Received your letter yesterday, and must say that it raised my morale one hundred percent.

Right now I am in pretty good shape and able to get up and walk around quite a lot. But am afraid I won't be quite up to my old badminton form. I have lost about 30 pounds since getting hit. Can't tell you about getting hit, because I don't remember a thing about it. It put me out like a light and I stayed that way for about four days. When I woke up, I had already been operated on and was in an Army Hospital at a nearby base. They took good care of me there—the nurses were exceptionally pretty. They're also pretty nice here at this Naval Hospital. Corpsmen are on the ball, too. As a result, I have received very good care and am ready to start back to the States. I'll be leaving here in about three days. Soon as I land in California, I'll call my folks and tell them I have arrived. Don't know what hospital I'll go to on the mainland, but hope it is Hutchinson or Olathe Naval Hospital (Good old Kansas).

When your letter arrived, I couldn't figure out from the return address who it was from—I guess I had forgotten your name was Moore. I certainly hope Keith is all right which I am sure he is. If you'll pardon me for saying so, the Navy is a safe outfit. That is excluding carriers, who take a beating. One of my roommates here was aboard a carrier when a Jap suicide plane dived into it. He had shrapnel wounds all over himself. The guy left for home a week ago.

Now I have a Naval aviator with me. He caught flak in both thighs off the coast of Japan. He flew a medium bomber. The pilot of the plane (he was the copilot) lost one of his legs and was clear out. So one of the crew, an enlisted man flew the plane clear back to Iwo Jima. The kid is up for DFC. Probably will get it. My roommate, the co-pilot is going back to the States—he's from Boston. Quite a character. He trained six months in Hutchinson, but didn't know where Wellington was. How about that! Used to make it to Wichita on liberty, too.

I received a letter from your mother several days ago, which I didn't answer—as yet, but will very soon. Did I know Mary Schnitzler? I don't believe I did. She must have been there after I left. Believe me when I get back to the States, I'm going to get all the time off I can. Thirty days convalescence and thirty days leave if possible. That will give me time to do a lot of things at home. Visit school, go out, go to W.U., go out, visit relatives, go out, etc. What a boring life that will be! Ho hum! I can hardly wait.

---

[1] This letter was written to John's cousin, Mary Margaret Felt (Mrs. Keith Moore). I know he was making little of the danger that her husband was in to make her feel a littler better. Keith was aboard the *USS Chauncey* and saw action at Okinawa. LH

As soon as I get in a stateside hospital, a metal plate will have to be put on my skull to cover up and protect the wound. Actually, I am very surprised to be alive now—for a while my brain was hanging out the hole in my head. Right now my head is infected. I get shot with penicillin every 4 hours. Have had around 260 shots since being wounded. Am just like a pin cushion all over—sore as a boil. I can't even sit on a hard chair anymore!

Enough of this chatter. I must close now.

As ever,
Johnny

The *USS Chauncey* DD 667 was a Fletcher-Class destroyer, the third Navy ship named for Commodore Isaac Chauncey (1779-1840). The *Chauncey* was a part of Task Force 58 commanded by Vice Admiral Mark Mitscher. The task force shielded our invasion forces during the three month battle for Okinawa. Ships of the task force suffered serious losses from the Japanese suicide strategy using kamikaze planes. The *Chauncey* earned seven battle stars during her service in World War II. MV

LETTER 123

Postmarked April 27, 1945
Received May 2, 1945

April 19, 1945

Dearest Folks,

A day or so ago I received a letter from Mother wanting to know why I hadn't written. That's mainly because it was hard to write while I was in bed. Now that I can get up, dress, etc., it is a little easier. Also I have written to a good many different people. I had a letter from Frank Garner—he said you had sent him a copy of my letter. Said he realized my injury had been very serious at first, but was glad to know I was getting along so well.

It's good to hear that the Red Cross sent you all a notice that I was getting along "as well as could be expected." You might say that I got along a whale of a lot better than that! In fact, while I was in the Army hospital –it's a wonder I lived what with part of my brain sticking out. Guess that was the closest shave I'll ever live to tell about.—A very intelligent looking brain I have too!!

I haven't left for the States yet, but expect to most any day. They've finally got the ball rolling in that respect. Miss Counsell wrote me a letter which arrived here yesterday. Also Catherine Murphy. They wrote very interesting letters, too. Catherine is a good gal—said Don Jones sent her a bottle of perfume from Paris. It thrilled her to death! So she said. Miss Counsell told me that she had just happened to drop down to Wellington one day—ran into Dorothy someplace and Dorothy told her the story. That was the day my long letter arrived.

By the way, is Bertha Clark still teaching at Wellington High? I've been wondering about that for some time. Her Christmas card had a Winfield return address on it. Mrs. Jones wrote me the other day. Said Don was still all right and with the 9th Army—Simpson's outfit. They seem to be leading the way over there. Wonder when it will be over, so the Army can come over here. Maybe I won't have to come back out if they move to the Pacific and take over. Sure hope they do decide to finish up Japan and China. Those are two tough spots that I want no part of. Your life would be worth about two cents on those operations. It wasn't even worth that much on Iwo Jima.

It was certainly too bad about President Roosevelt, wasn't it? Well Mother, guess you really called that incident. Hope Truman doesn't have any trouble doing the job. Some over in Washington may lead him astray.

So the 2 kids have really grown up, eh? The difference will probably be a shock to me. Hope I can recognize them! Jerry is the one that slays me with all that size. Next fall he should really make the football team. With that build, they should put him at end. The young Apollo of W.H.! I guess Dorothy is quite the young belle too. She has more dates than you can shake a stick at, it seems to me. With very nice boys too—isn't that right? Tell her I said to be prepared to scratch my back till her hands are worn out, just like she said she would in the cute letter she wrote from study hall one day. That was quite a letter and I really enjoyed it. Pictures for words and all that sort of thing.

I was sorry to hear that Wellington was beaten by the poorest team in the league. El Dorado was pretty poor this year, I guess. Not quite up to their old standards—used to be awfully good every year. They beat heck out of us several times. So W.H. has a pretty good track team—how far can Jerry throw the javelin? I used to be pretty good with that thing myself. Placed with it a couple of times at W.H. Dual meets of course—schools like Emporia and Washburn. Jerry must have had a pretty good time in Wichita. His letter sounded like it. The "Barber Shop Quartet Kid". Can he sing solo worth a darn? The day I ship out of here for the States, I'll do plenty of singing. Happy Day may it be soon!!

At the minute, I'm very sleepy. Got a sleeping pill tonight and it's starting to take effect. I better stop before I fall out of this chair on my face.

Much love to you all,

LETTER 124

Postmarked April 27th Rec'd May 2, 1945

April 23, 1945

Dear Folks,

Just received a letter from Mother this evening. It was good to hear again—Good to know that you've had two more letters already.

Yes, I remember Frank Dashler very well—but am sorry to hear he was killed. I knew him when I went that one semester in the seventh grade in Wellington.

So the Red Cross said I would have a long convalescence—hope they know what they are talking about. As soon as I am dismissed from the hospital in the States, I'm going to try and get thirty days convalescence plus a thirty day leave. Sixty days at home! How about that?

Received a letter from Mr. Schnider today. He wants me to use their home as headquarters when I hit Wichita. That I will do. After all, a free room for the night there will be great. Better than paying several dollars at one of the hotels.

Your package hasn't arrived yet, but might before I leave. It'll have to get here in the next couple of days though, because I'll be pulling out about Wednesday. Today is Monday. I should be back in California by next Wednesday or Tuesday. Will try to call the day I get back.

I won't need that money you sent because I got paid again today. Of course, I just drew $50 dollars, but that will last pretty well as long as I am confined to a hospital. I believe I have overdrawn my account now. Hope I don't get in any trouble over it. But not having my transfer pay account, there is no way of knowing how much I've got coming. I have drawn two emergency payments while here at the Naval Hospital. The first one disappeared the night I got it. I can't figure out what happened to it. In my pajama pocket when I went to sleep and gone the next morning. I looked all over the bed for it. Fifty dollars gone to pot!

Begging your pardon, I was on the Rock 18 days. I did land on D-day as I already told you. Vox Pop Johnson got his finger shot off.[1] Bill Granell,[2] who went all the way through training with me is not here! In fact, I don't believe he was ever wounded—they never did assign him to an outfit. Left him to work the beach. What a lucky guy he turned out to be. We landed on the same boat and spent the first two nights together. What cold, miserable nights they were, too! We had a foxhole that was hardly big enough for one person. Talk about being cramped up—and we were expecting a counter attack, too! Boy, some of those nights, especially in the front lines were really mean. I hope I never spend another night like them!

You may be right about me never having to go to combat again, but I'm not so sure. The Marine Corps is a little different than the Army.. Tell that to your friends who say I won't have to go back. Why six

---
[1] See Bill Johnson's letters to Lois written in 2003 on page 208-212.
[2] See more about Bill Grannel on page 192.

months from the time I get back, they'll put me in the 127 Replacement Draft and send me out again. That's one experience I'm not looking forward to.

All I want to do now is ship out from here to the Golden Gate in Frisco. Then to a Kansas hospital, preferably Hutchinson. It's within easy reach of home. On liberty from there, I would go to Wichita and even Wellington. Idle dreams! Knock it off J. Spencer!!!! In Wichita I would like very much to see Mel Binford at W.U. and Miss Counsell at W. East--also the people up at Stanolind Oil and Gas Co. I wonder if that place is the same. It should be—nobody there is in danger of being drafted. Except maybe the boss himself. He was pretty young when I was there. And should still be almost the same age. Of course, he may have aged a great deal since I left, I think most people did.

The War was pretty tough on the folks back in the States, I hear. The servicemen stationed there are going nuts to get out here and we out here are going nuts to get back. It's a vicious circle any way you look at it.

Love
John (over)

April 24, 1945

Folks, Guess what I am leaving tomorrow morning by (blank been erased).

That's a load off my mind. Going back as an "up" patient and should enjoy myself thoroughly. Sit out on deck and all that sort of thing. I'll get to watch the Golden Gate as we come to it, that is, if we go to Frisco. We're liable to dock anyplace. But I hope it turns out to be San Francisco. When I left there, I didn't expect to see the "Golden Gate" for at least two years.

Today I received 29 old letters with a lot of your letters. It took me most of the morning to read the mail. There was very nice letter from Betty Payne with the bunch! Also a couple from Joanne Wallace and there was one from West. Don't believe Mary Ann will ever give up.

[2]**Bill Granell** went ashore with John on D-Day. He was wounded twice on March 19 on the north end of the island. His wounds were not considered serious enough for evacuation and he went to the 5th Division Hospital on Iwo. Bill received a Letter of Commendation w/v and two Purple Hearts. After the war, he was president of the 5th Marine Division Association., Bill was chairman and CEO of several wholesale supply companies in Denver, Colorado and retired in 1994. He now resides in South Fork, Colorado. LH

PART IV. STATESIDE HOSPITALS

SAN DIEGO NAVAL HOSPITAL

RANCHO SANTA FE CONVALESCENT HOSPITAL

LETTER 125

Postmarked May 7, 1945
Saturday May 5, 1945

Dear Folks,

It's great feeling to be back in the States again. Even if I am in a hospital.. This is a regular country club—plenty nice. They don't even make me stay in the sack. I can go about pretty much as I please. Can't go out on liberty yet, as I lost my identification card on Iwo Jima. However, I'm having a new one made now, which will take about a week.

Yesterday I called the Allyns on the phone and talked to Inez for about fifteen minutes. They'll be down to see me tomorrow. I hope my phone call home didn't cost you folks too much. Sorry I had to call collect, but the nurse brought a phone to my room and plugged it in. Then there was no way to pay for the call myself. At least I didn't think there was until yesterday when I called Eagle Rock—the operator asked if I wanted to pay for the call myself. I said yes, so they came around this morning and collected $3.94 for five minutes plus ten minutes overtime.

Also I sent a wire to Don Hollar who is at Camp Pendleton now. Hope he gets it and comes down here soon. I'd like to talk to him before he goes overseas. A word to the wise is sufficient! Or should be. Hope he is more careful than I was. When you come right down to it, I was taking very foolish chances. Got away with it for quite awhile, but finally they caught up with me.

My roommate here is a young Navy doctor who was attached to the Marines on Iwo Jima. He caught shrapnel in the shoulder while eating chow in his foxhole.

The trip to (from) Pearl Harbor to San Diego was comfortable, but discouragingly slow. I thought we'd never make it. Do you remember Jim Tout? He is now a full lieutenant in the Navy Air Corps. He rode back with me. He had completed 18 months overseas, so was in good condition and eager to get home to his wife—a girl from Texas. He had written her to meet him in San Diego on the 1st of May, but it was the 3rd before we arrived. He was sort of worried for fear she had gone back to Texas! I haven't heard yet whether or not he found her. I do know that he plans to come see me here at the hospital. He hasn't shown up yet, but should Sunday. I was very surprised to see him on the ship. Ran into him quite by accident the first day aboard. He recognized my face, but couldn't remember my name.

There is one favor you can do for me, please. That is, send whatever officer's uniforms I happen to have at home to me. Including the barracks hat with the tan cover. You may leave the green cover on it, but enclose the extra cover to wear home on furlough. I believe the only uniforms I have at home are:

1. One pr. Green trousers
2. One tropical worsted blouse
3. One barracks hat

Everything else is missing. In order to buy the rest of my uniforms, you will have to send me whatever money I happen to have. I sent home about $400, so if there is $300 left, please send it immediately. The money you sent to Pearl Harbor never did arrive there, but may catch up with me here.

In case you haven't already guessed what hospitals I was in, here they are. Number one: Army General Hospital #204, Guam; and Navy Hospital #10 at Aiea Heights on Oahu—near Pearl Harbor Navy Yards.

When I first arrived overseas, I landed at Maui, Territory of Hawaii, where I spent ten wonderful days. Then I was moved to Hilo, Hawaii, where our draft was billeted at the Naval Air Station. I boarded ship to go to Iwo Jima, January 5; made practice landings with 4th Division on Maui, then spent a week in port at Honolulu—that's where I mailed several letters to you all. From Honolulu we sailed by convoy to Kwajalein[1] (the name of the aircraft carrier I came to the States in), then to Saipan where I mailed a letter and finally to Iwo Jima.

By the way, did you clip the picture of the fallen Marine you thought was me? I would like to see it very much. Want to check the resemblance!

Think I've written enough, so will close for now.

Love
John

P.S. Don't forget the uniforms and money. It looks like I'll stay here to be operated on. The doctor says this is the closest Neurosurgical Center to Kansas. Plenty of L.A. liberty here, too.

John

---

[1] The *USS Kwajalein*, CVE 98 was an escort carrier. Whenever a ship in the Pacific returned to a US port, men were transported back to the states. A carrier with its large medical staff and sick bay would be a natural choice for sending wounded men home. MV

LETTER 126

Postmarked May 21, 1945

Dear Folks,

Received the money in good condition and will go downtown to buy uniforms tomorrow. I am almost positive that I won't get a discharge. But will go easy anyway.

Just had a visit from Marsha's daughter who works in the telephone office at night. I guess she never has lived in Wellington because she doesn't know very many people there. She's lived here six years and says she doesn't particularly want to go back. I believe everyone who lives in California truly loves the state. Kind of like (it) myself.

Say by the way Daddy, can you make my excuses about any possible speeches on Iwo? I will still have to be careful about what I say. And no doubt some Daily News representative will be at a Rotary meeting. I was given definite orders not to be interviewed by the press without first seeing a Navy Public Relations Officer to have my speech or story cleared. I doubt if there is one of those gizmos around Wellington.

Well, I just heard some bad news from the brain surgeon here. He looked at my head awhile ago and gave me his verdict. Here it is: there is a bunch of dead bone embedded in the wound which must be taken out this week, Then it will take 2 or 3 months for my head to heal up enough for them to put in the plate. To add insult to injury, I'm back on penicillin again. I'm hoping to get my leave at home during the interlude, but that might not be possible. Just hoping!

It does look like I'll be seeing a lot of hospital duty. Might last until Christmas. I don't think I could hold out much longer than that. But as long as I am able to get up and get around, it shouldn't be too bad. I'd sure hate that much sack duty. Probably would wither to nothing. About 60 pounds.

After a slight interruption of conversation with a retired Naval Officer, I am back. This guy enlisted in the Navy in 1894 at 16 years of age. Really an old salt. He builds historical ship models. More patience than I'll ever have. He sure has a lot of sea stories to tell. In his day few sailors could read or write, but many could speak several languages as they had served on ships of many countries.

May 19, 1945

After a 5 day delay, with a reminder from Daddy on the phone last nite, I shall continue this epistle. The main reason I haven't written as frequently as overseas, is because there is so little to write about—spending all your time in a hospital. It's very tiring and boring, to say the least.

I do have some news now which I am going to call you about this evening. This morning, I made a trip to surgery, which was a cinch. They didn't give me ether or anything of the sort—just a local like the dentist does the teeth. The doc sure got a lot of dead bone out of there. Broke it up in little pieces which half filled a small glass. Also he found a piece of shrapnel there. It wasn't shown to me, but was pretty big, I guess.

However, I felt fine though. Should be able to get up again in a couple of days. I could right now, but they won't let me—darn the luck. If there's anything I hate, it's being tied down to the sack. Especially when I'm able to get up and get around. Monday, I intend to get up, go downtown and pick up the new uniform I bought. I spent $100 for clothing, so have a lot left. But as soon as they get in some tropical worsted, I intend to buy trousers for the blouse I already have--the one you sent me. There's no need for you to send the enlisted blouse, because I'll never need it again. An officer wearing those clothes would look slightly silly--or at least feel silly.

May 20, 1945

Good news—I'm up again! And going to the show in a few minutes. Your delicious cake just arrived and I've eaten most of it already with the help of my roommate, a corpsman and nurse. They all liked it very much. Must close now.

Love
John

P.S. Mother, I'm awfully sorry I didn't write or call on Mother's Day, but I was in Los Angeles at the time and broke. Couldn't call or wire either. Didn't make it out to see the folks because I met a family from Carthage, Missouri, who entertained me thoroughly. The bandage on my head made everyone take notice. Tomorrow, I'm going to start work on a convalescent leave, so might be home before long.

Goodbye for now.

John

Rancho de Santa Fe Convalescent Home.
The Bishop House at Rancho Santa Fe was designed by architect Sylvanus Marston in 1929 for the Reverend Ellis Bishop. The two story house is replete with lots of balconies, patios, balustrades, and plenty of grill work. The estate includes fountains, a huge swimming pool, tennis court. The property was bought in 1936 by John Burnham, the son of the famous Chicago architect, Daniel Burnham.. During WWII, the property was leased to the US Navy as a convalescent hospital. John was stationed here during his recovery from the shrapnel wound in his head and while recovering from the operation placing the titanium plate over the wound.

LETTER 127

Postmarked June 4, 1945

May 25, 1945

Dear Folks,

Just a short line to remind you that I am fine and in very good health. Went to see Don Hollar last nite and found Gunnar Hald and Ralph Abell there too. So we had a big reunion and bull session. All the Notre Dame "Cavaliers" are in California except Kessler and Abrams—the footballer from Missouri. The other boys seem to think Kessler has already shipped out because he was in the 54th draft and the 65th is standing by to leave now. They have no idea where Abrams is, because he never writes anybody. All they know is that he isn't at New River anymore. Grant Hall, the boy I met out here last fall—a member of the Cavaliers—is still at Pendleton. And I looked all over for him at Iwo Jima.

May 26, 1945

Good news—I'm to get leave before the next operation. But will have to wait until the wound heals up before getting it. At first, I thought they were going to operate three months from now, but I was wrong. They are going to wait 2 or 3 months after it heals—so the furlough.

Just received a long letter from Mother. She says I've neglected you all, which is probably true—but I do have a terrible time thinking of something to write about. So Jerry is singing solo now—I'd like to hear him. That's something I could never have done.

Sunday noon

Just got back from church. The Chaplain who preached was very good. There was a pretty large crowd because almost everyone here is a wounded veteran and a faithful churchgoer.

Days later (one week).

Since I stopped writing Sunday, I have spent 72 hours with Don at San Clemente. Received your package and the $25 that you sent to Pearl Harbor as well as Kate Murphy's package. There were several kinds of candy—all good and all gone.

I want to apologize for this letter. It is really quite a mess, and I've been a long time writing it. But it's really the best I can do, considering that I'm in a hospital. Personally, I hate San Diego and I can't wait to get a furlough to go home. It may not be too long because I have an appointment in the morning with the surgeon who pulled the dead bone out of my head. Maybe he will be able to tell me how soon it will be, but doubt if he'll know -- he didn't. Just saw I was nearer ready than before. However, my guess is that it'll be well over a month. May be not, though. I certainly hope not. Don't ever worry about me getting sold on California, because I never will, as long as I'm in San Diego. It is without a doubt the poorest town in America. Even worse than Honolulu, which was pretty bad.

No more scoop for now so will close. From now on my letter will be short, but more frequent.

Love
John

LETTER 128

Postmarked June 9, 1945

June 4, 1945
Dear Folks,

Please allow me to thank you for the lovely Christmas box. After all these months, it finally arrived—in good shape too. I hope the cigarettes are good as I'm giving them to Don and Barbara. Expect she'll need them when he goes overseas and she goes back to Kansas. I have another 72, so am going back up there tomorrow—maybe I'll take part of the pass in L. A. with the Allyn's. I must get up to see them as soon as possible. They've been halfway expecting me ever since I've arrived in California.

Just got back from an evening with a Lt. Commander in the British Royal Navy. And a very "jolly bloke" he is too. Pip pip. Met some of the other officers from his ship and was invited to lunch tomorrow aboard their aircraft carrier.

They are cleaning up our room now for inspection. When inspection day comes around it means everything, and patients mean practically nothing. A man died yesterday while they were holding field day and they didn't know it until a visitor came and found him.

By the way, are they expecting Don Jones home soon—and has Harlan Altman ever gotten home? I'm hoping they'll be home when I get there. Remember the time I got home in 1943—Don got there about the same time. A very fortunate situation to say the least. We could have a wonderful time together at home. But I must write him because I have received several letters while in the hospital. Most were written to the 27th Draft before he knew I was hurt. Hold on, just got another from him written in May. Now he knows all about it—but says he doesn't think much of Marine tactics. That is, throwing a few men into something that the Army would use hundreds to do. I don't agree with him—we lose men to do a job quick while the army loses the same amount over a period of time. I'll wager that if all 6 Marine Divisions had landed on Okinawa things would be secured long before—maybe within a month's time.

Whenever the movie short "To the Shores Of Iwo Jima" comes to Wellington, don't miss it. It shows exactly what a hell hole the place was and you will really appreciate what we went through. I imagine you already do. Don't you think it's worse to sit home and imagine what's happening, than to be actually on the scene where you are too busy to worry? I know I certainly didn't worry for one minute, except at night. That's when I said all my prayers—everyone else, too, for that matter. Nites were horrible with the smell of dead Nips and Marines, danger of attacks, mortar fire, infiltration and air raids. Also if you moved, you were subject to fire from friendly troops. We were ordered to kill anything that moved with grenades or rifles, preferably grenades to keep our position hidden. If they ever found your exact position, you were a dead pigeon. (Of course, when we advanced in the daytime they could see us.) That's what made it so cursed bloody.

Well, I'm going to take off on liberty pretty soon, so must close.
Love, John

P.S. I changed to pencil because the pen is terrible to write with.

LETTER 129

Postmarked June 10, 1945

June 9, 1945

Dear Folks,

Today I'm turning over a new leaf. From now on I intend—and I mean it—to write short and frequent notes. I hope it keeps you happy as so many of your letters do me. Several of your letters addressed to "B" Company, 28th Marines got here today. You didn't sound too worried although one was written about a day before you received my first letter. Both you and Daddy hoped I was back in a rest camp and all that. No, I didn't know this Corporal Wilson who was a cousin of Maude's, but I did know a Captain Wilson[1]—also killed.

Sorry I wasn't here when you called Tuesday nite, but that nite I spent with Don—as well as part of Wednesday. Then I went on up to Los Angeles, but wasn't there long enough to see Perce and family. I intend to see them next trip.

The trip—aboard Santa Fe train—from L.A. to San Diego—is really beautiful. We passed by grove after grove of orange trees—I wanted to jump right out the window into the middle of them. That was near Santa Ana. Then the route followed right along the ocean through Laguna Beach, San Clemente, Oceanside, Del Mar and San Diego.

While in L.A. I was walking down the street and some lady walked up to me and asked if I knew a Captain Moore of the 5th Division. Of course, I did as he was my skipper while I was still part of the shore party. He has since been promoted to Major and is executive officer of the 5th Pioneer Bn. At the time he was Co. Commander of "C" Company, 5th Pioneers.

Hey, just had a visitor from Wellington. It was a girl named Mary Hill—who I just faintly remember. Believe she was quite a bit behind me. Must be married though, as she was carrying a baby with her. Do you know whom she married?

Just saw a very fine movie. Bette Davis in "The Corn Is Green".

It was good to hear that you are all fine. I am too!!!

Love

John

---

[1] Captain Wilson was CO of the Battalion Headquarters Company. When the COs of the line companies were wounded or killed, he replaced one of them. The casualty rate among platoon and company commanders was high. MV

LETTER 130

Postmarked June 11, 1945

June 10, 1945

Dear Folks,

Still trying to keep my promise, I will knock off another letter to you tonight. There really isn't anything to say, but I will do my best anyway. I just don't want you to worry about me in any way. Tomorrow morning I have another appointment with the brain surgeon who wants to check up on my head at least once a week. This time maybe he can tell me when I can come home. He's better be able to anyway. Or I'll give him the word—after all, he's only a Commander in the Navy! -- equal to a Lt. Colonel in the Marine Corps. By the way, have you heard anything from or about Brig. Gen. Thomas. He's a very fine man and an excellent speaker. You probably remember that he made the graduation speech the time I got my commission. Everybody liked him too, but he didn't recognize my name. I got another letter from Don Jones the other day and he said he was leaving Europe some time this month, so he might be home when I get there. I should be there by July anyway. That's being a little pessimistic, but you can't count on anything in the Naval service. Personally, I can't wait to get home, but might be ready to come back before my thirty days are up. I've about given up the idea of sixty days, because I rather doubt if the Navy will see things my way. So please don't expect me to be home for that long. Although I'd go wild if they should give me that much. Think I'll ask for it anyway—they can't do any more than say no.

You know, I'm going to have to go to bed pretty quick as it is after eleven p.m. My bed time is long past.

I've got to get up at seven in the morning in order to make my appointment on time. The last time I went over to his office he was already out making sick call and I had to wait an hour for him. He's sure a hard man to find when you haven't an appointment—always in surgery! I think the man does more operations than any other doctor here. Did I tell you that Capt. Gray, chief of surgery at the hospital at Pearl Harbor, is here now as chief of surgery. He used to hold the same job at the Mayo Clinic, so must be a very fine surgeon. At least he has plenty of experience. But won't put the plate in my head as his specialty is abdominal operations. However, the other doctor is a very fine surgeon and is sure to do a good job on me.

You all wanted to know the dimensions of the hole in my head; well, here they are approximately: 3 inches long, 1½ inches wide and about an inch deep. You can see the scar when I get home. In fact, it will be more than a scar—there still will be a depression. But not as deep as the original hole. Please don't let the size bother you because I have never suffered any pain with it. I just had to stay in bed for a while until my strength began to come back. Finally I got tired waiting for permission to get up, so I got up on my own and went to the head. I must close now as it is very late.

All my love,

John

LETTER 131

Postmarked June 13 1945

Dear Folks,

Once again I sit down to this faithful typewriter to knock out a letter to you all. I am fine and happy, but anxious to get home. Is Don Jones (home) yet? It would be nice to get home at the same time he does. Yesterday evening some Air Corps lieutenant called out here saying he was a friend of Kate Murphy. Can't figure out who it could be as he didn't leave his name. Maybe he'll be out this afternoon. Anyway I hope so as I am anxious to see someone I know. Might not know him anyway.

So Judy Van finally got married. I was beginning to wonder if she'd ever marry that guy. Wonder if he is the same guy I met at Notre Dame as a Midshipman. That's been a long time ago--he's had to get in all his service. You know I'm starved to death right now---the period between breakfast and lunch around here is much too long. There is a lapse of six hours between the two meals and only a lapse of four hours until dinner. Irregular meals kill me although they are very good at this place, especially at noon when the hospital staff eats here. It is a regular mess hall with cafeteria style service. A head-waiter to show you to your seat, a lady to take care of the tray, and girls to clean up the tables after we finish eating.

My pay accounts have arrived at the Marine Base in San Diego, so I went out to collect my money yesterday. Was shocked to find I had $350 dollars coming. Bought a tropical worsted uniform yesterday which I intend to wear home. It cost me $50 which isn't too expensive. I also bought a gabardine shirt and tie to go with the gabardine trousers that I got when first here.

Am going to a movie this afternoon---don't know what it is, but it's a good way to pass the time away. Time does go slow in hospitals as you probably know. In fact, I think I'd go nuts if I had to stay here without going home on leave. Going nuts right now as a matter of fact, but keeping it a secret. No doubt will be stark raving mad by the time I arrive in Wellington. I plan to catch a Navy Transport when leaving on furlough. Probably will take me to Olathe or Hutchinson where I can catch a bus or train. If it's Olathe, I'll probably drop up to Independence and see Dott. Has she told you she plans to marry next Fall? Maybe I'll be a civilian by that time---hope so anyway. Although I might decide to turn down a discharge and stay in. If I should get out it would certainly give me a head start in finishing school and all that but I don't think I'm in a very big hurry. What is your opinion on a medical survey? Should I take it or not? I'll do what ever you say.

Don Jones tells me not to be foolish enough to turn it down. He says I've done my share, but I don't believe one campaign is quite enough. Especially when I see boys with 3 and 4 battle stars on their Asiatic-Pacific ribbon. They are the ones who really deserve to get out. Not me.

Honest to goodness, I am feeling fine again, so don't worry about me. I certainly don't. There's still a little spot about the size of a dime which is raw down in my skull. As soon as that heals over, I'll be home for sure.

Will close for now. I am sorry about the dull letter.

All my love,
John

LETTERS FROM FRIENDS

John's letters ended with Letter 131. He was granted convascelent leave to Wellington, Kansas from June 30 to July 30, 1945. I don't know what happened to letters written after his first leave home since November 1943. He returned to San Diego where a tantalum plate was inserted on August 22. 1945 to cover the loss of bone in his skull. He had another leave Nov.1, 1945 and when he returned he was Sent to Rancho Santa Fe north of San Diego.[1] This was a convalescent home for officers not needing hospitalization, but not fit for duty. The home was a mansion[1] loaned by the owner to the Navy during the war. It had a swimming pool and tennis courts.

On April 1, 1946, John was retired as a second lieutenant by act of congress for disability.

Over the years that I have been working on these letters and trying to find shipmates and friends from his childhood through WWII. I was able to locate and correspond with a few of them. Their letters follow.

Lois Hyndman

---

[1] See the drawing on page 197.

LETTER FROM WALT EBY

November 11, 1996

Fraternity brother and good friend of John's.
I dated him before I met John.

Lois:

Your call was purely wonderful. Helen and I wondered about you and John. In fact, while working in the garden one hot humid August day, I for some reason began thinking of you and John. Later I asked Helen if she had your address, but we couldn't find it in our file. I hope that we will stay in touch.

As to your question of when I was on Iwo, I found what I think is the dates that I was on the Island the first time. As you may know the Island was exactly halfway between the B-29 bases and Japan., This caused two important changes in the methods used to fly to Japan. The first one was that all missions left the bases by at least 2:00 A.M. The second was to fly between 100 and 200 feet above the water. This meant that we flew below their radar and their night fight fighters were at a great disadvantage in finding us. In doing this we were using more fuel than if we were at high altitude. You ask, well why didn't you fly higher. We could not because the normal mission lasted from 13 1/2 to 15 hours. The plane was not equipped to supply 11 men for that length of time. Plus the fact that if we had flown at 10,000 ft. the Japs would have been all over us! I may be wrong, but I seem to recall that more lives on the lost planes exceed those that were lost taking Iwo. In the final analysis, it became how much damage did we want to sustain bombing Japan.

All of this doesn't answer your question, but it might give you some insight as to why. Anyway, on the 8th of March 1945 after obtaining all the pictures that were required, we headed for home. An hour out of Japan we had an engine failure. Losing an engine is normally not a big problem, but ours was a runaway engine. This means that there is no way that the speed can be controlled. When this occurs, the propeller shaft either breaks off or burns off. This caused the prop to fly forward of the plane, then lose speed and come back toward the plane. When a plane is hit at the altitude we're flying at, the plane explodes. In our case, the prop missed us by a couple of feet. All this time we had used so much fuel that we knew that we would not make it back to the base. We knew that the Iwo field was not finished and that it was doubtful that we could land there. We had either land or ditch the plane along a coastline. A couple of hours later we made Iwo and finally made radio contact. The word was that if we landed it would be our responsibility. We made several fly-bys and finally decided to attempt a landing. We then informed our base as to what was going on. They informed us that a plane would be sent to pick up the film and review the plane. So we landed and what a landing!! A B29 was not made to land on a piece of scraped real estate. We dusted off everybody between the mountain and midway the length of the Island. I was in the nose and I never saw so many people diving for cover. Later we found out that we finally stopped approximately 30' from the American lines and that the only reason we had not been hit by enemy fire was we couldn't be seen due to the dust storm. We added to the dust by turning around and heading back to the mountain.

We were there about a week before we could take off. Until then we had to move the plane about every 15 min. After awhile the interval was 1/2 hr., 45 min., then no movement was required. At first we used the aircraft engines to move the plane, but "grunts" were complaining about the dust. It bothered their environment and gave the Japs an aiming point. So we were finally given a crew to move the plane by using a bulldozer plus chains. There is a lot more that I could tell you about our visit on Iwo, but that's another tale, I hope that I have answered your question. But if I haven't let me know.

As always

Helen and Walter.

LETTER FROM NOTRE DAME FRIEND GRANT HALL

Boise. Idaho, 17 Aug. 2006

Dear Lois,

I appreciate the phone call and letter and it brought back long memories of the past. Many names you referred to bring back memories by name, but no real information about many of them.

After Notre Dame, I went to Parris Island, S.C. to boot camp, then Lejuene, N.C. From there to Quantico, Va. And commissioned 2nd Lt., Camp Pendleton for infantry training, then transferred to Amphibian tractors at Boat Basin by Pendleton.

Was Amphib instructor for our troops and English officers. Finally sent to Hawaii, then to Maui to join the 5th Amphib Battalion. We were training and about ready to load out for Iwo for maneuvers when the war ended.

We spent much time in cleaning equipment and tractors then dumping them in the ocean. I was in the 5th Amphib battalion which was kept in contact so we eventually came back to Boat Basin..They wouldn't release me until a replacement was available, but finally it came, just before the unit was sent to the East Coast.

I stayed in the Reserves and went back to school at the University of Idaho. I was appointed Herdsman of the University Dairy Herd so had house to live in -- a full time job and could take 6 hrs. course work. After graduation was hired as a County Agriculture agent in Bonners Ferry. Idaho—from there to Caldwell, Id. Then to Boise, Id. As a supervisor over a dozen county staff. I finally got in the only Reserve unit in Idaho, but had attended 2 weeks active summer camp at Pendleton prior to the Boise unit. I was C.O. at Boise, then left and returned to school for a masters degree, but could never get back in the unit because I was senior.

I was discharged a captain but was short 1 ½ years for retirement.

Thanks for the pictures and memories.

LETTER FROM BOB ALLEN

```
                                        Bob Allen
                                        P. O. Box 331
                                        Snellville, Ga 30078
                                        August 27, 1999
```

Mrs. F. Trevitt
P. O. Box 65
Mediapolis, IA 52637-0065

Dear Margaret,

    I am delighted to know that Lt. Hutchcroft's note book is now in the hands of his family. I have been in possession of it since sometime in April of 1945. I had been notified some of my personal effects which I had abandoned on March 11 had been recovered and were being held at Company Headquarters. When I picked up my possessions, I noticed this note book in the trash and retrieved it. They had apparently salvaged Lt. Hutchcroft's pack and had discarded the notes since they were of a military nature. I assume his personal things were forwarded to his parents.

    As I remember, a group of us were trapped on top of a ridge on the northern end of Iwo in the "Band Lands." We had three dead and two wounded, all victims of sniper and machine gun fire. We discarded all our gear, except our rifles, in order to remove the dead and wounded from the ridge. I am quite certain Lt. Hutchcroft was one of the dead since that is where we suffered most of our casualties on the 11th.

    I was an 18 year old private fresh out of boot camp, and I joined B Company from the 31st Replacement Battalion on February 23 shortly before the patrol from E Company raised the flag atop Suribachi. Lt. Hutchcroft joined our company on March 5 after we returned to Suribachi from the battle of Hill 362A and Nishi Ridge. Originally, Lt. Hutchcroft assumed command of the mortar platoon of B Company, relieving 2nd Lt. Daniel Ginsburgh in order for Lt. Ginsburgh to assume control of the First Platoon. Lt. Ginsburgh had joined B Company on February 27 along with a large group of other replacements from the 27th and 31st Replacement Battalions.

    Shortly after we went back into the assault lines on March 8, Lt. Ginsburgh was killed. The next day Lt. Hutchcroft turned the mortar platoon over to PFC Rolla G. Henry and took command of Lt. Ginsburgh's platoon from an enlisted man. On March 9th Lt. John S. Hyndman, who had joined our company on March 5, received severe concussion from a mortar blast and was evacuated. Hyndman was in command of the Second Platoon. Cpl. Bernard Mueller took over and led the Second Platoon for two days. On March 11, shortly before he was killed, Lt. Hutchcroft assumed command of both the First and Second Platoons.

    I was a member of a machine gun squad which was attached to the Third Platoon lead by Lt. Clarke King. Lt. King commanded the Third Platoon from February 27 until he was wounded on March 13. Lt. King, also, came from the 27th Replacement Battalion and, no doubt, knew Lt. Hutchcroft. Clarke is still around, and I have corresponded with him during the past few years.

Lt. Hutchcroft's notes were invaluable to me. With only 8 weeks "boot camp," I knew little more than how to use a rifle. When I became a machine gunner on Iwo, I had never fired a machine gun and did not even know how to replace a barrel. I had once tossed a "dummy" hand grenade in "boot camp." Suffering only minor injuries from "friendly fire," I was the only member of my squad to survive Iwo, and I continued to serve as the gunner after we returned to Hawaii. Most everything I needed to know about being a Marine I learned from Lt. Hutchcroft's notes.

Of the seven officers joining B Company from the 27th Replacement Battalion two were killed and four were wounded. Only Captain Puckett survived unscathed. I would suspect your parents received a letter from Captain Puckett with details of Lt. Hutchcroft's death. Captain Puckett became the commanding officer of B Company on Iwo and continued in that capacity until the 28th Marines returned to the U. S. in December 1945. Captain Puckett passed away not long ago, and Clarke King is the only former officer of B Company I am still in contact with.

I am not sure what Lt. Hutchcroft's activities were between February 19 and March 5. On February 19 (D Day) he was either part of a ship's company, supervising the unloading of a ship, or a member of the shore party, helping unload supplies on the beach. If he was part of the shore party, he probably landed at about 10:00 o'clock (H-hour +1). If he was part of the ship's company, he remained aboard ship until the fourth or fifth day until after his ship was unloaded. At that time he would have joined the shore party on the beach. Being a member of the shore party was no picnic. My four days on the beach with the shore party were probably my most terrifying days.

Your daughter must be something special. It's hard to imagine why someone would leave Georgia and move to Iowa. (Just kidding, of course.) I have a number of distant kin in Iowa. Both my Bilbrey and Provow lines migrated west from Tennessee during the 1800s and some of them settled in Iowa. Some are still in the DeMoines area. I correspond with a distant cousin, Douglas Provow, who lives in Ames.

Several years ago our youngest daughter, Janie, did summer stock at Western Illinois in Macomb. One Sunday afternoon we drove across the Iowa state line just to say we had been in Iowa. We sat in the car a few minutes and listened to the corn grow. Then we drove back to Macomb. We couldn't see Iowa for the corn. On our farm in South Georgia (Thomasville), we thought we had a bumper crop if we made 50 bushels to the acre.

It is not likely I am telling you anything your family doesn't already know, but would you pass this information on to the person in your family who is preserving your family history?

Sincerely,

Bob Allen

PS: The attached is the information I lifted from the internet on your family. I notice Lt. Hutchcroft's date of death is incorrect on his data sheet. He was definitely killed on March 11, not March 16. By March 16 Lt. Fouch, Lt. Hutchcroft's successor, had been in control of both the 1st and 2nd Platoons five days.

Bob Allen was a member of the platoon that John and Lester Hutchroft led in the final days of cleaning out the Japs from the Northwest corner of Iwo. His letter to Hutchroft's sister describes what the battle was like as fought by a depleted platoon in the rugged terrain of Iwo. MV

LETTERS FROM BILL JOHNSON

Jan 16, 2003

Dear Lois,

Really enjoyed hearing from you this Christmas - New Year season. It should be a good time to write, but I'm spoiled — as my wife "M.F." (Mary Frances) writes so well, so I don't... much.

Our life is busy with ranch, farm, renting houses, children, grandchildren, politics in our newly incorporated village, and our church activities. You can fill in the gaps of these -- but I love most to go build something, carve wood, go to some beach, etc.

Yes, have read "We Few" -- A good report on our group. I went from U. of Texas, to Engineering Detachment V-12 at U. of Colo, to Parris Island, to New River, to SOCS to Calif., to Maui (4th), to Hawaii (5th). Think John & I were together, maybe from P.I. on —

209

Hope your medical problems and moving chores are over for awhile -- and that you can continue to enjoy the grandchildren.
Happy New Year -- and love,

from Bill Johnson

Dear Lois

Thanks' for your nice letter -- which resurfaced on my desk today. Glad you're still keeping up with Marine friends.

Without digging up old Marine Corps stuff, I'll answer your questions as best as I can.

I was one of the few marines from Iwo who didn't land on first boat in first wave! Saw John on the beach once -- usual conversation of who got shot. I was probably wounded about 10 days after the landing going up, always up, hill 362 something A,B,C,D -? Spent time in a 'shell hole -- Eventually able to head back for help -- with my good left arm helping a buddy with one good leg -- An endless walk -- too open -- lots of mortar rounds -- Flag on Suribachi didn't comfort us much! Ended up on cot in tent -- ended up in sand when 155s or 105s opened up their barrages ... no corpsmen, etc as we in that tent weren't "head, stomach" men. Next day, afternoon, loaded onto DUWK to a 3rd Div. transport ship (Capt.s son was a USMC

Sergeant who died as we left Iwo area... to Guam (for a week or so) with gas-gangrene shot reaction (hives) for a week... Ship to Oahu.— Saw John at Aiea Heights hospital, where he was well cared for, but had little to say. Home, finished at U. Tex., married, 5 children. Discharged 1950 ±

Was 1st Plt, B Co, 1st Bn, 27th Reg, 5th Div...

Summary -- enjoyed life with Hyndman, Hatchcroft, Humphries, D. Jones, etc. WWII was the last war - when we knew the enemy, and our country is still worth fighting for!

Appreciate you, Lou —

Bill Johnson

LETTER FROM MARGARET TREWITT

May 22, 2007

Dear Lois,

Thank you again for sending the book and letters. As I told you on the phone it is not easy for me to read about Iwo. Am enclosing a copy the last letter that Bill (Lester) wrote home to the folks. And also a copy of a letter I received from Bob Allen who found me on the internet. The other page is a copy of a page from a book about Iwo that my sister borrowed from our library.

Here is a list of the names that were mentioned in some of Bill's letters.

Jack D. Culley – Nickolas Knezervich, Jr. – John Hyndman – John Huffman – Bob Humphreys (who wrote the book "We are Not Barbarians") – Bill Johnson – Dick Kelly – 2nd Lt. Rhudoff - James D. Harris

As I told you on the phone, I am the last of seven children (one brother died before I was born) There were four boys and three girls. My younger sister died at the age of 47. Because of a heart murmer my oldest brother was not in the service. Another brother was a pilot in the Air Force and the same day that my folks received a telegram that Bill was killed they received another saying Harold's plane had been shot down but that he had survived the crash. My other sister and I were very close. She died three years ago. Needless to say I miss them all and often wonder why I'm the last.

Frank and I have been married 61 years and have three children. A son and two daughters. 9 grandchildren (5 of them are bonuses) 13 great grandchildren, 6 of whom are bonuses (I don't care for the term step children. Therefore the bonus)

This is probably more information that you wanted to know so I will close and get this in the mail.

Margaret

LETTERS FROM JIM TOUT[1]

Saturday, 17 FEB. (2007)

Dear Lois,

I enjoyed receiving your letter, the memoriam and the copies of letters written by John. I've read the letters I think three times.

John was in the class behind me in Wellington and our acquaintance was primarily as members of the football squad. However, when we ran into each other on our way back to the states it was a feeling I'll never forget. I had reported for active duty as an aviation cadet during March of 1942 and since that time I had never run on to a single person that I had know before the war. That was a good feeling.

After getting my wings and commission during November of 1942 I spent one year being trained to direct pilots in their approaches and landings upon aircraft carriers. Then in October of 1943 I went aboard the USS Enterprise (CV-6) as a Landing Signal Officer. From then until the last of April 1945 the Enterprise participated in every island hopping campaign including Iwo Jima, although the Enterprise was hit by Kamakazies (sp/) my war years were really easy. I was awarded the Bronze Star for bringing planes aboard while the carrier was being straffed, however, it was after the event that I learned that I been in any danger. The guns on the carrier were all going off and I was thinking the Jap planes would all be shot down before they got near the carrier.

After the war I returned to college and upon graduation I returned to active duty until I retired in 1969. During those years I would spend one tour at sea in a squadron then a tour training pilots. The highlight of my career was as commanding officer of a squadron that was accident free--carrier operations and all weather flights. My last tour of duty was as Executive Officer (second senior) of Naval Air Station, Kingsville.

After the Navy we moved to Woodland Park, Colorado (20 miles up Ute Pass from Colorado Springs) where we bought some vacation cabins. 12 cabins, 1, 2, and 3 bedrooms with kitchenetts and fireplaces. We operated like a motel during summer and rented them out by the month during the winter. After 10 years the beauty of the area was gradually replaced by had work so we sold the lodge (the name of the business was Woodland Hills Lodge and move here to Round Rock. That was in 1980 and I started playing golf three and four times a week. That was great until February of 2004 when I had to undergo treatment for vocal cord cancer. My cancer was cleared and I'm still OK but a month after my radiation treatments I threw out my left hip out and again 28 days later. I had had it replaced 1978. Now the doctors keep me slowed down because if I throw my hip out again they say it might be really had news. No more golf!!!

I've been married twice, 23 years and now 40 years. Three children. I hate to admit that one is a lawyer in Houston, another with a career with the IRS, and the third, my favorite has not settled down yet. I guess that's it. Again, I enjoyed receiving the news of John.

The very best,

Jim Tout.

The brother of my wife was also at Iwo Jima. He was in the 3rd Marine Division and saw the first flag being raised, not the one in pictures. He was hit by shrapnel and had his jaw broken and teeth knocked out. He killed one jap that was attacking him with a bayonet. The jap had a Japanese flag on him and some identification. Years later the Japanese family was located and the flag was returned to them

---

[1]

Monday, 5 March 07

Dear Lois, First to answer your questions.

When we arrived in San Diego, I met my wife that I had not seen for nearly 22 months. AS I remember we departed for Texas the following day. That was an emotional upside-down period and the last I saw John was I think the evening before we arrived in San Diego.

My father was a doctor and opened practice in Wellington before I was in kindergarten. He and a partner opened a hospital when I was a freshman in high school. He later sold his ownership in the hospital and moved to Texas when I was a freshman at Kansas Univ.

I remember the name Mary Margret Felt but she was not in my class. Kieth Moore and I were close friends during grade school and junior high. We lived next door to each other on Poplar Street. Later I became close with Kieth's older brother Phillip. Phillip married Rheba Helm who was in my class and we have seen each other during our high school reunions.

The brother of my wife is Robert Shaefer. He was in the 3rd Marine Division and was in on landings in both Guam and Iwo Jima. I think it was shrapnel in the knee during the Guam invasion and shrapnel in the jaw that knocked his teeth out during Iwo Jima. My wife called him this morning to get more information but he is in such bad shape physically that he did not want to talk and told he was "ready to go."

I was stationed in Kingsville from 56 to 58, New Iberia LA from 61 to 63 and again in Kingsville from 68 to 69. During each tour I made regular visits to the Navy staff in Corpus.

My Navy experience during the Iwo Jima operation was no different than many other days in the Pacific. I was a Landing Signal Officer aboard the USS Enterprise (CV-6). My job was to stand on a platform over the catwalk on the left side and hear the rear of the flight deck. With a paddle in each hand I assisted the pilots as they approached they ship for landing with their speed, altitude and lineup. If all was OK as they approached the ship I gave them a "cut: which meant they we ti OK'd iff the throttle and land. If all was not OK I gave them a wave off and they would try again. From November 43 through June of 45 we threw strikes on islands from the Gilbert Islands to Tokyo which included strikes at Iwo Jima from the 19th of Feb, 1945 through 9th of March. There was nothing really romantic about my experience because the wake of the ship and the planes approaching for a landing looked all the same. My job as to see that the pilots made a safe landing and where they were coming from or what they have been doing made no difference to me.

Over the years I made 690 carrier landings myself and that is what I wanted from the Landing Signal Officer, just get me aboard safely.

So as important as Iwo Jima was during the war, those days during Feb and March of 45 were all the same to me.

I hope this letter has been a little enlightening.

John was one of those that gave it his all and had a really rough time. Sometimes it is kind a embarrassing to me that even though I was there, my WWII was a piece of cake.

Wishing your the very best

Jim Tout

If I were to try and type a letter without errors I's never get it in t he mail.

TAPS

September 11, 1990

On November 19, 1990, John Hyndman's ashes were buried at Arlington with full military honors by the Marine Corps. The Marine Corp Band, a contingent of Marines with a horse drawn caisson wove through the cemetery from the headquarters building to the grave site (3581) shown on the enclosed map. John's children (two of whom had been Marines also) chose a metal ammunition box to hold his ashes.

A DVD of the entire ceremony is available from members of the family.

John S. Hyndman
October 22, 1922 -- September 11, 1990
In Memoriam

Forty two years ago, John Hyndman became an important part of our oil and gas exploration community. He died at his residence in Corpus Christi, Texas on September 11, 1990 after a short illness.

John was born October 20, 1922 in Wichita, Kansas and reared in Mayfield and Wellington, Kansas. He obtained a Bachelor of Arts degree in Petroleum Geology at Wichita State University in 1947. While at Wichita State, he lettered in three sports: basketball, football, and track, and was an active member of Phi Sigma fraternity. He attended the Navy V-12 school at Notre Dame University and was commissioned as a lieutenant in the United States Marine Crops. He commanded the 1st Platoon of Company B of the 5th Marine Division and was critically wounded during the Marine offensive on Iwo Jima during World War II. Many of his experiences were depicted in Richard Newcomb's book, "Iwo Jima." While recovering from his injuries, he spent one year in the San Diego Naval Hospital until he was retired from the USMC for his disabilities. John was an officer in the Corpus Christi Chapter of the Military Order of the World Wars and always gave his time and talents when asked to serve his country. He was active in the Marine Corps League, serving as its representative on the Mayor's Council of Veterans Affairs. In 1985, John was invited to the White House and honored along with other Iwo Jima veterans by President Ronald Reagan.

After graduation from Wichita State University, John was employed by Stanolind Oil and Gas (now Amoco) and worked as a senior geologist with Tom Barber and Caldwell Starkey, District Geologist with offices in the Kaffie Building in Corpus Christi. He remained with AMOCO until 1960, when he formed his own consulting firm in petroleum geology. My first professional contact with John was about 1950, when I was an open hole logging engineer with Halliburton. John was the field geologist supervising the development of Luby Field, Nueces County, Texas. John was friendly, technically excellent and a joy to work with. He did consulting work for Varn Petroleum, Corpus Christi Management Company, Tom Allen and many others for over thirty years. He was an active member of the Corpus Christi Geological Society (1948), the American Association of Petroleum Geologist (1948), Society of Independent Earth Scientists and certified by the American Institute of Professional Geologists.

John was efficient and professional in his work which he performed for operators throughout North America. He took time to provide guidance and direction to all who worked with him. He was an honor to his profession and his country. John was a devoted Christian and a Bible student of Colonel R.

B. Thiem's Worldwide Ministry of Berachah Church in Houston. This strong faith which sustained him through his many health problems over the years, also gave him the strength to enjoy his family and friends to the very last day of his life, even though critically ill.

Memorial services were conducted Monday, September 17, 1990, at the Protestant Chapel at the Corpus Christi Naval Air Station. Burial was in the National Cemetery in Arlington, Va. on November 5, with full military honors. Survivors include: his wife of 43 years, Lois Williams, formerly of Wichita, Kansas, two sons and a daughter, John S. Hyndman, Jr. of Corpus Christi, Gerald A. Hyndman of San Antonio, Texas, Jeanne Barber of Tampa, Florida; a brother Colonel Gerald S. Hyndman of Falls Church, Va., a sister, Dorothy Rogers of Wichita Falls, Texas; and his three grandchildren. His mother, Madge Hyndman died in Wichita Falls, Texas just three days after John's death. John's death at 67 ended a distinguished life of duty to God, country, family and his profession. He will be missed by his family, his friends and members of his profession, all of whom hold fond memories of him.

C. E. Jacobs
Corpus Christi

Photo Taken in 1960 for Newspaper Article about Opening His Own Business in Corpus Christi, TX

Memorial Service
for
Second Lieutenant

John Spencer Hyndman, USMC Ret.

17 September 1990
Protestant Chapel
Naval Air Station, Corpus Christi

++

Post the Colors	Color Guard
Eulogy	Mr. Mark Cameron
Presentation of Marine Corps Emblem	Joe A. Benairdes Commandant of Marine Corps League
Firing Party	
Taps	
Presentation of Flag	Col. Peter L. Perkins, USMC
Retire the Colors	Color Guard

Christian Death

This isn't death, it's glory.
This isn't dark, it's light.
It isn't stumbling, groping,
Or even faith, it's sight!
This isn't grief,
It's having my last tear wiped away.
It's sunrise and it's morning
Of my eternal day.
It isn't even praying,
It's speaking face to face;
It's listening and it's glimsing
The wonders of His grace.
For this is the end of pleading
For strength to bear my pain;
Not even pains dark memory
Will ever live again!
How did I bear that earth life
Before I came up higher;
Before my soul was granted
Its every deep desire.
Before I knew this rapture
Of meeting face to face
The One Who sought me, saved me,
And kept me by His grace!

by M. S. N.

Memorial Service for John Hyndman, 17 September 1990.

Caisson with Casket Containing Ashes.

Marine Band and Honor Guard.

View from Grave site.

Grave of John Spencer Hyndman, Arlington National Cemetery.

John's Grave Site

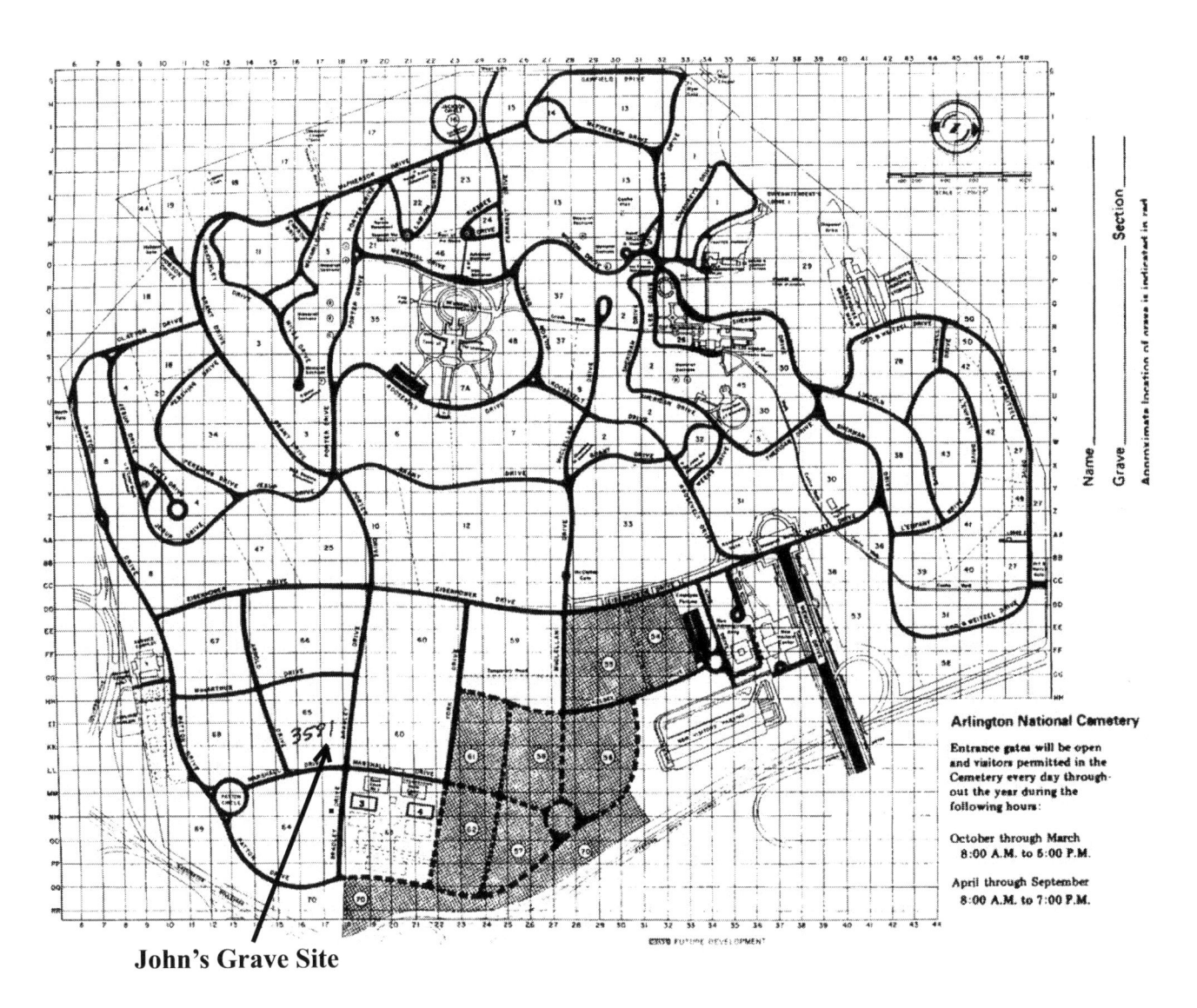

The Navy Hymn

Eternal Father strong to save.
Whose arm hath bound the restless wave,
Who biddest the mighty ocean deep
Its own appointed limits keep;
Oh, hear us when we cry to Thee
For those in peril on the sea!

Oh Christ, whose voice the waters heard
And hushed their raging at Thy Word.
Who walked on the foaming deep,
And calm amidst its rage dids't sleep;
Oh hear us when we cry to Thee,
For those in peril on the sea!

Most Holy Spirit! who dids't brood
Upon the chaos dark and rude,
And bid its angry tumult cease,
And give, for wild confusion, peace:
Oh hear us when we cry to Thee
For those in peril on the sea!

Oh, Trinity of love and power!
Our family should in danger's hour:
From rock and tempest, fire and foe,
Protect us wheresoever we go;
Thus evermore shall rise to Thee
Glad hymns of praise from land and sea.

A Marine Band played the Navy Hymn at John's funeral at Arlington Cemetery.

Washington

The President of the United States takes pleasure in presenting the PRESIDENTIAL UNIT CITATION to

ASSAULT TROOPS OF THE FIFTH AMPHIBIOUS CORPS, REINFORCED
UNITED STATES FLEET MARINE FORCE

for services as set forth in the following

CITATION:

"For extraordinay heroism in action during the seizure of enemy Japanese-held Iwo Jima, Volcano Islands, February 19 to 28, 1945. Landing against resistance which rapidly increased in fury as the Japanese pounded the beaches with artillery, rocket and mortar fire, the Assault Troops of the FIFTH Amphibious Corps inched ahead through shifting black volcanic sands, over heavily mined terrain, toward a garrison of jagged cliffs barricaded by an interlocking system of caves, pillboxes and blockhouses commanding all approaches. Often driven back with terrific losses in fierce hand-to-hand combat, the Assault Troops repeatedly hurled back the enemy's counterattacks to regain and hold lost positions, and continued the unrelenting drive to high ground and Motoyama Airfield No. 1, captured by the end of the second day. By their individual acts of heroism and their unfailing teamwork, these gallant officers and men fought against their own battle-fatigue and shock to advance in the face of the enemy's fanatical resistance; they charged each strongpoint, one by one, blasting out the hidden Japanese troops or sealing them in; within four days they had occupied the southern part of Motoyama Airfield No 2; simultaneously they stormed the steep slopes of Mount Suribachi to raise the United States Flag, and they seized the strongly defended hills to silence guns commanding the beaches and insure the conquest of Iwo Jima a vital inner defense of the Japanese Empire."

The following Assault Troops of the FIFTH Amphibious Corps, United States Fleet Marine Force, participated in the Iwo Jima Operation from February 19 to 28, 1945:

9th Marines; 21st Marines; 3rd Engineer Battalion (less detachment); 3rd Tank Battalion; 3rd Joint Assault Signal Company (less detachment); Reconnaissance Company, Headquarters Battalion, THIRD Marine Division; Liaison and Forward Observer Parties, 12th Marines; Pilots and Air Observers, Marine Observation Squadron 1; 23rd Marines; 24th Marines; 25th Marines; Companies A, B, and C, 4th Tank Battalion : Companies A, B, and C, 4th Engineer Battalion; 1st Joint Assault Signal Company; 1st, 2nd, 3rd Platoons, Military Police Company, Headquarters Battalion, FOURTH Marine Division: Companies A, B, and C, 4th Pioneer Battalion 10th Amphibian Tractor Battalion: 5th Amphibian Tractor Battalion: Reconnaissance Company, Headquarters Battalion FOURTH Marine Division: Companies A and B and Detachment, Headquarters Company, 2nd Armored Amphibian Battalion; 7th Marine War Dog Platoon: Pilots and Air Observers, Marine Observation Squadron 4; Liaison and Forward Observer Parties, 14th Marines; 1st Provisional Rocket Detachment; 26th Marines, 27th Marines, 28th Marines; 5th Engineer Battalion: 5th Tank Battalion: 6th War Dog Platoon: 5th Joint Assault Signal Company; 3rd Amphibian Tractor Battalion; 11th Amphibian Tractor Battalion; Companies A, B, and C, 5th Pioneer Battalion: Reconnaissance Company, Headquarters Battalion FIFTH Marine Division; 1st, 2nd, 3rd Platoons, Military Police Company, Headquarters Battalion, FIFTH Marine Division, 3rd Provisional Rocket Detachment; Pilots and Air Observers, Marine Observation Squadron 5; Liaison and Forward Observer Parties, 13th Marines: Companies C, D, and Detachment Headquarters Company, 2nd Armored Amphibian Battalion.

For the President,

John L. Sullivan
Secretary of the Navy

MEDALS AND RIBBONS.

KEY: MEDALS AND RIBBONS

Top Row Left to Right:

Purple Heart   **American Theater**   **Asiatic Pacific Theater**   **Victory Medal**
                                                             with one battle star

Ribbons: Left to Right:

Combat Action Ribbon   **Navy Unit Commendation**   **Presidential Unit Citation**

The Spearhead
Shoulder Patch of the Fifth Marine Division

2nd Lt. Gold Bars   **2nd Lt. Gold Bars**

Rifle Badge EXPERT   **Marine Corps Emblem**   **Dog Tag**[1]

[1] A Marine Dog Tag provided the following information: Name, Serial Number, Date of Tetanus Shot, Blood Type, Branch of Service:USMC or USCR.-

APPENDIX I. SPECIAL OFFICER CANDIDATES' SCHOOL

CAMP LEJEUNE, G.I.

SOCS Graduates Complete Sti[nt]

PAGE EIGHT

SCHOOLS REGIMENT

Tradition Of Marine Corps Being Handed On To Sons

By MARION A. ALLEN

That the Marine Corps tradition is being carried on into the second generation is definitely substantiated by the number of Marine Corps Juniors who have reported for the College Training Program. Pfc. Merritt A. Edson Jr., son of the well-known Brig. Gen. Merritt A. Edson, is with Company "A" of the V-12's. Brig. Gen. Lewie G. Merritt's son, Pvt. Lewie G. Merritt Jr., is teeing off on the college training program in Company "G." The sons of Col. E. A. Pollock, Col. Eugene F. C. Collier and Maj. Reginald G. Sauls III are "doing the three R's" together for the second time. Pvt. Erwin Allen Pollock, Tom Collier and Reginald G. Sauls IV. came through the Post School. T. F. Swearengen, is also a Marine Junior—son of Sgt. Maj. Charles C. Swearengen. Now Cpl. Swearengen is putting his former Post School cohorts through their paces as the D. I. for their platoon.

Last Saturday night, Battalion is in the groove on the recreation program. Company "A" and their WR guests danced to the syncopated rhythm of Montford Point Band, from the jitterbug to waltzes. The ready, willing and able chefs in the galley very capably took care of the refreshments.

F Company had a workout on the assault course last Friday evening—in the form of a stag period. The softball stars and enthusiasts worked up an appetite with several innings of friendly competition. The enthusiasm with which these fellows can attack food is little short of miraculous. Every lusty baritone, mellow tenor and basso-profundo gave forth with a bit of harmony in the song fest

Making Officers

ROSTER OF GRAD[UATES]

Allen, Robert D.
Allen, Robt W.
Allert, William J.
Alley, Lesley R.
Anderson, John O.
Armiger, John G.
Baade, John H.
Baigas, Joseph F. Jr.
Bailey, Almarion S.
Bailey, Richard C.
Baker, William L.
Banta, James S.
Barbarotto, Nicholas J.
Barnes, Edwin A. Jr.
Barrett, James B.
Berry, Richard P.
Berthelot, Paul D. Jr.
Billeaud, Roy J. Jr.
Bilotti, Anthony G.
Bittig, John A.
Blankenship, D.
Bloch, Edward
Blount, Earl E. Jr.
Bosworth, Frank K., Jr.
Bowdan, Stewart
Bradford, Jack T.
Bradley, Robert J.
Brandt, Fred A. Jr.
Breckenridge, Charles M.
Bressoud, Marius L., Jr.
Brooks, Edward J.
Brown, Fred V. Jr.
Brown, Robert R.
Brundage, Robert P.
Bruning, Glen A.
Rubeck, Arlin E.
Bunker, William W.
Burchard, Albert S.
Burke, John L., Jr.
Burress, Richard T.
Busch, William M.
Cabrall, Francis P., Jr.
Cardick, Thomas R.
Carnes, Webb McN., Jr.
Carney, Matthew J.
Carrell, Jeptha J.
Carter, William H.
Catterton, Elijah D., Jr.
Cavallini, Edward
Clement, Joseph F.

Clement, Mark A., Jr.
Clemmer, Joseph D.
Cline, John E.
Cohen, Erwin R.
Collins, Preston M.
Condley, Walter H.
Conlon, John M., Jr.
Connick, Louis, Jr.
Cook, Thomas C.
Cooper, Manly W. Jr.
Cowger, Harold V., Jr.
Craig, James
Craig, Robert P.
Crane, Duncan McL.
Crowton, Robert F.
Cunrad, Earl M., Jr.
Cunuff, John A.
Curtis, John A.
Dacus, Melvin O.
Dahl, John M.
Davis, Dick L.
Davis, Donald B.
Davis, Harold L.
Day, Scott, Jr
Dean, Robert L.
Deland, R.
DeLong, Robert A.
De Mange, Ewing A.
Denebeim, James E.
De Rose, Louis J.
De Vante, Earl H.
Dewhirst, Joseph F.
Dibble, Gordon K.
Dieffenderfer, James H.
Dillof, Henry
Ditto, William M.
Donnelly, Patrick R.
Drum, David G.
Dugger, William L., Jr.
Dunlap, Samuel A.
Dunn, James F., Jr.
Dunning, Charles W.
Eberhardt, Charles L.
Eckert, John A., III
Egbert, Eugene R.
Ehrisman, Richard D.
Elliott, Norman
English, Homer C.
Eubank, Joe C.
Euler, Robert C.
Evangelist, Nicholas C.
Everson, Virgil M.
Fajardo, Theodore C.
Falcon, Lawless C.
Fallon, John M.
Fansler, Jack W.

Helm, James B.
Helms, Frank J., Jr.
Henderson, Byron S., Jr.
Henderson, Eugene
Herwehe, Donald H.
Higgin, Wilfrid L., Jr.
Higgins, Bernard J.
Higgins, John B.
Hodgson, Robert D.
Holmes, Robert D.
Hourcade, Aime J.
Huck, John P.
Huffman, John M.
Hughes, Robert W., Jr.
Humphrey, Robert L.
Hungate, William J.
Hunt, Roy F., Jr.
Hurson, Daniel F.
Hutchcroft, Lester E.
Hyndman, John S.
Jackson, Murray T., Jr.
Jans, Ralph T.
Johnson, Horace L. V.
Johnson, Robert E. V.
Johnson, Robert R. T.
Johnson, William P., Jr.
Jones, Dunbar.
Jones, Henry J.
Jones, Robert E.
Jordan, Robert L.
Kalish, Norbert
Kearns, John V.
Keeley, John M.
Kelley, James D.
Kelly, Hugh S.
Kelly, William D.
Kenny, Henry B., Jr.
Kennedy, Frederick R.
Kerley, James J.
Key, William P.
Kimball, Peter R.
King, Clark.
Kitchen, Richard S.
Kleinman, Myron D.
Klingelhofer, Benjamin W.
Koehler, John L.
Koppitz, Paul N.
LaHood, Thomas J.
Lamport, Harry B., Jr
Landrigan, James M.
Larkin, John F.
Lauck, John H.
Leach, Edmund L.
Lee, Robert E.
Leggat, John E.

Some of the Netherlands Marines really kept the other members of the company on their toes trying to understand the lyrics of several Dutch songs . . . It takes more than ten easy lessons to do it . . .

Capt. G. W. Gage is the new officer candidates battalion recreation officer, replacing Ld. Gerard T. Chirazzi.

The Infantry Schools Battalion is anticipating another dance in the near future . . . PMSgt. Frank H. Bahm is now going through the Rifle Indoctrination Course. Soon he will be brushed up on rifle techniques to equal his chow calls. FM 1/c James W. Givin is replacing Sgt. Bahm with Headquarters and Service Company. Givin really blows a smooth bugle!

HE'LL HAVE TO WAIT

Officer Candidate James Dodd Eppright will have to wait a few weeks before receiving his gold bars.

Eppright completed the required training and study and has qualified for a commission —but he lacks a few weeks of being 19 years old. So arrangements were./made to award Eppright his commission on his 19th birthday on 19 October.

Pierro, Arthur A.
Fisher, William P.
Fitzgerald, Jack D.
Flanders, Alvan R., Jr.
Folks, Ray J., Jr.
Forman, William B.
Fortier, David R.
Fouch, Franklin W.
Franzman, Frederick L.
Friend, Emery H.
Frye, Robert E.
Fussell, Milton H. III.
Gagen, Joseph W.
Gaillard, Edward McC.
Gallagher, George G.
Gailiford, Walter T. Jr.
Garcia, Alberto.
Geagan, William J. Jr.
Ginsburg, Daniel.
Glase, Wayne R.
Golan, Leonard W.
Goodman, Marvin R.
Goodspeed, Neil C.
Goodwin, Robert R.
Grannell, William E.
Graustein, Ernest J.
Groome, Roland C.
Hanson, James F. Jr.
Harrington, Charles E. Jr.
Harris, James D.
Harris, Richard E.
Hart, John L.
Hartman, Burton A.
Hawkins, William B.
Hebert, Junius J.
Heilshorn, Kenneth N.
Heller, Carl A. Jr.

Lennan, Craig R.
Lennox, Grant H.
Leonard, Frederick C., Jr.
Lepore, Louis R., Jr.
Levy, David J.
Long, LeRoy C.
Louviere, Clarence J., Jr.
Lowell, Hervey W.
Lowry, Alan E.
Luchetti, Lawrence L.
Ludwig, Verle E.
Mackey, Willard C., Jr.
Madigan, Patrick R.
Mallet, Frederick J., Jr.
Marben, Arthur E.
Martineau, Fortune H.
Mason, Quintin.
Matthews, Donald V.
Matthews, Joseph O.
Mayer, George N.
McCaffrey, J.
McCormick, James J., II.
McCoy, Paul D.
McCreary, Kenneth G.
McDaniel, Charles P., Jr.
McDaniel, Frank, Jr.
McGinley, William J.
McNamee, Gerald G.
McNulty, Edward P.
McQuaid, Richard W.
Mearkle, James
Melcher, Thomas J.
Menzefos, Soterios J.
Mertens, Harry L.
Metzler, Robert J.
Middleton, George W., Jr.
Miller, Harold E.

WED., SEPT. 27, 1944 PAGE NINE

Course To Win Commissions

First Male OC Class At Camp Lejeune To Graduate Saturday

Climaxing eleven weeks of rugged training and intensive study, some 375 Marines of the Special Officer Candidate School will be commissioned as second lieutenants at graduation exercises Saturday, 30th October. The program will be held at the Rifle Range Theater and will begin at 1000 Saturday morning.

This group, which trained as a unit of the Schools Regiment, Training Command, FMF, is the first male OC class to be commissioned at Camp Lejeune.

The graduates will receive their commissions from Brig. Gen. Gerald C. Thomas, OinC of the Plans and Policies Section of HQMC. Gen. Thomas will deliver the address for the occasion. The complete program for the exercises is given elsewhere on this page.

On Friday morning, 29 September, there will be a promotion ceremony at which the officers-to-be will be promoted to platoon sergeant. This ceremony will be combined with the rehearsal for the graduation exercises. Lt. Col. M. A. Fawcett, OinC of SOCS and Maj. I. J. Irwin, Executive Officer, will officiate.

TRAINING RECORD

These are no "ninety-day won-ders" who have finished this eleven weeks "blitz" course. Their training record includes eight months of V-12 college work, nine weeks of boot camp at Parris Island and at Camp Lejeune, nine weeks of Officer Candidate Applicant training topped by the eleven weeks SOCS course which won them their gold bars. Thus, this particular group will have held active Officer Candidate rating for 15 months.

The term "blitz" is aptly applied to the course. Practically every day for eleven weeks the candidates were on the go from reveille until "lights out." A 40-hour-week would have seemed like a vacation in comparison to their work week which ran from 62 to 66 hours. And the training was really rugged, as evidenced by the pictures on these pages.

An average day's program, picked at random from the jam-packed schedule, ran something like this:

Classes in weapons from 0730 to 0930, classes in rifle platoon tactics from 0930 to 1130, classes on Naval law from 1230 to 1330, inspection at 1330, extended order drill from 1430 to 1530, classes in map reading from 1630 to 1845, field exercise in scouting and patrolling from 1845 to 2145.

The first phase of the course was devoted principally to the study of weapons and basic military fundamentals. The second phase gave them intensive training in tactics and field work and the third phase stressed field problems and combined the elements of all previous training.

STIFF COURSE

In both the classroom and field the candidates dug into such subjects as technique of fire, scouting and patrolling, jungle warfare, signal communications, interior guard duty, administration and organization, combat principles — to name only a few.

The ystudied not only Marine Corps weapons but learned to field strip and operate Jap weapons as well. They gained knowledge on how to take care of themselves and their equipment in the field, they learned to handle demolitions, to build and camouflage field fortifications; they went thru field exercises and landing problems.

Thus, these are well trained Marines who Saturday will receive their commissions and prepare to join, sooner or later, Marine units whose ultimate destination is Tokyo!

GRADUATION PROGRAM

Invocation by Capt. F. L. Albert, USN, Camp Chaplain.
Lt. Col. W. R. Williams, CO of Schools Regiment, will introduce the speaker, Brig. Gen. Gerald C. Thomas, OinC of Plans and Policies, HQMC.
Gen. Thomas will address the graduates and present their commissions.
Lt. Col. M. A. Fawcett, OinC of SOCS, will administer the oath of office.
Benediction by Lt. Camdr. J. P. Murphy, USNR, Senior Catholic Chaplain.

The Hard Way

Urgent Need For Anesthetists At Onslow Hospital

Wives of Lejeune Marines who have had experience as nurse anesthetists are sought by officials of the Onslow County Hospital in Jacksonville where an urgent need for such personnel exists.

Mr. Fletcher Little, manager of

GATES

Miller, Lloyd L.
Miller, Paul LeR.
Millspaugh, William H.
Mitchell, Owen H., Jr.
Monnett, Charles G., Jr.
Moore, Edgar F., Jr.
Moore, Myron L., Jr.
Morgan, Herbert J., Jr.
Morris, Hugh R.
Morrow, Joseph M.
Mottola, Vincent V.
Mruk, Leonard J.
Mueller, Donald E.
Muir, William M.
Mulligan, Francis J., Jr.
Munroe, Richard P.
Murphy, Dean G.
Murphy, Joseph C.
Myers, Curtis.
Nelson, William O.
Nichols, Carl W., Jr.
Nickels, Matthew J., Jr.
Nield, Ralph P.
Noble, Ralph W., II.
Nordmark, Elving C.
Norris, Williams S., Jr.
Novak, Anthony.
Nowicki, Joseph F.; X.
O'Neill, Emmet J., Jr.
Ossowski, Theo L.; R.
Overton, Timothy M.
Pace, Sidney B.
Pakradooni, Aram P.
Paulus, Firmin A.
Pawlyshyn, John.
Pearce, Harry P.
Penton, Hugh V.
Perrigo, Robert E.
Perrin, James R.
Peterson, William C.
Phillips, Kenneth L.
Pitman, John C.
Potts, Rand E.
Prescott, Karl J.
Primoff, Leon R.
Qualls, James L.
Randall, John W.
Raphael, Milton L.
Ray, Stanley.
Record, Walter R., Jr.
Reynolds, Robert A.
Rodgers, Wayne A.
Ronayne, James A.

Stroh, Alvin L.
Stubbs, Sidney J., Jr.
Tarter, James R.
Taylor, Ben L., Jr.
Taylor, Edward R.
Tenney, Henry M., Jr.
Teutschel, Charles A., Jr.
Thomas, Charles P.
Thomas, George L.
Thompson, Robert C.
Tobias, John E.
Todd, George K.
Tomkinson, Richard P.
Tomlinson, Thomas A.
Tongate, Ernest L., Jr.

Ross, Daniel M.
Royce, Harrison S., Jr.
Rubenstein, Albert.
Rubinow, Gerald M.
Ryan, Gerald C., Jr.
Ryan, Joseph J.
Ryan, Lawrence V.
Rybarsyk, Jack E.
Sadowski, George F.
Salwasser, Mervin J.
Samuels, Edward R.
Saperstein, S.
Savage, Harry L.
Schlegel, William L.
Schwartz, John L.
Scott, Gordon G.
Scott, Robert B.
Shaffner, Robert R., Jr.
Shean, Richard T.
Shearer, John F.
Sheridan, George R.
Shepard, John R.
Shinkarik, Michael.
Sieben, Paul T., Jr.
Simmons, Roy.
Sink, Kester A.
Smiley, Ernest T.
Smith, David R.
Smith, Edward W.
Smolkin, William.
Sockett, Charles S., Jr.
Soyars, William B., Jr.
Speary, William A.
Spencer, Dave C.
Steck, William P., Jr.
Stengle, William B.
Stevens, James H.
Stevenson, Peter C.
Stone, John W., Jr.
Strasenburgh, Edwin G., Jr.

Trehey, Harold L.
Tsigouns, Stanley A.
Turner, William A.
Vanseious, Kenneth C.
Vessie, William A.
Villaret, George C.
Vorys, Arthur T.
Wahlberg, Robert H.
Walker, Gordon P.
Ware, John A., Jr.
Warner, Johnathan S.
Wasserberg, Sidney.
Watto, John S.
Webb, Billy J.
Weiser, Elwood V.
Weiss, Richard L.
Wells, James H.
Westfeldt, Wallace O., Jr.
White, Robert O.
Wilson, Robert J.
Winant, John H.
Winfrey, Frank N.
Winter, Robert M.
Woll, Seneker.
Woodworth, Henry D., Jr.
Woog, John F.
Young, Eugene M.
Young, Vilas E.

TOUGH JAP

SAN DIEGO, Calif.—One of the "toughest" Japs he encountered in five campaigns in the South and Central Pacific was one on whom he and a buddy expended 10 rounds of ammunition before they killed him on Saipan, according to Marine Corporal Powell Michael Elrod Jr., of Detroit, Mich.

ienced in giving general anesthesia, who might be available. The position offers an excellent salary with living quarters if desired, he states.

Wives or other members of Marine families here who have had such experience and are interested in the position are requested to contact Mr. Little at the Onslow County Hospital in Jacksonville.

New Color Added To Marine Slanguage

SOMEWHERE IN THE SOUTHWEST PACIFIC—(Delayed) — Though much has been written about the slanguage of the lingo-loving Leathernecks new expressions are coined as Marines in the South Pacific find themselves in new surroundings and situations.

"Gook" he means a native of a tropical island. At most places Leathernecks hit-the-sack when they're ready for bed. In the South Pacific they "get under the net" (mosquito netting). He will boast to his buddies, "I'm a short-timer," to tell them he put in his time overseas and is waiting for transportation to the States.—By S/Sgt. E. L. Volk.

Ross, Daniel M.
Royce, Harrison S., Jr.
Rubenstein, Albert.
Rubinow, Gerald M.
Ryan, Gerald C., Jr.
Ryan, Joseph J.
Ryan, Lawrence V.
Rybaryk, Jack E.
Sadowski, George P.
Salwasser, Mervin J.
Samuels, Edward R.
Saperstein, S.
Savage, Harry L.
Schlegel, William L.
Schwartz, John L.
Scott, Gordon G.
Scott, Robert B.
Shaffner, Robert R., Jr.
Shean, Richard T.
Shearer, John.
Sheridan, George R.
Shepard, John R.
Shinkarik, Michael.
Sieben, Paul T., Jr.
Simmons, Roy.
Sink, Kester A.
Smiley, Ernest T.
Smith, David R.
Smith, Edward W.
Smolkin, William.
Sockett, Charles S.
Soyars, William B., Jr.
Speary, William A.
Spencer, Dave C.
Steck, William F., Jr.
Stengle, William B.
Stevens, James H.
Stevenson, Peter C.
Stone, John W., Jr.
Strasenburgh, Edwin G., Jr.

Trehey, Harold L.
Tsigounis, Stanley A.
Turner, William A.
Vanseious, Kenneth C.
Vessie, William A.
Villaret, George C.
Vorys, Arthur T.
Wahlberg, Robert H.
Walker, Gordon P.
Ware, John A., Jr.
Warner, Johnathan S.
Wasserberg, Sidney.
Watto, John S.
Webb, Billy J.
Weiser, Elwood V.
Weiss, Richard L.
Wells, James H.
Westfeldt, Wallace O., Jr.
White, Robert O.
Wilson, Robert J.
Winant, John H.
Winfrey, Frank N.
Winter, Robert M.
Woll, Seneker.
Woodworth, Henry D., Jr.
Woog, John F.
Young, Eugene M.
Young, Vilas E.

...enced in giving general anesthesia, who might be available. The position offers an excellent salary with living quarters if desired, he states.

Wives or other members of Marine families here who have had such experience and are interested in the position are requested to contact Mr. Little at the Onslow County Hospital in Jacksonville.

New Color Added To Marine Slanguage

SOMEWHERE IN THE SOUTHWEST PACIFIC—(Delayed) — Though much has been written about the slanguage of the lingo-loving Leathernecks new expressions are coined as Marines in the South Pacific find themselves in new surroundings and situations.

When a Marine talks about a "Gook" he means a native of a tropical island. At most places Leathernecks hit-the-sack when they're ready for bed. In the South Pacific they "get under the net" (mosquito netting). He will boast to his buddies, "I'm a short-timer," to tell them he put in his time overseas and is waiting for transportation to the States.—By S/Sgt. E. L. Volk.

TOUGH JAP

SAN DIEGO, Calif.—One of the "toughest" Japs he encountered in five campaigns in the South and Central Pacific was one on whom he and a buddy expended 10 rounds of ammunition before they killed him on Saipan, according to Marine Corporal Powell Michael Elrod Jr., of Detroit, Mich.

APPENDIX II.

In 1944, the pace of our attack against the Japanese in the Central Pacific quickened. The Marshall Islands were invaded in January-February, Saipan in June, Tinian and Guam in July-August, Pelilu in September, and finally Leyte in October. The Marines were primarily responsible for the first five and casualties were heavy, especially among platoon leaders. Many of the second lieutenants who survived these battles had been promoted. Four new regiments, 26th, 27th, 28th, and 29th were formed which required a full complement of platoon leaders. The Officer Candidate School at Quantico was filled .

A Special Officer Candidate School at Camp Lejeune was established in order to meet this heavy demand for new officers. The story of the "Marine Corps 400" is told in an article from the Marine Corps Gazette, October 1990.

All of the men in the SOCS were from the V-12 College Training Program and all had completed Boot Camp at Parris Island. Although still privates, the "college boys' had completed several months of rigorous physical and military training unlike new recruits. John's letters tell about being shipped to the candidates detachment at Camp Lejeune. As the V-12's finished boot camp, the number of potential candidates was larger than could he accommodated at Quantico. Three hundred and seventy five out of 400 received their commission on the rifle Range at Camp Lejeune. Lt. General Victor H. Krulak once said: of the SOCS *It was the finest class of second lieutenants that the U.S. Marine Corps ever produced.*

J. Fred Clement in his book, *The SCOS 400*, tells the story of this special group of Marine 2nd Lieutenants and the part they played in the last two operations of the war. In pages 184 through 191, Clement covers the period from 9 March through 12 March, when John took over the 1st platoon, B Company and was wounded. He brings the story alive by quoting accounts by Marines who led the attack. Here are the stories of John Hyndman and Lester Hutchcroft.

> John Hyndman (B/1/28 - PH) I went ashore on D-day with classmate Bill Grannell (F/2/26 - LOC w/V & PH w/star). We had been together in the Notre Dame V-12 unit, Boot Camp, and Camp Lejeune. The Japs waited until we hit the beach and then opened up on us. It was mighty hot for a few days. A very good friend, Bob Holmes (A/1/27 - PH w/2 stars), was killed by a mortar burst on D-day.
>
> We had to throw all of our plans to the wind. My how we did work! I've never worked like that in all my life. And 24 hours a day with no sleep.
>
> I spent the first two weeks on the beach supervising men in my Replacement Draft (used as a Shore Party) until I was assigned to go forward as a replacement officer in a rifle platoon. I was beginning to feel like a slacker since I was still on the beach. I made that short trip with five other classmates. Three of them were killed and the other two wounded. I picked up the 1st platoon in B/1/28 and five minutes later moved out in an attack. I didn't know a soul in the platoon. That's really doing things the hard way. I picked up a 15-man platoon - all that was left of the original 50. When we got through that first day, I only had 12 left. I had 3 machine-gun squads attached - lost 4 of those boys, too. All to one well hidden sniper. Snipers were really mean - very accurate, too!
>
> We stayed on the line all that day and that night. The next morning we were relieved by another outfit and marched back to the other end of the island. It was only a two mile walk, but after three days on the front, the boys were pretty tired. They had put in an extra day up there.

> We rested for three days and moved back up again on the 8th. We had finally received replacements from the shore parties. Some of my old men joined my platoon. I hated to see that as they were awfully green - didn't know the scoop. A lot of those boys were killed on the lines - more from their own ignorance or stupidity than anything else. Didn't realize there could be snipers behind them as well as in front. Or didn't realize the accuracy with which Japs fire their mortars. Knee mortars were a terrible thing - as well as their 90-mm., 150-mm. and 240-mm. mortars. Our largest mortar was the 81-mm. and it doled out a lot of trouble.

That little rock was really an arsenal. The terrain was terrific for defensive purposes. We had three divisions on a line that was two miles wide at the island's widest point. No room to maneuver - it was all just straight ahead into Nambu's (light machine guns) and snipers. The small caliber bullets don't do much damage at long ranges. The Japanese were good marksmen though. Their hits were right in the head, neck, chest or stomach almost every time. I got awfully tired of seeing it happen. It's a feeling you can't imagine to see one of your men hit. Also always wondering when I'd get hit while walking around careless-as-hell.

Finally, my second day back on the line, a large mortar fragment creased my cranium and I did a complete blackout. The next thing I knew, I was in an army hospital where I spent eight days. I'll always wonder who took over my platoon. I had a corporal acting as platoon sergeant. My only sergeant was hit the day we went back on the line.

The nurses were wonderful except when they shot me with penicillin or morphine. There wasn't an "unstuck" place on my body. Everything was sore clear down to my toes. There is always an exception to the nice ones and ours was one very efficient race horse. She was very sharp with the tongue - had been known to very thoroughly read off half dead patients. She did give-me-the-devil a couple of times. I talked right back to the ole' gal. Harass the patients - that's her motto. And that she does! That is everybody but my roommate and myself. He and I stay right on an even keel with her. No harsh words, no blows exchanged, no nothing.

In the room next to me was a 1st lieutenant from Idaho. He was a forward observer for the artillery. He spent nine of his eleven days in the front lines. Usually with an assault platoon. He received a terrific thigh wound from a sniper. They operated on him here and he now has two incisions almost a foot long in his leg.

When the doctor changed my dressing, with the other doctors observing, they asked me all kinds of questions. Such as: "When were you wounded? When were you operated on? How long were you unconscious? Do you have any pain?" I couldn't answer any of the questions except the last one - the answer to that one was "No pain."

A lot of people got hurt on this operation, especially officers. We were very vulnerable You couldn't see for heck where they (Japanese) were shooting from. Their pill boxes are wonders to behold. You can sit right on top of one and never see it. They really had the beach covered. Boy, it was murder. For fifteen days I watched guys all around get hit - killed or wounded. Some had terrible wounds. Lost legs, arms, fingers, heads and every other thing that was attached to their bodies. Bullets through the stomach, chest, face, heart, arms, legs, neck, fanny, and all those places combined. The Japs used a bullet like the .22 hollow-point that made a small hole going in and a huge one going out. One guy here got hit in the chest and it came out his back injuring his backbone and spinal column. He's paralyzed from the waist down to his toes. Has no control over his urine and bowels. The doctors thought I too might be paralyzed. As one stuck me with a pin up and down the legs I could feel it, believe me! I almost lost control of my urine and they threatened me with a tile drainage system for my bed. I had wet it too many times. So they had to change my sheets and pajamas too frequently - very embarrassing. Now they ask ever ten minutes if I need a "duck" (urinal). Of course, I never had to ride the silver saddle (stainless steel bedpan) anymore. All that duty is done in my trips to the head. Such is life. I've only been on a bedpan once since being confined to the sack. Then they gave me an enema - *very* unsatisfactory.

Note: Much of the information in this account is taken from John's Letter 117.

In B/1/28 was another SOCSer - **2nd Lt. Les Hutchcroft.** Hutch spent less than two weeks working with a Shore Party on the beach before he was called forward. He was to last only three days. His last command is described briefly in a 1965 book about Iwo Jima as follows:

> "**Second Lieutenant Lester E. Hutchcroft** and Second Lieutenant **Ginsburg** had started out together in the 27th Replacement Draft. Every time someone was killed at the top, **Ginsburg** moved up a notch and **Hutchcroft** followed him. **Ginsburg** got to the front March 5 at the head of the 2nd Platoon, Company B, 1/28, and three days later was killed. **Hutchcroft** got to the front on March 9, taking over the 1st Platoon as its fifth commander. Two days later there was little left of the 2nd Platoon, and he took that one over too, from Corporal Mueller. The same day (12 March 1945) **Hutchcroft** was killed. So depleted were the ranks now, that both platoons fell to privates first class." (Newcomb, 1965)

27th Replacement Battalion

► OFFICERS

Aughey, Robert M, 2 Lt
Compton, Joseph O, 2 Lt
Domeier, Dwayne H, 2 Lt
Fortier, David R, 2 Lt
Fouch, Franklin W, 2 Lt
Franzman, Frederick L, 2 Lt
Friend, Emery D II, 2 Lt
KIA Garcia, Alberto, 2 Lt
KIA Ginsburg, Daniel, 2 Lt
Glase, Wayne R, 2 Lt
Goodman, Marvin R, 2 Lt
Goodspeed, Neil C, 2 Lt
Graham, Thomas B, 2 Lt
W Grannell, William E, 2 Lt
KIA Harrington, Charles E Jr, 2 Lt
KIA Harris, James D, 2 Lt
KIA Hawkins, William B, 2 Lt
W Hebert, Junius J, 2 Lt
Helms, Frank J Jr, 2 Lt
KIA Henderson, Eugene, 2 Lt
Higgins, Bernard J, 2 Lt
Higgs, Donald V, 2 Lt
Hosmer, Milbur J, 2 Lt
W Huffman, John M, 2 Lt
W Humphrey, Robert L, 2 Lt
KIA Hutchcroft, Lester E, 2 Lt
W Hyndman, John S, 2 Lt
James, Stewart R, 2 Lt
Johnson, Robert E V, 2 Lt
W Johnson, William P Jr, 2 Lt
Kelley, Richard G, 2 Lt
Kelly, William D, 2 Lt
W King, Clark, 2 Lt
Kitchen, Richard S, 2 Lt
Kleinfelder, William Jr, 2 Lt
KIA Lamport, Harry B Jr, 2 Lt
W Lauck, John H, 2 Lt
KIA Leach, Edmund L, 2 Lt
W Leman, Craig B, 2 Lt
Lepore, Louis R Jr, 2 Lt
KIA Long, Philip I, 2 Lt
KIA Louviere, Clarence J Jr, 2 Lt
KIA Lowell, Hervey W, 2 Lt
W Lowry, Alan E, 2 Lt
McCaffrey, John, 2 Lt
Metcalfe, Robert B, 2 Lt
W Metzler, Robert J, 2 Lt
Parrett, Robert E, 2 Lt
Puckett, Charles R, Capt
Ramus, Victor J, 2 Lt
Shields, Robert F, 2 Lt
Sockett, Charles S, 2 Lt
KIA Walsh, James P, 2 Lt
W Welke, Roy A, 2 Lt

► ENLISTED MEN

Abel, Leland L, Pvt
W Abrams, James, Pvt
W Adams, Harold D, Pfc
W Adams, Henry L, Pvt
KIA Adams, Milton E, Pvt
W Addleman, Lee E, Pvt
KIA Agray, Henry, Pvt
KIA Aguzzoli, Mario A, Pvt
Akins, Loval M, Pvt
Alcorn, Raymond S, Pvt
W Aldridge, Hubert O, Pvt
W Alford, Floyd G, Pvt
W Allen, Darrell L, Pvt
Allen, James R, Pvt
W Allen, Osborne M Sr, Pvt
Altosino, Michael J, Pvt
W Alvarez, Manuel, Pvt
KIA Alvey, Norman E, Pvt
W Amerine, Cecil F, Pvt
KIA Amiot, Lloyd J, Pvt
TOW Anderson, Raymond P, Pvt
KIA Anderson, Ben E, Pvt
W Anderson, Ernest Le R, Pvt
KIA Anderson, Ervin R, Pvt
W Anderson, Gail S, Pvt
W Anderson, George LeR, Pvt
Anderson, Howard L, Pvt
W Anderson, Jack R, Pvt
W Anderson, Miles E, Pvt
W Anderson, Neville, Pvt
KIA Andreason, George H, Pvt
W Apolzan, George, Pvt
KIA Arabie, Rudolph J, Pvt
Aubusci, James A, Pfc
Arelt, Charles R, Pvt
Arendt, Raymond F, Pfc
Arledge, Joseph N, Pfc
Aremedariz, Roberto S, Pvt
W Arnold, Jack T, Pvt
W Arntson, Robert H, Pvt
W Arthur, Charles A, Pvt
Asbjornson, Carvel O, Pfc
Ashley, Nicholas, Pfc
Asper, Harold R, Pvt
Atterson, George H, Pfc
Ayers, George D, Pvt
W Ayers, Robert L, Pvt
Aymes, John O, Pvt
Babos, Robert J, Pvt
Baca, Valentin, Pvt
Bailey, Joseph W III, Pvt
Bailey, Leonard C, Pvt
Baird, Lewis R, Pvt
W Baker, Elmer E, Pvt
Baker, John S, Cpl
W Baker, Martin B, Pvt
Baker, Paul J, Pvt
W Baldwin, Jack Jr, Pvt
W Bandeen, James G, Cpl
W Banks, Woodrow W, Pvt
W Barber, William B, Pvt

Barkhurst, Jack V, Pvt
W Barlow, Riley M, Pvt
Barnes, Fred E, Pvt
KIA Barra, Calvin C, Pvt
W Barragree, Lawrence J, Pfc
Barrett, J L Sr, Pvt
Barth, Arthur, Pvt
W Barton, Clarence A, Pvt
Bartsch, Arthur G,
Bauer, Conard F, Pvt
W Baxter, Kenneth H, Pvt
Beattie, Warren R, Pvt
Beck, Alfred N, Pvt
Beck, Francis R, Pvt
W Becker, Marvin L, Pvt
KIA Bedois, John S, Pvt
KIA Beeler, Philip L, Pvt
W Belcher, Henry C Jr, Cpl
Belknap, Leland N, Pvt
W Bell, Donald A, Pvt
Bell, Eugene L, Pvt
Bell, James H Jr, Pvt
Bellini, Anthony W, Cpl
W Bemis, John H, Pvt
W Bennett, Carl E, Pvt
W Benston, Homer D, Pvt
W Berg, Mens O, Pvt
Bergdall, Richard S, Pvt
KIA Bergeson, Donald, Pvt
W Bernard, Louis E, Pvt
KIA Berry, Stanley R, Pvt
KIA Betley, Chester J, Pvt
Betts, Wm H, Pfc
Bieloh, George E, Pvt
W Biesman, Edward C, Pvt
W Bieszcak, Edward, Pvt
Billings, Gerald E, Pfc
W Binkie, Chester R, Pvt
KIA Bischoff, Henry F, Pvt
Bishop, William C, Pvt
W Bisson, Marcel H, Pvt
KIA Bivens, Arthur LeR, Pvt
Bixler, Alfred J, Pfc
Black, Jack C, Pvt
W Black, Norman L, Pvt
Blair, Edwin J, Pvt
Blank, Harold J, Pvt
Blankenship, Robert E, Pvt
W Boatright, Thomas C, Pvt
Boeckel, Edgar R, Pvt
Boehlke, Fred W, Pfc
Bordson, Richard V, Pvt
Born, Peter A, Pvt
W Bosher, Frank I, Pvt
Boswell, Elmer J, Pvt
KIA Bosworth, Lee S, Pvt
W Bott, Robert, Pvt
Bottorff, Cecil K Jr, Pvt
W Bowers, Rex J, Pvt
Bowery, Ernest, SSgt

W Boyers, Charles LaV, Pvt
W Bradford, Elmer F, Pvt
KIA Brandt, Albert E, Pvt
Brandt, Ralph W, Pfc
Brassfield, Jack A, Pvt
W Braymer, Velden D, Pvt
Breaux, Dave, Pvt
Bremer, Henry F, Pvt
Brendler, Wm A, Pfc
KIA Bridger, Charles H Jr, Pvt
Brieger, Curtis, L, Pfc
Brightwelle, Bob J, Pfc
W Briscoe, Donald M, Pvt
W Brittian, Jay, Pvt
W Brossia, Robert A, Pvt
W Brown, Arthur, Pfc
W Brown, Billy J, Pvt
W Brown, Clifford K, Pvt
KIA Brown, Cloyd M, Pfc
W Brown, Floyd A, Pvt
W Brown, Frank T, Pvt
KIA Brown, Louis, Pvt
KIA Brown, Louis E, Pfc
KIA Browne, William C, Pvt
W Bruce, Oscar O, Pvt
Brunner, John E, Cpl
Bryant, Lester M, Pvt
KIA Bryson, Robert D, Pvt
W Buck, Virgil G, Pfc
W Buckingham, Vincent D, Pvt
Budde, Arnold G R, Cpl
W Budge, George H, Pvt
Budris, Victor, Pvt
W Bull, Dwight E, Pvt
W Burba, Michael M, Pvt
W Burchfield, Joseph L, Pvt
Burgeis, Dean J, Pvt
W Burnett, Bruce E, Pvt
W Busby, Delmer E, Pvt
Buse, Raymond C, Pfc
W Butler, Charles R, Pvt
W Byers, Raymon M, Pvt
Bylski, James A, Pvt
W Byrne, Wm G, Pvt
W Cafarelli, Pete R, Cpl
KIA Caldwell, Kenneth C, Pfc
Calkins, Maurice E, Cpl
DOW Calvert, Robert W, Pvt
Campbell, Alfred, Pfc
W Campiran, Arthur, Pvt
Canard, Harvey C, Pvt
Cannon, John R, Pfc
Cantelmi, Umbert, Pvt
W Carder, Clyde E Jr, Pvt
KIA Cargill, Iroy G, Pvt
KIA Carlson, Russell E, Pfc
KIA Carmona, Philip E, Pvt
W Carrico, George W, Pvt
Carroll, Paul R, Pvt
Carter, Charles R, Pvt

233

W Gilbert, Russell J, Pvt
Gillespie, Stanley R, Pvt
W Gillis, Leslie R, Pfc
W Ginter, Walter M, Pvt
Glass, Robbie H, Pvt
Godfrey, Wilbert W Sr, Pvt
Godsey, Jack D Sr, Pvt
Goegel, Robert J, Pvt
Goldhagen, Andrew W, Pvt
Gomez, Roberto, Pvt
W Gore, Donald W, Pvt
Goswick, Frank, Pfc
Gottfried, Julius A, Pvt
W Gower, Hubert M, Pvt
Goyt, Kenneth R, Pvt
Graham, Kenneth R, Pvt
W Grant, Frank D, Pvt
Gray, Robert D, Pvt
Gray, Robert D, Jr, Pfc
Greathouse, Wm C, Pfc
W Green, Harry R, Pvt
W Green, John R, Pvt
W Green, Walter I, Sgt
Greer, Jack E, Cpl
W Gregory, George H Jr, Pfc
W Gregory, Robert, Pvt
KIA Gribble, Jesse W, Pvt
Griego, David, Pvt
Griego, Serafin C, Pvt
Griffin, Gerald H, Pfc
W Griner, Edward R, Pvt
Griswold, James W, Pvt
Growbner, Bernard A, Pvt
W Gross, Benny J, Pvt
KIA Gross, Malcolm, Pfc
KIA Gross, Robert J, Cpl
Grove, Daniel I, Pvt
W Grubb, Willie D, Pvt
W Gruenwald, Dean J L, Pvt
Grunstrup, Erling J, Pvt
W Grunerud, Ralph H, Pvt
DcW Grushey, George E, Pfc
Guderian, Elmer K, Pvt
Guedel, Harry T Sr, Pvt
Guinn, Omer, Pvt
Gunter, Howard E, Pvt
Harry C, Pvt

Mc
McKn.
McMahf.
McMurtre
McNabb, Be
McRill, Freddi
Nault, Leo J, Pfc
Nealy, Thomas V
Neaman, Bernard L
Nelson, Walk   Pfc
Ness, Roller   Pvt
Nettles, Arthur L J, Cpl
Newton, Edmund Jr, Sgt

W Hansen, Raymond A, Pvt
Hansely, Roy A, Pvt
Hanson, Eugene C, Pvt
W Hanson, Merle LeR, Pvt
Hautig, Kenneth W, Pvt
Hanzal, Albert R, Pvt
Harbison, John W, Pvt
Hardcastle, Herman, Pfc
W Hardyman, Tom B, Sgt
DoW Harmon, Samuel F, Pvt
Harness, Milton, Pvt
Harper, Albert H, Pvt
W Harper, James H, Pvt
KIA Harper, Marvin W Jr, Pvt
W Harrington, Charles E, Pvt
Harrington, Robert L, Pvt
Harris, Emmit W Jr, Pvt
KIA Harris, Thelmer D, Pvt
Harrison, Horace R, Pfc
W Harrison, William T, Pvt
W Hartley, Joseph B Sr, Pvt
Harwood, Arthur W, Pvt
W Hasse, Glenn M, Pvt
W Hatcher, Charles W, Pvt
W Hatzke, Albert A, Pvt
W Havenstrite, Harry W, Pvt
Haws, Kenneth R, Pvt
Hayes, Arturo, Pvt
Hayes, Robert L Jr, Pvt
W Haynes, Lavern W, Pvt
W Hazel, George W Jr, Pvt
W Head, James R, Pvt
Heaton, Donald F, Pvt
KIA Hebron, Samuel J, Pfc
Hedgwood, Edward, Pvt
Hedison, Haig H, Pvt
Heinrich, John M Jr, SSgt
KIA Hellem, Norman M, Pvt
KIA Helton, Eugene S Sr, Pvt
W Henderson, Raymond E, Pvt
Heneger, John A, Pfc
Henry, Fred N, Pvt
Henry, James E, Pvt
W Henry, Kenneth L, Pvt
Henson, Edward L, Pvt
Heron, Charles L, Pvt
W Harrington, Gaddis N, Pvt
Hesse, Siegel G, Pfc
Waldo J, Pvt
Pvt

W Holmes, Robert L, Pvt
KIA Holmes, Roy E, Pvt
Holt, Dayton V B, Pvt
W Holthusen, Harry H, Pvt
Hoover, Lawrence R, Pvt
W Horcasitas, Juan T, Pvt
W Horn, Harold A, Pfc
W Horne, Robert, Pvt
Houdashelt, David A, Pvt
Housman, Ralph J, Pvt
W Howard, George E, Pvt
W Howard, Leo M, Pvt
Howard, William H Jr, Pvt
W Howe, Clarence G, Pvt
W Howell, Bonnie J, Pvt
Hoyt, Donald J, Sgt
W Hubbard, James C, Pvt
W Hudson, Clyde E, Pvt
Hugh, Ivan C, Pvt
Hull, Henry, Pvt
W Hunnicutt, Roy L, Pvt
DcW Hunter, Clarence R, Pvt
W Hyde, Robert C Jr, Pvt
DoW Icaza, Frank X, Pvt
Impellizeri, Leo F, Cpl
Ingham, Edwin J, Cpl
Insalaco, Thomas, Pvt
W Iovan, Peter, Pvt
Iverson, Gordon P, Pvt
Jackson, Andrew J, Pfc
KIA Jackson, Duane S, Pvt
W Jacobson, Burton LeR, Pvt
Jakupcak, Stephen R, Pvt
James, Alfred W, Pvt
Jans, Jerome J, Pvt
Jarr, Harlan H, Pvt
W Jenkins, Glen E, Pvt
Jenkins, Joe W, Pvt
W Jensen, Junior N, Pvt
Jeselard, Charles V, Pvt
Jesmok, John S, Pvt
W Johns, Lawrence C, Pvt
Johnson, Orville L, Pfc
Johnson, Ovie H, Pfc
W Johnson, Walter C, Pvt
KIA Johnson, William E, Pvt
Johnston, Clyde Jr, Pfc
W Jones, Carroll L, Pvt
Jones, Everett O, SSgt
W Jones, Harold L, Pvt
Jones, J P, Pvt
Jones, Joseph A Jr, Pvt
Jordan, Franklin L, Pvt
Jordan, Richard K, Pvt
Juberian, Edward L, Pvt
DoW Jurek, Alfred J, Pvt
Jurkiewicz, John J, Pfc
Kahles, Rudolph, Pvt
W Kahrs, Leonard G Sr, Pvt
KIA Kail, Wm E, Pfc
Kaiser, Philip J, Pvt
Kampff, Kenneth R, Pvt
Kane, Charles H, Pvt
Kapoun, Robert P, Pvt
Kathrein, Joseph L, Pfc

W Keidel, Harold H, Pvt
Keikkila, Russell E, Pfc
Kellerstrass, Earl O Sr, Pvt
Kelly, J C, Pvt
KIA Kelly, John D, FM1cl
Kemmler, Robert C III, Pvt
W Kendrick, Verlo E, Pvt
Kennady, Abner B Jr, SSgt
Keppler, Arthur C, Pvt
Kerezsi, Elmer E, Pvt
Kerr, James W, Pvt
Kersey, Ernest T, Pvt
Kersin, John M, Pvt
Keys, Walter J Jr, Pvt
Kier, Bob K, Pvt
Kifer, Lorin L, Pvt
W Killhoffer, Eugene M, Pvt
Kindley, Robert F Jr, Pvt
Kindy, Glen D, Pvt
King, Edward L, Pfc
King, Joseph E, Pvt
King, Martin L, Pfc
King, Richard, Pfc
King, Robert J, Sgt
W King, William E, Pvt
Kintz, Clyde LeR, Pvt
Kiphen, Henry G, Pvt
Kirk, Harold E, Pfc
Kirkpatrick, Charles E, Pvt
Kleist, Charles, Pvt
W Kline, Richard H, Pvt
Klimp, Jacob, Pfc
W Klopfenstein, Cecil LaV, Pvt
W Knapp, Richard A, Cpl
W Knickrehm, Albert B, Pvt
W Knoblich, Clarence, Pvt
W Knops, Duane W, Pvt
KIA Kohut, William E, Pvt
Kolar, John, Pfc
Komma, Fred H, Pfc
W Konesky, Paul L, Pvt
Korthais, Melvin G, Pvt
KIA Kouskie, Judson F, Pvt
Krayer, George H Jr, Pfc
Kriesel, Floyd J, Pvt
Krugis, Alfred W, Pfc
Krumanocker, James R, Pvt
KIA Krummer, Lloyd A, Pvt
Kusalo, Pete G, Pvt
Krydzka, Walter S Jr, Pvt
W Kuperus, John G, Pvt
Kuta, Raymond G, Pvt
Labre, Charles E, Pfc
Labreche, Earl J, Cpl
Lacy, Robert A, Pvt
Lacy, Robert B, MTSgt
Laesch, Robert G, Pvt
W Lafferty, George S Jr, Pfc
Lagios, George, Pfc
LaGrange, Robert I, Pvt
W Lain, Vernon L, Pvt
KIA Lamb, John D, Pvt
W Lambert, Clifford F, Pvt
Lancaster, Don D, Pvt
Land, George L, Cpl

234

Note: *I apologize for the messy copy., This page got folded over inadvertently. I can assure you that Lou Hindbaughs name is listed in the part covered up.*

APPENDIX III.

ACTION REPORT
LANDING TEAM 128
IWO JIMA OPERATION
19 February, 1945 to 26 March, 1945

Annex MIKE to CT-28 Action Report

UNCLASSIFIED

SECTION VII OPERATIONS ASHORE - NARRATIVE

Monday, February 19, 1945: D-Day.

All troops were afloat by 0730 and proceeded to their rendezvous areas. No difficulties were encountered getting the troops afloat, however, one LVT had some mechanical trouble, and it was necessary to transfer these troops into a reserve LVT.

The first wave consisted of eleven (11) LVT(A)'s.

The second wave, consisting of the assault platoons of Baker and Charlie Companies, hit beach GREEN - 1 at 0902. The fire on the beach was very light and continued light until the troops approached the second terrace where they encountered heavy machine gun and mortar fire.

The third wave carried the remainder of Baker and Charlie Companies with one platoon of Able Company, and landed at 0907. The fire on the beach was still light and the entire wave moved up and over the first terrace without any casualties.

Baker and Charlie Companies, immediately reorganized, and started pushing across the island, meeting the expected resistance; blockhouses, pillboxes, and dug in emplacements.

The fourth wave landed at 0912. It carried the remainder of Able Company, and one-half (½) of the CP personnel. The fire on the beach had increased, but was not heavy. Able Company immediately reorganized, and pushed forward and to the left to reinforce and secure Baker Company's left flank.

Able Company made contact with Baker Company and faced south towards Mount Suribachi. Baker and Charlie Companies continued to drive on across the island; Baker on the left, Charlie on the right.

The CP personnel started working towards a position on the right flank which had previously been designated by aerial photographs.

The 81mm mortar platoon plus the balance of the CP personnel, landed in the fifth wave at 0917. The mortars set up approximately 150 yards inland from the beach (Target Square 132 EASY FORTH) and prepared to give supporting fire. Communication men from the mortar platoon had landed with Baker and Charlie Companies, and dropped phone lines. This enabled the Companies to have communications with the mortars

SECTION VII OPERATIONS ASHORE - NARRATIVE (Cont'd)

SECTION VII OPERATIONS ASHORE - NARRATIVE (Cont'd)

ten (10) minutes after they hit the beach.

The CP set up in a knocked out emplacement. (Target Square 147 YOKE SOUTHWEST)

Baker and Charlie Companies continued to drive across the island. Able Company maintained contact with the right flank of Baker Company. They encountered a maze of mutually supporting blockhouses and pillboxes extending across the entire front.

The attack was accelerated by such deeds as that of Captain D. E. Mears, Company Commander of Baker Company, who personally assaulted a pillbox that was retarding the advance of his Company, armed with only a pistol. Captain Mears was seriously wounded in one of these attempts, but continued to direct his Company until he was too weak to talk. First Lieutenant Weaver assumed command of the Company. Lieutenant Weaver, prior to this time, had been a platoon leader in Baker Company.

On Baker Company's right flank, Captain P. E. Roach, Commanding Officer of Charlie Company, continued to drive forward maintaining the same rate of progress as Baker Company. Captain Roach was wounded leading his Company in the assault on a heavily fortified position. Captain Rice Executive Officer, Charlie Company, assumed command.

A liaison party from the R-2 section maintained contact between Charlie Company and Combat Team - 27, which was on Charlie Company's right flank.

The 60mm mortars fired continuously on Japanese which had been flushed out of emplacements, keeping the enemy ever on the run. Lieutenant Sandberg, mortar platoon leader, Able Company, flushed out a 90mm mortar squad and continued to harass them until they abandoned their weapon. Lieutenant Sandberg was firing a 60mm mortar without a baseplate with amazing accuracy. He was later evacuated after having been hit three (3) times by enemy fire.

The attack developed in such a manner that at times some elements were held up, but others could slash through and continue to drive towards the west beach. Consequently, some men were seperated from their platoons. These men, however, working independently, continued to push on across the island.

SECTION VII OPERATIONS ASHORE - NARRATIVE (Cont'd)

SECTION VII OPERATIONS ASHORE - NARRATIVE (Cont'd)

At 1035, Lieutenant Wright, platoon leader, 1st Platoon, Baker Company, reached the west beach along with four (4) of his men. Lieutenant Bates, platoon leader, 2nd platoon, Charlie Company, and six (6) men reached the west beach soon after and joined forces with Lieutenant Wright.

The attached 75mm half-track platoon, Weapons Company, under the command of Captain Rhoades, landed on schedule and set up about one hundred twenty five (125) yards in front of the beach (Target Square 138 EASY WEST). The 75's fired initially on targets south towards Mount Suribachi, they later shifted their fire to emplacements on the mountain. The 1st and 3rd 37mm platoon, Weapons Company, landed in the same wave and put their guns in to the rear of the 75's (Target Square 132 EASY CENTER). They fired to the south on targets of opportunity. Both platoons delivered excellent neutralization fire.

LT 128 suffered heavy casualties in its staff section and before 1400 had lost: Captain Gililland, Battalion - 3; First Lieutenant Dreyer, Battalion - 4; Second Lieutenant Thomey, assistant Battalion - 3, along with key enlisted personnel.

Baker and Charlie Companies continued to mop up with tanks which had been attached from Charlie Company, 5th Tank Battalion, in their zone of action. LT 226 had relieved one platoon of Able Company and this platoon joined in mopping up. Easy Company, which was Combat Team reserve, was released to LT 128 at 1335 and assisted in cleaning out by-passed positions. The casualties were reported to be over six hundred, but all afternoon, men that had been separated and lost continued to join their respective companies, and the MIA report decreased considerably.

The CP moved to a new location (TARGET SQUARE 132 ROGER EAST) and by 1730, Baker, Charlie, Easy, and one (1) platoon of Able Company, were dug in along the high ground on the west beach and around LT 128's CP.

The night was quiet except for sporadic mortar fire. No infiltration attempts were made.

Casualties sustained on 19 February, 1945 were: 2 officers KIA; 11 officers WIA; 42 enlisted KIA; 132 enlisted WIA; 2 enlisted DOW, previously WIA on 19 February, 1945; 4 enlisted sick, evacuated.

SECTION VII OPERATIONS ASHORE - NARRATIVE (Cont'd)

SECTION VII OPERATIONS ASHORE - NARRATIVE (Cont'd)

Tuesday, February 20, 1945: D-Day plus 1.

LT 128 received orders to mop up along west beach. EASY Company was released prior to King hour, and all of Able Company rejoined LT 128. Able, Baker, and Charlie Companies sent out patrols in force to mop up rear area and west beach. Pillboxes and emplacements which had been by-passed on the quick thrust across the island, were destroyed by using close supporting weapons such as flame throwers and demolitions. Seventy three (73) Japs were killed.

The companies were reorganized and resupplied with ammunition, food, and water. The WIA continued to return and many of them had joined other elements of CT - 28 on the afternoon of D-Day until they could find LT 128.

The CP remained in the same position all day while LT 228 and LT 328 attacked Mount Suribachi. Light sniper and mortar fire was received in and around the CP all day.

The night was filled with several infiltration attempts, and light mortar fire. At 2315, a Jap barge attempted to land personnel on the west beach. Thirty nine (39) were killed and none reached safety.

Casualties sustained on 20 February, 1945 were: 1 officer KIA; 1 officer DOW, previously WIA on 19 February, 1945; 4 enlisted KIA; 16 enlisted WIA.

Wednesday, February 21, 1945: D-Day plus 2.

Able Company was committed on the right flank of George Company, LT 328, to reduce George Company's front. Able Company jumped off at King hour, securing the area along the west beach up to the foot of Mount Suribachi, repulsing one counterattack along the way. This was the first counterattack experienced by LT 128 and more than one hundred and fifty (150) Japs participated.

The 37mm platoon was in position along west beach (TARGET Square 132 ABLE SOUTH) and fired into enemy emplacements ahead of Able Company. They were firing at about 600 yards, but required only one or two shots to get on the target. They destroyed eleven (11) known enemy positions during the day.

SECTION VII OPERATIONS ASHORE - NARRATIVE (Cont'd)

SECTION VII OPERATIONS ASHORE - NARRATIVE (Cont'd)

By 1100, Able Company had pushed to the base of Mount Suribachi and consolidated their lines. Baker and Charlie Companies followed up the attack, mopping up and clearing rear area of snipers.

LT 128's forward elements of the CP moved to the west beach (Target Square 147 QUEEN SOUTH WEST) at 1000, and the balance displaced to the new CP at 1400. Baker and Charlie Companies dug in around the CP for the night. Able Company remained on line.

Charlie Company killed 28 Japs attempting to move down the beach during the night, and Able Company received heavy mortar fire.

Casualties sustained on 21 February, 1945 were: 2 officers WIA; 3 enlisted KIA; 21 enlisted WIA; 2 enlisted DOW, previously WIA, on 19 February, 1945; 2 enlisted sick, evacuated.

Thursday, February 22, 1945: D-Day plus 3.

Able Company was relieved out of the lines and brought back around the CP to reorganize. Baker and Charlie Companies again sent out patrols to clean out snipers. One large emplacement was encountered in Target Square 147 MIKE North West. This position had evidently been reoccupied because many dead Japs that had been dead for two (2) or three (3) days were found in the area. Thirty one (31) Japs were killed in and around this area, and an additional sixteen (16) were killed along the west beach. Anti-personnel mines were found in (Target Square 147 HOW South West). They had not been planted as a mine field, but placed in trenches, however, none of the mines had the safety pins pulled.

The CP remained in the same position with all the Company's dug in around it. At 2330, Japs were seen off shore attempting to swim out to sea and up north; three (3) of them were killed.

Casualties sustained on 22 February, 1945 were: 1 officer WIA; 6 enlisted KIA; 18 enlisted WIA; 1 enlisted DOW, previously WIA on 19 February, 1945, 2 enlisted sick, evacuated.

Friday, February 23, 1945: D-Day plus 4.

LT 128 was ordered to relieve LT 328. Able Company went back into the lines, moved to the west base of Mount Suribachi, and continued around the west side mopping up as they went. Two men were lost when Able Company encountered a mine field; (Target Square 131 FAN CENTER) it was marked by

SECTION VII OPERATIONS ASHORE - NARRATIVE (Cont'd)

SECTION VII OPERATIONS ASHORE - NARRATIVE (Cont'd)

the Engineers, and by-passed. At 1015, Captain A. G. Wilkins, Company Commander, Able Company, made contact with LT 228 on the southern tip of the island. During the time the ground at the base of Mount Suribachi was being secured, patrols from LT 228 moved up the northern slope of Suribachi. The first patrol reached the top at 1020, and planted the American flag.

The Companies set up a defense around the base of Suribachi for the night. Able Company on the south, Baker Company on the west, and Charlie Company on the north, tying in with LT 228, which completed the circle around Mount Suribachi. A feeling of "well done" prevailed within the Landing Team.

The CP remained in the same position and during the night, Japs worked their way up the beach from the south, infiltrating into the CP. This was kept under control and twenty eight (28) dead Japs were counted the next morning.

Casualties sustained on 23 February, 1945 were: 2 enlisted KIA; 5 enlisted WIA; 1 enlisted DOW, previously WIA on 22 February, 1945; 1 enlisted sick, evacuated.

Saturday, February 24, 1945: D-Day plus 5.

Able, Baker, and Charlie Companies sent out patrols along the west beach and around the western side of Suribachi, closing caves. A squad of engineers were attached to each company, and they performed their duties well, blasting emplacements and caves. Bull-dozers were used to close large caves, enabling the companies to do the job in about one-half ($\frac{1}{2}$) the time it would have normally taken.

All companies returned to their original defensive positions around the CP for the night. The night was quiet.

Sunday, February 25, 1945: D-Day plus 6.

LT 128 continued to mop up and clean out its area along the west beach. Patrols were sent out from Baker Company to close caves on the west beach, the engineers accompanied them on their mission. Able Company and Charlie Company rested throughout the day, taking inventory of their shortages and making the necessary changes in personnel. The engineers cleared a route to the west beach and each man in LT 128 had the opportunity to take a bath. The CP and line companies occupied the same areas as they did the night before. The night was quiet. Casualties sustained on 25 February, 1945 were: 4 enlisted WIA; 4 enlisted sick, evacuated.

SECTION VII OPERATIONS ASHORE - NARRATIVE (Cont'd)

SECTION VII   OPERATIONS ASHORE - NARRATIVE (Cont'd)

Monday, February 26, 1945: D-Day plus 7.

Able Company with the Engineers attached sent out patrols to close caves, while the balance of LT 128 rested. The bull-dozers proved themselves to be very effective in clearing an area. The armored bull-dozers moved into areas which were still being harrassed by small arms fire and worked even before the areas were secured. Able Company moved down the west beach closing caves.

The CP remained in the same position. The companies remained in their same defensive positions as they had occupied the night before.

There was no night activity.

Casualties sustained on 26 February, 1945 were: 1 enlisted, WIA; 3 sick, evacuated.

Tuesday, February 27, 1945: D-Day plus 8.

LT 128 remained in the same position throughout the day. Able Company and Baker Company sent out patrols in and around the west side of Mount Suribachi and along the west beach. LT 128 blasted 209 caves during the four (4) day period they mopped up. These caves were all located in; (Target squares 147 QUEEN, ROGER, UNCLE, VICTOR, and WILLIAM; 132, ABLE, BAKER, and FOX; 131, EASY, ITEM, JIG, NAN, OPOE, SUGAR, and XRAY).

The CP remained in the same position.

The Companies defensive positions were the same as they had occupied the night before.

The night was quiet.

Casualties sustained on 27 February, 1945 were: 1 enlisted WIA; 1 enlisted sick, evacuated.

Wednesday, February 28, 1945: D-Day plus 9.

LT 128 received orders and moved to the northern sector. A route of approach had been reconnoitered and at 1200 Charlie Company moved out followed by Baker Company at 1230, and Able Company at 1300. The Headquarters Company and CP personnel moved out at 1330. The CP arrived at the new location (Target Square 181 UNCLE EAST) at 1530.

SECTION VII   OPERATIONS ASHORE - NARRATIVE (Cont'd)

SECTION VII OPERATIONS ASHORE - NARRATIVE (Cont'd)

LT 128 received 8 replacement officers and 65 enlisted men from CT - 28. A great deal of equipment was found in this area which had been abandoned by friendly troops. This equipment was salvaged and sent to the Division salvage section.
LT 128 received orders that it would relieve LT 327 in the morning. The Landing Team Commander, his staff, and the Company Commanders went forward to reconnoiter the sector where the landing team was to be committed. The Companies dug in around the CP for the night. No night activity.

Casualties for 28 February, 1945 were: 1 enlisted WIA.

Thursday, March 1, 1945: D-Day plus 10.

Able, Baker, and Charlie Companies moved out at 0530, and the CP started to displace forward at 0645 arriving at LT 327's CP around 0745. LT 128 moved into the same CP as LT 327 had occupied. (Target Square 199 GORGE NORTH EAST).

Companies Able, Baker, and Charlie relieved the companies of LT 327 and were in position to jump off in the attack by 0845. King hour was 0900. The companies jumped off on time and took Hill 362 (Target Square 216 ROGER and SUGAR). As the landing team pushed on north of Hill 362, it ran into exceptionally heavy machine gun and mortar fire. The terrain was very difficult to move over. The left flank moved up and started over Hill 362 but there was a sheer drop of at least 100 feet. Able Company, LT 128 reserve, was ordered to move around to the right and fan out over into the draw in front of the left flank. They met very stubborn resistance. Captain A. G. Wilkins, Able Company Commander, went forward with one of his front line squads, leading his company down into the draw. The resistance increased and Able Company received such heavy casualties that it was impossible to move over in front of the left flank. Captain Wilkins was killed in the assault and Captain R. J. Persons, Executive Officer, Able Company, assumed command. Captain Wilkins was the last original company commander. Captain Wilson, Company commander, Baker Company, was wounded as he attempted to work his way down into the draw on the left flank and, First Lieutenant Weaver assumed command of the company. LT 128 received 6 replacement officers and 31 enlisted men. They were all sent to the three line companies.

The left flank dug in on Hill 362 and the right flank was just forward of the hill for the night.

There were small infiltration attempts during the night. All were repulsed.

SECTION VII OPERATIONS ASHORE - NARRAVTIVE (Cont'd)

SECTION VII   OPERATIONS ASHORE - NARRATIVE (Cont'd)

Casualties sustained on 1 March, 1945 were: 2 officers KIA; 3 officers WIA; 18 enlisted KIA; 70 enlisted WIA; 4 enlisted sick, evacuated.

Friday, March 2, 1945: D-Day plus 11.

The companies prepared to continue the attack, King hour was 0845. The landing teams first POW was captured near Able Company at daylight and brought into the CP for questioning.

The companies jumped off on time and pushed forward over Hill 362 the terrain continued to be exceptionally rough. This whole sector consisted of nothing but a series of draws which the landing team was forced to cross in the attack. It was extremely difficult to drive forward because each time the companies pushed into a draw, it was met by fire coming from both front and rear. The reverse slopes, actually they were cliffs, were honeycombed with well concealed enemy implacements from which the enemy delivered withering small arms and machine gun fire into the rear of our troops.

The companies received heavy casualties, but continued to drive forward under a blanket of friendly mortar fire. By 1645 they had pushed forward four hundred (400) yards, north of Hill 362, where they dug in for the night.

During the day it was discovered that the CP was set up in an old Jap Aid Station, and upon investigation of caves nearby, forty (40) Jap dead were located, and two (2) wounded removed. One wounded ran out and was captured.

The night was quiet except for small infiltration attempts. All of these were repulsed.

Casualties sustained on 2 March, 1945 were: 1 officer WIA; 22 enlisted KIA; 86 enlisted WIA; 2 enlisted DOW, previously WIA on 19 February, 1945, 1 enlisted sick, evacuated.

Saturday, March 3, 1945: D-Day plus 12.

The companies jumped off at King hour, 0745, and met the same stubborn resistance as the day before. The casualties continued to mount as the companies drove through the maze of enemy emplacements hidden in the rugged terrain.

How Company, LT 328, was attached and relieved Baker Company at 1100, but an hour and a half (1½) later, Baker Company had to relieve How Company due to heavy casualties. The left flank was

SECTION VII   OPERATIONS ASHORE - NARRATIVE (Cont'd)

SECTION VII OPERATIONS ASHORE - NARRATIVE (Cont'd).

held up by a series of heavily fortified emplacements. Captain Rhoades, Company Commander, Baker Company, was wounded and Captain Puckett, a replacement officer, assumed command. Charlie Company ripped through enemy resistance and drove ahead five hundred (500) yards. There was a lateral gap of about two hundred (200) yards between Baker and Charlie Company. How Company moved into position to cover this gap by fire since they did not have the personnel to cover it physically. The companies started digging in at 1745. The CP moved up to Hill 362 at 1230 (Target Square 216 SUGAR WEST) A reserve Company, How Company, LT 327, was moved in behind our lines but it was not necessary to use them. The night was quiet except for the usual mortar fire and infiltration.

Casualties sustained on 3 March, 1945 were: 1 officer KIA; 3 officers WIA; 18 enlisted KIA; 55 enlisted WIA; 2 enlisted MIA; 3 enlisted sick, evacuated.

Sunday, March 4, 1945: D-Day plus 13.

LT 128 was relieved in the lines by LT 327 at 0730, and moved back to the base of Mount Suribachi, arriving there at 1100. LT 128 was released from CT-28 control and went into Corps reserve. Baker and Charlie Companies dug in at the base of the mountain on the north side, Able Company in reserve near the CP. The CP was located at (Target Square 132 HOW SOUTH WEST). The night was uneventful.

Casualties for 4 March, 1945 were: 4 enlisted WIA; 1 enlisted sick, evacuated.

Monday, March 5, 1945: D-Day plus 14.

LT 128 sent out patrols moving up the west beach from the foot of Suribachi to the Cross Island road. The companies returned to their respective areas around 1300. Patrols were sent out in the afternoon to scout over the mountain. They closed a total of nine (9) caves. The night was uneventful. Received one hundred and forty six (146) replacements, enlisted, from CT-28.

Casualties for 5 March, 1945 were: 2 enlisted WIA.

Tuesday, March 6, 1945: D-Day plus 15.

LT 128 sent out patrols around the mountain closing six (6) caves. At 1400 the Landing Team received orders north again, and preparations were made to leave the following morning. The night was quiet. No casualties were sustained on 6 March, 1945.

Wednesday, March 7, 1945: D-Day plus 16.

SECTION VII OPERATIONS ASHORE - NARRATIVE (C)

SECTION VII   OPERATIONS ASHORE - NARRATIVE (Cont'd)

LT 128 cleared camp and started to move north at 0700, arriving at new location three hundred (300) yards to rear of (Target Square 216 WILLIAM CENTER) Hill 362 at 0815. LT 128 was now in Division reserve and was ordered to go in a reserve position three hundred (300) yards to the right front of Hill 362 (Target Square 217 PETER). Arriving at new CP around 1100 and set up for the night. Received orders to relieve LT 327 from the lines the next day. The night was quiet. Casualties for 7 March, 1945 were: 3 enlisted sick, evacuated.

Thursday, March 8, 1945:   D-Day plus 17.

LT 128 relieved LT 327 at 0730. Baker and Charlie Companies went on the line, and Able Company was in reserve. The companies started to push forward immediately. Snipers dressed in Marine uniforms and armed with M.1's were encountered, also, it was discovered that the enemy were booby-trapping their dead. The resistance was heavy and the terrain difficult to move over. Baker Company received heavy casualties but continued to press the attack, keeping abreast of Charlie Company on the right. Both companies received heavy knee mortar fire and the 81mm mortars of the landing team fired all afternoon knocking out two possible mortar positions.

The CP displaced forward to a position about three hundred (300) yards behind the front lines, and set up in what appeared to have been a Jap Motor Park, arriving in the new position (Target Square 233 TARE) at 1545. The companies continued to attack until 1730 driving forward approximately three hundred (300) yards at which time they dug in for the night. The night was filled with small infiltration attempts resulting in hand grenade duels between our troops and the Japs. The 81mm mortar platoon fired harrassing fire all night. Casualties sustained on March 8, 1945 were: 1 officer KIA; 6 enlisted KIA; 36 enlisted WIA; 3 enlisted DOW, previously WIA on 8 March, 1945; 1 enlisted MIA; 1 enlisted sick, evacuated.

Friday, March 9, 1945:   D-Day plus 18.

LT 128 received orders to continue the attack, King hour was 0730. The companies jumped off at King hour and met bitter resistance. The terrain was very difficult to move over, being cut up into numerous small draws which were covered with exceptionally accurate small arms fire. The attack was delayed for an artillery barrage, and then an air strike. Captain Parsons,

SECTION VII   OPERATIONS ASHORE - NARRATIVE (Cont'd)

SECTION VII OPERATIONS ASHORE – NARRATIVE (Cont'd)

Commanding Able Company was wounded, and First Lieutenant Weaver of Baker Company was sent over to take command. LT 128 launched a coordinated attack at 1520, with Landing Team 326, which was on its right flank, and succeeded in pushing forward three hundred (300) yards. First Lieutenant Tanner, Charlie Company Commander, was killed; Major Wood, Landing Team Executive Officer, took charge of the Company. The CP remained in the same position. The night was relatively quiet with occasional mortar fire. Casualties for 9 March, 1945 were: 1 officer KIA; 3 officers WIA; 18 enlisted KIA; 32 enlisted WIA; 4 enlisted DOW, previously WIA on 9 March, 1945, 2 enlisted sick, evacuated.

Saturday, March 10, 1945: D-Day plus 19.

The Landing Team received orders to continue the attack, King hour was 0800. The companies jumped off at 0800 and started to push forward, advancing slowly under heavy machine gun and rifle fire. The terrain was still very rough and our progress had to be based on the Landing Team on our flanks since we were in the center. The same stubborn resistance confronted the Landing Team as in previous days. The Japs refused to abandon their position and it was necessary to move across their fields of fire to destroy these positions. Small gains, amounting to approximately fifty (50) yards on left flank to one hundred (100) yards on right flank were made by 1730, at which time the companies dug in for the night. The CP remained in the same place. The night was quiet with only small infiltration parties attempting to pass through our front lines. All attempts were repulsed.

Casualties for 10 March, 1945 were: 2 officers KIA; 17 enlisted KIA; 33 enlisted WIA; 2 enlisted DOW, previously WIA on 10 March, 1945, 4 enlisted sick, evacuated.

Sunday, March 11, 1945: D-Day plus 20.

Landing Team 128 received a Naval Gunfire and Artillery barrage from 0800 to 0830, and the companies pushed out immediately under the barrage and fought their way to the top of ridge (Targe Square 234 ITEM) by 1645. Our flanks, however, were exposed and the companies received heavy casualties due to heavy enfiladed fire. The CP remained in the same position. There was considerable activity during the night, consisting mainly of infiltration attempts and grenade duels between the Japs up on the ridge and our troops below.

Casualties for 11 March, 1945 were: 1 officer KIA; 1 officer WIA; 8 enlisted KIA; 43 enlisted WIA; 1 enlisted DOW, previously WIA on 10 March, 1945, 3 enlisted sick, evacuated.

Monday, March 12, 1945: D-Day plus 21.

SECTION VII OPERATIONS ASHORE – NARRATIVE (Cont'd)

SECTION VII OPERATIONS ASHORE - NARRATIVE (Cont'd)

Naval Gunfire and Artillery fired a preparation barrage and King hour was set for 0700. Able Company relieved Charlie Company in the lines. The companies jumped off and were immediately met by heavy resistance. Preparation fires were again laid down and companies attacked at 0900 but were again held up by heavy machine guns, rifle, and mortar fire. A road was cleared and tanks moved up to support the attack. The companies were not on the topographical crest of the ridge and spider traps with trenches leading back down into the draw to the north rained small arms and machine gun fire on the troops which were exposed as they moved up the hill. This type emplacement allowed the enemy to change positions often. A heavily fortified position on Able Company's right flank continued to harass the entire front. Our 81mm mortars and 4.5" rockets were used continually. The 81mm mortars seemed to be the only weapon which would get the Japs up and out of their holes. The 7.2" rockets were attached and were pulled into position near the front lines and fired. Lt. Colonel J. B. Butterfield, Landing Team Commander, directed the fire. The concussion effect was excellent. 1st Lieutenant Nolan assumed command of Charlie Company and Major Wood returned to the CP.

The Companies remained in approximately the same positions as the night before. One hundred (100) motor transport men with twelve (12) light machine guns, under the command of Captain Slocum, were brought up to reinforce the lines, however, they were to be used only in defense. The night was quiet except for usual infiltration attempts and mortar fire.

Casualties for 12 March, 1945 were: 4 enlisted KIA; 24 enlisted WIA; 1 enlisted DOW, previously WIA on 19 February, 1945; 1 enlisted DOW, previously WIA on 12 March, 1945; 8 enlisted sick, evacuated.

Tuesday, March 13, 1945: D-Day plus 22.

Landing Team 128 received orders to attack, King hour was 0730. The companies moved out on time but made very slight gains as the landing teams to our right and left were held up by strong resistance, leaving our flanks exposed to enfilade fire when it moved ahead. The companies remained in the same defensive positions they had occupied the previous night. The CP remained in the same position. The night was filled with the usual activity. The 81mm mortar platoon fired harassing fire all night.

Casualties for 13 March, 1945 were: 1 officer WIA; 1 enlisted WIA; 8 enlisted sick, evacuated.

SECTION VII OPERATIONS ASHORE - NARRATIVE (Cont'd)

SECTION VII OPERATIONS ASHORE - NARRATIVE (Cont'd)

Wednesday, March 14, 1945: D-Day plus 23.

The companies jumped off and pushed forward, the right flank of Able Company which was on the right flank, moved up to the top of the ridge (Target Square 234 ITEM and OBOE), the left flank of Able Company dropping back to tie in with Baker Company on the left. Able Company was two hundred (200) yards ahead of the Landing Team on our right. The Divison Reconnaissance Company was attached and used to fill in this gap. Baker Company was seventy-five (75) yards ahead of the Landing Team on our left. Charlie Company pulled up into the line to fill this gap. The CP remained in the same position.
Usual night activity.

Casualties for 14 March, 1945 were: 1 officer WIA; 7 enlisted KIA; 28 enlisted WIA; 1 enlisted DOW, previously WIA on 14 March.

Thrusday, March 15, 1945: D-Day plus 24.

Received orders to hold, and companies remained in same positions. Patrols sent out to clear out snipers who were in our rear. Division Reconnaissance Company sent out patrols to feel out the positions to their front. They encountered little physical resistance, but the avenues of approach to these positions were well convered by fire. The CP remained in same position. The front lines received considerable mortar and small arms fire during the night.

Casualties for 15 March, 1945 were: 2 enlisted KIA; 9 enlisted WIA; 2 enlisted DOW, previously WIA on 15 March, 1945; 1 enlisted sick, evacuated.

Friday, March 16, 1945: D-Day plus 25.

Received orders to continue to hold. Very little activity except close hand grenade exchanges. Mortar personnel in the Landing Team OP using an '03 rifle with a telescopic sight accounted for a number of snipers. Companies remained in position on ridge just above a large draw (Target Square 234 DOG, ITEM, and OBOE); other elements of the 5th Division were pushing up and around to encircle this draw where the enemy made its last stand. The CP remained in the same position. The night was filled with the usual activity.

Casualties for 16 March, 1945 were: 1 officer WIA; 4 enlisted KIA; 14 enlisted WIA; 4 enlisted sick, evacuated.

SECTION VII OPERATIONS ASHORE - NARRATIVE (Cont'd)

SECTION VII   OPERATIONS ASHORE - NARRATIVE (Cont'd)

Saturday, March 17, 1945:   D-Day plus 26.

LT 128 held its position on the ridge on order and supported by fire other elements of the 5th Division as they swung around the north end of the island. Charlie Company pulled out of the line and mopped up snipers in rear areas, going back into positions at night. Able, Baker, and Reconnaissance Company remained in their same positions. There was some activity during the night, mostly hand grenade duels.

Casualties for 17 March, 1945 were: 2 enlisted KIA; 5 enlisted WIA; 2 enlisted sick, evacuated, 1 enlisted DOW, previously wounded in action on 16 March, 1945.

Sunday, March 18, 1945:   D-Day plus 27.

LT 128 received orders to continue to hold present position. The other units had completed their swing and were in position along northern side of the draw. Flame thrower tanks tried to work into draw with limited success. The CP remained in the same position. During the night a good number of infiltration attempts were made, all were repulsed and forty-eight (48) Japs were counted dead where these attempts had been made.

Casualties for 18 March were: 1 enlisted KIA; 3 enlisted sick, evacuated.

Monday, March 19, 1945:   D-Day plus 28.

LT 128 was ordered to remain in same position. Because of the position of our lines in relation to the attacking units our lines received a large amount of friendly fire, ranging from 81mm to small arms. The CP remained in the same position. The night was quiet except for a little friendly mortar fire falling in Able Company's lines.

Casualties for 19 March, 1945 were: 6 enlisted WIA; 1 enlisted DOW; previously WIA on 19 March, 1945, 1 enlisted sick, evacuated.

Tuesday, March 20, 1945:   D-Day plus 29.

Able and Baker Companies remained in position holding the ridge. Charlie Company pulled into the rear and mopped up with aid of attached Engineers. They blew fifty-two (52) caves bringing the landing team total to over four hundred

SECTION VII   OPERATIONS ASHORE - NARRATIVE (Cont'd)

SECTION VII OPERATIONS ASHORE - NARRATIVE (Cont'd)

(400) caves blown since it had gone back into the lines on March 8. The CP remained in the same position. A total of twenty (20) Japs were killed during the night attempting to infiltrate.

Casualties for March 20, 1945 were: No casualties.

Wednesday, March 21, 1945: D-Day plus 30.

The LT 128 received orders to hold the high ground they occupied. Able and Baker Companies stayed in position, and Charlie Company pulled out and came back to the CP to rest, arriving at 1030. The Division Reconnaissance Company was by-passed and pulled back into LT 128 reserve at 1035. At 1330, LT 128 received orders to push to the very edge of the cliff, which meant advancing ten (10) yards on the right flank and approximately fifty (50) yards on the left flank. Charlie Company left to go back into the lines for the push, King hour was 1545. All companies were on the edge of the ridge by 1700 and digging in for the night. The left flank platoon of Baker Company had been badly hit and the Division Reconnaissance Company was ordered to move into the area this platoon had occupied. During the night thirteen (13) Japs were killed on the left flank, while Able Company on the right flank, dropped charges over the cliff closing a number of caves and fired bazookas into emplacements, accounting for an estimated one hundred fifty (150) Japs. The CP remained in the same area. Able Company also sent out patrols into the draw and knocked out six (6) or eight (8) emplacements capturing four (4) heavy machine guns.

Casualties for 21 March were: 1 officer WIA; 1 enlisted KIA; 5 enlisted WIA; 2 enlisted sick, evacuated.

Thrusday, March 22, 1945: D-Day plus 31.

LT 128 remained on the cliff's edge giving supporting fire to LT 327 advancing down the draw across our front. By 1725 Able and Baker Companies had been by-passed and withdrawn one hundred fifty (150) yards in rear of the cliff, where they dug in for the night. Charlie Company and the Division Reconnaissance Company were left in the line. LT 327 had previously by-passed both Charlie Company and the Reconnaissance Company but were forced to withdraw under heavy fire, tying in with the right flank of the Reconnaissance Company for the night. The night was quiet.

SECTION VII OPERATIONS ASHORE - NARRATIVE (Cont'd)

SECTION VII   OPERATIONS ASHORE - NARRATIVE (Cont'd)

Casualties for 22 March, 1945 were: 6 enlisted WIA; 1 enlisted DOW, previously WIA on 21 March, 1945.

Friday, March 23, 1945:   D-Day plus 32.

Baker Company mopped up in area assigned the landing team. Able Company relieved the Division Reconnaissance Company in line at 1000. Able Company cleaned out remaining emplacements on edge of cliff killing twelve (12) Japs. All elements of the LT 128 were squeezed out by 1300, and came back approximately two hundred (200) yards back of the ridge where they dug in for the night. The Division Reconnaissance Company was detached from LT 128 at 1740. The CP remained in the same position and the night was quiet.

Casualties for 23 March, 1945 were: 1 enlisted KIA; 2 enlisted WIA.

Saturday, March 24, 1945:   D-Day plus 33.

Headquarters Company sent out working detail to clean up the area CT-28 had assigned us while the line companies policed up their immediate areas, encountering no enemy activity except an occasional sniper. The CP remained in the same position and the night was quiet.

Casualties for 24 March, 1945 were: 1 enlisted KIA.

Sunday, March 25, 1945:   D-Day plus 34.

The entire Landing Team spent all day cleaning and policing up its assigned area. The area was put in good order and a considerable amount of equipment salvaged. The landing team received orders to evacuate the area by 0730 the following morning and moved to WHITE BEACH-1. The CP remained in the same position and the night was quiet.

Casualties for 25 March were: 1 enlisted WIA.

Monday, March 26, 1945:   D-Day plus 35.

The landing team moved out at 0730 starting back to the beach. Packs and equipment were grounded and LT 128 proceeded to the 5th Division's cemetery for the 28th Marines Memorial Service. Services were brief but portrayed the homage and respect be-

SECTION VII   OPERATIONS ASHORE - NARRATIVE (Cont'd)

SECTION VII   OPERATIONS ASHORE – NARRATIVE (Cont'd)

fitting those who had paid the supreme sacrifice for the capture of Iwo Jima. The landing team then returned and picked up its gear and stood by to embark.

At 1430 the Landing Team commenced loading aboard an LCT which retracted from the beach at 1535. The troops embarked aboard the USS ZEILIN (PA-3) at 1630. No casualties.

BY ORDER OF LIEUTENANT COLONEL BUTTERFIELD

W. A. WOOD,
Major, USMC,
Executive Officer.

O F F I C I A L

W. R. HENDERSON,
1stLt., USMCR,
Bn-3.

SECTION VII   OPERATIONS ASHORE – NARRATIVE

APPENDIX IV. RECORDS

HEADQUARTERS, 27TH REPLACEMENT DRAFT,
TRAINING COMMAND, FLEET MARINE FORCE, SAN DIEGO AREA,
CAMP JOSEPH H. PENDLETON, OCEANSIDE, CALIFORNIA

2 November, 1944.

MEMORANDUM TO: All Officers.

Subject: Staff Duty Officer Watch, assignment of.

1. The following officers are assigned Staff Duty Officer Watch on the dates mentioned:

2nd Lt. FORTIER, David Roch	2 November, 1944
2nd Lt. FOUCH, Franklin Wheeler	3 November, 1944
2nd Lt. GARCIA, Alberto	4 November, 1944
2nd Lt. GINSBURG, Daniel	5 November, 1944
2nd Lt. GLASE, Wayne Raymond	6 November, 1944
2nd Lt. GOODMAN, Marvin Roy	7 November, 1944
2nd Lt. GOODSPEED, Neil Calvin	8 November, 1944
2nd Lt. GOODWIN, Robert Ray	9 November, 1944
2nd Lt. GRANNELL, William Edward	10 November, 1944
2nd Lt. HARRINGTON, Charles Edwin Jr.	11 November, 1944
2nd Lt. HARRIS, James Dudley	12 November, 1944
2nd Lt. HAWKINS, William Blair	13 November, 1944
2nd Lt. HEBERT, Junius Joseph	14 November, 1944
2nd Lt. HELMS, Frank John	15 November, 1944
2nd Lt. HENDERSON, Eugene	16 November, 1944
2nd Lt. HIGGINS, Bernard Joseph	17 November, 1944
2nd Lt. HOLMES, Robert Duncan	18 November, 1944
2nd Lt. HOURCADE, Aime Jean	19 November, 1944
2nd Lt. HUFFMAN, John Miles	20 November, 1944
2nd Lt. HUMPHREY, Robert Lee	21 November, 1944
2nd Lt. HURSON, Daniel Joseph	22 November, 1944
2nd Lt. HUTCHCROFT, Lester Earl	23 November, 1944
2nd Lt. HYNDMAN, John Spencer	24 November, 1944
2nd Lt. JOHNSON, Horace Lee Jr.	25 November, 1944
2nd Lt. JOHNSON, Robert "E", "V"	26 November, 1944
2nd Lt. JOHNSON, William Parks Jr.	27 November, 1944
2nd Lt. JONES, Dunbar	28 November, 1944
2nd Lt. KELLY, William Dixon	29 November, 1944
2nd Lt. KING, Clark	30 November, 1944

2. The tour of duty will be from 1630 until 0730.

3. Throughout the tour of duty, the Staff Duty will remain on the reservation.

4. There will be no unauthorized exchanges of watch.

RICHARD S. KITCHEN.

DIST: CO Staging Area (1); Each officer concerned (1); Co. A (1); Co B (1); Co C (1); Co D (1); Co E (1); FILE.

HEADQUARTERS, TRAINING COMMAND, FLEET MARINE FORCE,
SAN DIEGO AREA, CAMP JOSEPH H. PENDLETON,
OCEANSIDE, CALIFORNIA.

RESTRICTED
10 November, 1944.

From: The Commanding General.
To: First Lieutenant Leonard LUDTKE, 09101, USMC, (0600).

Subject: Change of station.

References: (a) CMC Serial 003D28744, dated 16 October, 1944.
(b) CG, FMF, SDA Serial 60004, dated 2 November, 1944.
(c) S O P G R O, dated 19 June 1944.

1. On or about 14 November, 1944, you and the below named officers will stand detached from the Training Command, FMF, SDA, Camp Joseph H. Pendleton, Oceanside, California. You will report with these officers to the Port Director, Naval Transportation Service, 11th Naval District, for transportation to FRAY. Upon arrival at that place, you will report with your detail to the Senior Fleet Marine Force Ground Commander present, for duty.

Rank		Name	Number	Branch	Code
Lt DC-V(G)		WELSH, Elvin A.	135514	USNR	
Lt(jg) DC-V(G)		CALDWELL, Gilbert L.	347814	USNR	
2dLt		AUGHEY, Robert M.	034180	USMCR	0200-154-
2dLt		COMPTON, Joseph O.	036388	USMC	1331-1542
2dLt		DOMEIER, Dwayne H.	036796	USMCR	4805
2dLt		FORTIER, David R.	041847	USMCR	1542
2dLt		FOUCH, Franklin W.	041848	USMCR	1542
2dLt		FRANZMAN, Frederick L.	041849	USMCR	1542
2dLt		GARCIA, Alberto	041857	USMCR	1542
2dLt		GLASE, Wayne R.	041861	USMCR	1542
2dLt		GINSBURG, Daniel	041860	USMCR	1542
2dLt		GOODMAN, Marvin R.	041863	USMCR	1542
2dLt		GOODSPEED, Neil C.	041864	USMCR	1542
2dLt		GRANNELL, William E.	041866	USMCR	1542
2dLt		HARRINGTON, Charles E.	041873	USMCR	1542
2dLt		HARRIS, James D.	041874	USMCR	1542
2dLt		HAWKINS, William B.	041878	USMCR	1542
2dLt		HEBERT, Junius J.	041879	USMCR	1542
2dLt		HELMS, Frank J., Jr.	041883	USMCR	1542
2dLt		HENDERSON, Eugene	041885	USMCR	1542
2dLt		HIGGINS, Bernard J.	041888	USMCR	1542
2dLt		HIGGS, Donald V.	032378	USMCR	0200-1542
2dLt	KIA	HOLMES, Robert D.	041891	USMCR	1542
2dLt		HOSMER, Wilbur J.	038413	USMCR	1542
2dLt		HUFFMAN, John M.	041894	USMCR	1542
2dLt		HUMPHREY, Robert L.	041896	USMCR	1542
2dLt	KIA	HUTCHCROFT, Lester E.	041900	USMCR	1542
2dLt	WIA	HYNDMAN, John S.	041901	USMCR	1542
2dLt	KIA	JAMES, Stewart R.	034364	USMCR	0200-1542
2dLt		JOHNSON, William P.	041910	USMCR	1542
2dLt		KELLEY, Richard G.	038424	USMCR	1542
2dLt		KELLY, William D.	041920	USMCR	1542
2dLt		KLEINFELDER, William, Jr.	036462	USMCR	9953-1542
2dLt		LAMPORT, Harry B.	041934	USMCR	1542

Subject: Change of station.

2dLt	LOWELL, Harvey W.	041948	USMCR	1542
2dLt	LOWRY, Alan E.	041949	USMCR	1542
2dLt	MC CAFFREY, John	041962	USMCR	1542
2dLt	METCALFE, Robert B.	039605	USMCR	7314-1542
2dLt	METZLER, Robert J.	041977	USMCR	1542
2dLt	PARRETT, Robert E.	032023	USMCR	4801
2dLt	SHIELDS, Robert F.	038494	USMCR	1542
2dLt	SOCKETT, Charles S.	042067	USMCR	1542

2. You will confer with this Headquarters as to time and other details of embarkation.

3. "Safe Arrival Cards" will be turned into this office prior to departure.

4. The present address of members of this detail will continue to be used until departure from their present stations for embarkation. After embarkation, letters will be mailed only through a Navy Censor. After sailing, the address will be 27th Replacement Draft, FMF, C/o Fleet Post Office, San Francisco, California. Correspondents should be instructed in letters or post cards written after sailing to address mail only as stated on the "Safe Arrival Cards" to be received by them.

5. These orders will constitute permanent change of station to duty beyond the seas.

6. There being no Government transportation available for dependents within a reasonable time, rail transportation to such point within the continental limits of the United States as each officer entitled to transportation for dependents may select for the residence of his dependents during his tour of duty abroad is authorized for such dependents. The location of your next permanent station is omitted from these orders for security reasons. Transportation beyond the continental limits of the United States is not authorized for dependents.

7. Change of station certificates will be furnished the Post Transportation Officer, Building 24-A-1, for each officer for which transportation for dependents is required.

8. The travel herein enjoined is necessary in the public service.

G. L. OWENS,
By direction.

Copy to: CMC   QM   PM   CG, FMF, SDA-2
CG, Dept. of Pacific   PM, TrngCommand
CG, ProvHq, FMF, Pacific   Post Transportation Off,
Fleet Post Office   CO, 27thReplaceDraft
                              F I L E

S E C R E T   5TH PIONEER BATTALION,
5TH MARINE DIVISION, FLEET MARINE FORCE,
C/O FLEET POST OFFICE, SAN FRANCISCO, CALIFORNIA.

NAME	RANK	SERIAL	REMARKS
CECCHIN, Anthony W.	Corp.	910930	
CLIFFORD, Edward M.	Sgt.	902142	
EVERETT, John N.	PFC	543221	
HAGEN, Burton L.	Corp.	895630	
MENDOZA, Tony R.	PFC	544244	
MOTTA, William J.	FldCk.	896659	
NUCKLES, William N.	Sgt.	286374	
PETERSON, Kenneth A.	Corp.	934659	
ROBINSON, Joseph F.	Corp.	920318	
WILSON, Goode D., Jr.	FldCk.	365517	

27TH REPLACEMENT BATTALION,
5TH MARINE DIVISION, FLEET MARINE FORCE,
C/O FLEET POST OFFICE, SAN FRANCISCO, CALIFORNIA.

NAME	RANK	SERIAL
GRANNELL, William	2dLt.	041866
HUTCHCROFT, Lester E.	2dLt.	041900
JOHNSON, William P.	2dLt.	041910
KELLEY, Richard G.	2dLt.	038424
DONNELLY, Jack A.	Sgt.	395095
FERRIS, Donald L.	Corp.	859362
FISCHER, James P.	Pvt.	823838
FISHER, Glen A.	Pvt.	828812
FISHER, Sam P.	Pvt.	990589
FISHER, Stanley M.	Pvt.	828896
FLECHLER, John E.	Pvt.	965249
FLEISH, Henry R.	Pvt.	990656
FLEGIEL, Chester S.	Pvt.	973265
FLORES, Jonias J.	Pvt.	959199
FLOWERS, Joseph M., Jr.	Pvt.	977160
FLOYD, Charles L.	Pvt.	557115
FLYNN, Harold E.	Pvt.	984907
FOGG, William B.	Pvt.	981619
FOLER, John M.	Pvt.	982245
FORD, Henry A.	Pvt.	822940
FORD, James A.	Pvt.	981690
FORD, Mac "B"	Pvt.	954741
FORSHEY, Clarence E.	Pvt.	989183
FOSMO, Edwin O.	Pvt.	978911
FOWLER, Delmar W.	Pvt.	887170
FOWLER, Ford F.	Corp.	865705
FRANCIS, Claude K.	Pvt.	569093
FRANCOIS, Otis R.	Pvt.	997976
FRANKS, Henry A.	Pvt.	822421
FRAZIER, Hoyle W.	Pvt.	965592
FRIDGE, Charles D., Jr.	Pvt.	961784
FRIESWYK, Calvin W.	Pvt.	072560

NM8—Form M
(1910)
Serial No: A45-579

REPORT OF MEDICAL SURVEY

Place **U.S. NAVAL HOSPITAL, Aiea Heights, T.H.** Date **20 April 1945**
(Name of hospital, ship, or station where survey is held)

From: Board of Medical Survey.
To: Commanding Officer.
For Transmission to the Bureau of Medicine and Surgery

Name **HYNDMAN, John Spencer** Rank or rate **2nd Lt. USMCR**
(In full, surname first)
Born: Place **Wichita, Kansas** Date **28 October 1922**
(Name of place and State or county)
Enlisted or appointed: Date **19 March 1942** Place **Kansas City, Missouri**
Total service: Navy **NONE** Marine Corps **3 yrs. 1 mo.** Army **NONE**

PRESENT HISTORY OF CASE

Admitted from **CO "B", 1BN., 26TH MARINES, 5TH DIVISION #2529** Date **9 March 1945**
Diagnosis **FRACTURE, COMPOUND, COMMINUTED, SKULL** Key letter **"K"** Specialty letter
(From navy nomenclature, under which carried on sick list)
Disability **is not** the result of his own misconduct and **was** incurred in line of duty
(Is or is not) (Was or was not)
Existed prior to enlistment **No** If "Yes," was condition aggravated by service?
(Yes or No)
Present condition **Unfit for duty** Probable future duration **Indefinite**
Recommendation **That he be transferred to a U.S. Naval Hospital on the mainland for further treatment and disposition.**

FACTS ARE AS FOLLOWS:

This officer was admitted to the sick list on 2 March 1945 from Company "B", 1st Bn. 26th Marines with the diagnosis of Fracture Compound, Skull, circumstances: (1) Within command. (2) Work. (3) Negligence not apparent. (4) While on forward line of battle on Iwo Jima he was hit by mortar shell. He was unconscious for four days, but has good memory of events preceding injury.

Examination shows large open wound of fronto-parietal region extending more to right frontal region. There is a large pulsating mass into wound. This wound has been debrided, and there is no loss of spinal fluid. Neuro-surgical consultant thinks no immediate surgical procedure should be attempted at this time.

Since he is not fit for duty and will need prolonged treatment, it is the opinion of this Board that he should not be retained at this hospital and the patient is so advised.

H. K. GRAY, P. W. DAY, E. B. WALKER,
CAPT. (MC), U. S. Navy. COMDR. (MC), U. S. Navy. COMDR. (MC), U. S. Navy.
Senior Member of Board. Member. Member.

AJG/JSH/fp.

MARINE DETACHMENT, U.S. NAVAL HOSPITAL
SAN DIEGO 34, CALIFORNIA.

3 May 1945.

From: Second Lieutenant John S. HYNDMAN, (041901),
U. S. Marine Corps Reserve.
To: The Commandant of the Marine Corps.
Via: (1) The Commanding Officer, Marine Detachment.
(2) The Commanding General, Department of the Pacific.

Subject: Report of arrival for treatment at hospital.

Reference: (a) Article 10-12(1), Marine Corps Manual.

1. In accordance with reference (a), the following report is submitted.

 (a) Detached from: Transient Center FMF, Pac.

 (b) Date Detached: 24 April 1945.

 (c) Authority: CG, FMF, Pac.

 (d) Conveyance: USS KWAJALEIN (CVE-98).

 (e) Date embarked: 26 April 1945.

 (f) Date sailed: 26 April 1945.

 (g) Port of embarkation: Pearl Harbor, T. H.

 (h) Date of arrival: 3 May 1945.

 (i) Date disembarked: 3 May 1945.

 (j) Port disembarked: San Diego, California.

 (k) Date admitted to hospital, etc: 3 May 1945.

JOHN S. HYNDMAN.

OO/AJG-fp. (041901). 1st Endorsement   3 May 1945
MARINE DETACHMENT, U.S. NAVAL HOSPITAL, SAN DIEGO 34, CALIFORNIA.
(5517).
From: The Commanding Officer.
To: The Commanding General, Department of the Pacific.

1. Forwarded.

HEADQUARTERS DEPARTMENT OF THE PACIFIC,
San Francisco, California
17.ba-O-
Dept Comdr   by dir.
CMC

ADMISSION OR DISCHARGE ORDER
NAVMED-HF-1 (REV. 1-45)

U. S. NAVAL HOSPITAL, San Diego, 34, Calif.
DATE 15 June 1945

TO: ☐ Chief of Naval Personnel (Pers-31)
☒ Commandant, U. S. Marine Corps
  Hdqs. F.M.F., Pacific Restricted

REF: Orders 2445-40/850-70, 0142-393 (28233), dated 24 April 1945

NAME OF OFFICER		FILE NO.
HYNDMAN, John Spencer		041901

RANK	CLASS	DATE OF BIRTH
2nd Lt. USMCR		10-20-22

PERMANENT DUTY STATION: Transient Center, Fleet Marine Force, Base Hospital #10

ADMISSION

DATE ADMITTED	DIAGNOSIS
5-3-45	Fracture, compound, skull
	CODE 2529

STATION FROM WHICH ADMITTED: Transient Center, Fleet Marine Force, Base Hospital #10

PROBABLE LENGTH OF HOSPITALIZATION (DAYS)	PROBABLE LENGTH OF SICK LEAVE (DAYS)
Indefinite	Undetermined

PROBABLY FIT TO RETURN TO— Undetermined
☐ FULL DUTY ☐ LIMITED DUTY ☐ INACTIVE DUTY OR MEDICAL DISCHARGE

DISCHARGE

DATE DISCHARGED	DISCHARGED TO—
	☐ PERMANENT DUTY ☐ TEMPORARY DUTY

STATION TO WHICH DISCHARGED:

CONSIDERED TO BE FIT FOR—
☐ ALL DUTY ☐ ADVANCE BASE OR U. S. SHORE ☐ U. S. SHORE ONLY

LENGTH OF HOSPITALIZATION (DAYS) LENGTH OF SICK LEAVE (DAYS)

REMARKS:

By direction of MOinC, NavHosp, SanDiego, Calif.

E. McElwee
E. MC ELWEE, ENS, H(W) USNR

(M.C.), U.S.N.

Copy to FLEET FORCE or AREA COMMANDER—When patient is received from or discharged to an activity located outside continental United States

U. S. NAVAL HOSPITAL
SAN DIEGO, CALIFORNIA

DATE: June 27, 1945

FROM: 2nd Lt. John S. Hyndman, USMCR #041901
TO: The Medical Officer in Command.

Subject; Leave, request for.

1. It is requested that I be granted ____30____ days of leave of absence beginning __June 29, 1945__ to expire at 2400 __July 30, 1945__.
   Date

2. Reason for request ____Convalescent leave.____

3. If granted my address will be: Wellington, Kansas

Ward Medical Officer

N.S.Klmquist, Lt.Cdr., (MC) USNR

Officer in Charge of SOQ

J.W.Porter, (MC) USNR, Cdr.

U. S. NAVAL HOSPITAL
SAN DIEGO, CALIFORNIA

NH16/OO   June 27, 1945

FROM: The Medical Officer in Command.
TO: 2nd Lt. John S. Hyndman, USMCR #041901

1. Returned, granted. Your leave expires at 2400 __July 30, 1945__.

                                         J.R.Fulton
                            J.W. Allen, by direction

Before departure and upon return from leave check "out" and "in" with the following:

                        Upon Departure   Upon Return

Admission Nurse SOQ _____   _____

Patient Officer's Office _____   _____

Officer of the Day _____   _____

1st Endorsement

From: Commanding Officer.
To: BUREAU OF MEDICINE & SURGERY, Washington, D.C.
(Officer convening board)

Date 27 AUG 1945
By direction of the MO i/c

H.K. GRAY, CAPT., MC, USNR

2d Endorsement

From:
To:

Date

(Signature)

Endorsement

From: Bureau of Medicine and Surgery.
To: ~~COMMANDANT, U.S. MARINE CORPS~~

Date 5 SEP 1945

1. Forwarded: *Recommendation of Board Approved.*

ROSS T. McINTIRE
Chief of Bureau

J.N. MARQUIS
By direction

(Signature)

041301-1
DFA-904-rcc

3rd Endorsement

HEADQUARTERS MARINE CORPS, WASHINGTON.
From: Commandant of the Marine Corps.
To: The Medical Officer in Command, Naval Hospital, San Diego, Calif.
Via: The Commanding General, Department of the Pacific, Marine Corps.

Date 10 SEPTEMBER, 1945.

1. Returned.

Copy to M&S.

FILE

L.C. Hays, Jr.,
By direction.

U. S. NAVAL HOSPITAL
SAN DIEGO, CALIFORNIA

DATE: October 19, 1945

FROM: 2nd Lt. John S. Hyndman, USMCR #041901
TO: The Medical Officer in Command.

Subject: Leave, request for.

1. It is requested that I be granted __30__ days of leave of absence beginning __Oct. 23, 1945__ to expire at 2400 __Nov. 21, 1945__.
   Date

2. Reason for request __Sick leave in accordance with BuPers letter -Q9-MLB 18-1/00 dated 12 September 1945.__

3. If granted my address will be: 624 No. Washington St.
                                    Wellington, Kansas

Ward Medical Officer
F.A.Faileis, Lt.(MC) USNR

Officer in Charge of SOQ
J.M.Porter, Cdr.,(MC) USNR

U. S. NAVAL HOSPITAL
SAN DIEGO, CALIFORNIA   Oct. 19, 1945

SN16/00

FROM: The Medical Officer in Command.
TO: 2nd Lt. John S. Hyndman, USMCR #041901

1. Returned, granted. Your leave expires at 2400 __Nov. 22, 1945__.

                                    E.F.Kunkel
                        J.W. Allen , by direction

Before departure and upon return from leave check "out" and "in" with the following:

	Upon Departure	Upon Return
Admission Nurse SOQ		
Patient Officer's Office		
Officer of the Day		

REPORT OF MEDICAL SURVEY

Place U.S. NAVAL HOSPITAL, San Diego 54, California Date 27 AUG 1945
(Name of hospital, ship, or station where survey is held)

From: Board of Medical Survey.

To: Commanding Officer.
For Transmission to the Bureau of Medicine and Surgery

Name **HYNEMAN, John Spencer** Number **041901** Rank or rate **2nd Lt. USMCR**
(In full, surname first) (File or service No.)

Born: Place **Kansas** Date **October 20, 1922**
(Name of place and State or county)

Enlisted or appointed: Date **September 30, 1944** Place **North Carolina**

Reported for active duty, USMCR: Date **Oct. 7, 1944** Place **Camp Pendleton, California**

Total service: Navy _____ Marine Corps A.D. **10 mos.** Army _____
Res. **none**
PRESENT HISTORY Prior **1 yr. 3 mos.**

Admitted from U.S.N.H. Aiea Heights, T.H. Date **May 3, 1945**

Diagnosis **FRACTURE, COMPOUND, COMMINUTED, SKULL** #2529 letter "K" Specialty letter _____
(From navy nomenclature, under which carried on sick list)

Summary of case history: 1. Within command. 2. Work. 3. Negligence not apparent. 4. Injured in action against an organized enemy.

This officer was previously surveyed at the U.S. Naval Hospital, Aiea Heights, T.H. on April 20, 1945 with the diagnosis fracture, compound, comminuted, skull and the approved recommendation that he be transferred to a USN Hospital on the mainland for further treatment and disposition.

He was first admitted to the sick list on March 9, 1945 at Co. "A" Med. Bn. VAC, FMF in the field with a gunshot wound of the frontal region of the skull. The wound was debrided, hemostasis was obtained, the wound was dressed and penicillin and sulfonamide therapy was instituted. He was transferred via various government facilities to this hospital.

On admission to this hospital on May 3, 1945, the physical examination revealed a large open wound of the frontal region of the skull approximately 6 by 3 cm. in size, with one large bone fragment exposed and not covered with granulation tissue. On May 4, 1945 the patient was seen by the neurosurgical consultant who removed several small bone sequestra from the wound and advised penicillin therapy. X-ray examination of the skull revealed a defect of the frontal bone 2 by 5 cm. in size and about 5 cm. above the right supra orbital ridge. There was a radiating fracture extending downward and laterally to the left temporal fossa, and one extending upward and posteriorly parallel to the saggital suture. A neurological examination on May 9, 1945 was negative. On May 19, 1945 a sequestrectomy was performed followed by an uneventful recovery. All remaining laboratory procedures were normal.

At the present time the skull wound is healed and the skull defect is covered over with firm healthy tissue. The neurosurgical consultants have advised that a tantalum plate cranioplasty be performed in the near future and that he be retained for further treatment. His ultimate return to duty is anticipated.

_____ is not _____ the result of his own misconduct and **was** incurred in line of duty.
(Was or was not)

Existed prior to appointment or enlistment? **No** If "Yes," was condition aggravated by service? _____
(Yes or No) (Yes or No)

Present condition **Unfit for duty** Probable future duration **Indefinite**

Recommendation: That he be retained for further treatment.

C.H. DICKERSON, CAPT., MC, USNR   J.F. PORTER, CMDR. MC, USNR   H.S. LITTLUIST, LT. CMDR.
Senior Member of Board.   Member.   MC, USNR, U.S.N.
                                                              Member.

JAN FEB MAR APR MAY JUN JUL AUG SEP OCT NOV DEC JAN FEB MAR APR MAY JUN JUL AUG SEP OCT NOV DEC

MARINE CORPS BASE SAN DIEGO CALIFORNIA: (onDet at USN SDA Calif)
(CasCo#3, GdBn)

FEB. 1946: 1, Joined; 1-28, Convalescent Leave.

MARINE CORPS BASE, SAN DIEGO CALIFORNIA (On Det Ort at USN Diego Calif)
(CasCo #3 GdBn) (1Mar46, DC)

MAR. 1946: 1April46, RETIRED.

Placed on the retired list as Second Lieutenant in the Marine Corps Reserve on 1 April 1946 by reason of physical disability.

041901   RETIRED   390888 RESERVE

NAVMC 545A-OP

RECORD OF .... HYNDMAN, John Spencer .... MARINE CORPS   SHEET ....

Date and place of birth ..... 20 October 1922, Wichita, Kansas.
Usual residence ..... 624 N. Washington, Wellington, Kansas.
Next of kin ..... FATHER - Eugene B. Hyndman, same address.
Single or married ..... SINGLE.
Prior service ..... Enl. USMCR:19Mar42to29Sep44.

Appointed from ..... KANSAS.

Appointed a Second Lieutenant in the Marine Corps Reserve for temporary service 30 September 1944, with rank from 30 September 1944, pursuant to the provisions of the Act of 24 July 1941 as amended.

Acknowledged appointment on 30 September 1944.

Upon acknowledgement, assigned to active duty at

CAMP LEJEUNE, NORTH CAROLINA
     (Spec OCC, FRegt, TC, FMF)

SEP. 1944: 30, Joined.

OCT. 1944: 1, detached to

FLEET MARINE FORCE, SAN DIEGO AREA
     (H-Co, InfTR, FRegt, TC, Camp Pendleton, Calif)

OCT. 1944: 6, Joined: 1-5, enroute; 6-29, Student Troop Leaders Class; 30, detached to

27thReplDraft, StagingArea, TrngComd, Post

30, Joined.

NOV. 1944: 1-12, Company Officer; 13-30, temporary duty with
     Twenty-fourth Replacement Draft.

FLEET MARINE FORCES, PACIFIC
     (27thReplacement Draft, SerTrps, 5thMarDiv)   (2Dec44, Design ch

DEC. 1944: 1-2, Temporary duty with the 24th Replacement Draft; 3-31, Company Officer; 13Nov44, embarked on board the USS GENERAL R. E. CALLAN; 14Nov44, sailed from San Diego, California; 15-22Nov44, at sea; 23Nov44, arrived and disembarked at Kahului, T.H.

JAN. 1945: Draft Officer; 7, embarked aboard USS DICKENS (APA 161); 8, sailed from Hilo, Hawaii, T.H.

APPENDIX V. THE CAVALIERS & OTHER SHIPMATES

VERLIE F. (ABE) ABRAMS

His Story

Abrams spent his early years on the streets of Chicago. After teaching Abe to fight the boys that bullied him, his mother, unable supervise him while she worked, put him in Catholic School so that he would not grow up to be a thug or get killed. He didn't like Catholic School and after a few years, ran away to live with his Uncle's family in Webb City. He stayed in high school only so he could play football. When he went to the University of Missouri, again it was only to play football. Nevertheless, those early teachings from Catholic School led him to the want to know more about bible teachings so he was drawn together with friends to this very special bible study group. The bible study group, the Catholic School and of course football made him the man that he was to become.

After college. he didn't personally participate in organized religion, but the principles, ethics and values previously learned stayed with him throughout his life.

He was determined that his children go to Sunday School so he made it his top priority to see that his children started back to Sunday school as soon as they moved into a new community.

He was a champion to many, but most of his accomplishments were unknown to most unless they happened to be specifically involved in an incident and they happened to see him as a protector of the underdog. Abe rarely spoke of his good deeds which were more important to him than his many outwardly known successes…well except for his occasional success chasing and swinging at the little white ball.

Most of his co-workers never knew of his previous football career and outside of his work relationships, friends did not know he was considered a national expert in the area of work force initiatives and job development.

He represented DuPont for several meetings at the prestigious Business Roundtable, which at the time consisted one executive representative from each of the 35 largest U.S. corporation whose purpose was to addresses the economic well being of the nation. The Business

Roundtable believes the basic interest of business closely parallel the interest of the American Workers so it's not surprising that Abrams efforts were desired by this group.

His children were always amazed that within a few months of moving to a new town, everyone seemed to know him and wanted to talk with him. On Saturday's, Abe would take his oldest daughter downtown to buy her an ice cream cone. He chatted with a man digging a drainage ditch for the city. Then he would stop to tell the trash collector what an important job he was doing and how his work made such a difference. It seemed he would chat everyone: the Governor, the Mayor, a ministers, a bankers, a lawyers, a firemen, a policemen, a farmers, cherry pickers, a solders, etc. Almost always by the time the drug store was reached, he would have chatted with a very socially and economically diverse group, most of which would to join Abe for sandwiches and of course, an ice cream cone for his daughter.

Missouri teammates and spectators would cheer for "Abie Baby", with most never knowing the story behind the nickname. Abe returning to school from his part-time job, saved several very young black girls, from being attacked by some older boys. Seeing the incident, someone reported it to one of his teammates and so began the "Abie Baby" chant because he had saved these children. Throughout his adult life, he was constantly making a difference by defending the rights of others and would not stand for prejudice based on race, color, religion, sex, age or economics.

While climbing the ladder of achievement, he never hesitated to take time to help others. Perhaps, that is the reason he was a successful labor negotiator. He held out for contracts that were just and fair for union members and management.

Teamster leadership wanted him dead. He received death threats. His family lived in another city during one six month negotiation. He wore a very large ugly metal belt for protection. He held his position and finally when the contract negotiation were completed, it was a good contract for the Teamsters, labor and Management. His reputation was built as a result of this contract and while his Teamster's negotiations would continue hot and heavy in future years, the death threats did not. There was finally a respect built among all the negotiators.

His real victory for both labor and management came years later when he trained management in multiple industries and trades to hold out for common expiration dates in contracts. This was a planned activity that he instigated. It was probably the most important change in union-management relationships in the 20th century. Prior to companies utilizing common expiration dates for contracts, each trade would close down or threaten to close down a facility at its contract expiration date. When a contract was resolved, another trade would close down that facility. While utilizing common expiration dates for contracts may this seemed to be a victory for management, it was really a victory for all the trades. Employees of all trades would have more opportunities to work steadily without having to worry about lay-offs because a supporting trade was negotiating its contract.

DuPont employees introduced him to golf. He played golf all over the country. When TV introduced Monday night football, he would be on the greens. The same would be true of Saturdays and Sundays. Rain, snow and heat would not chase him away from his pursuit of the little white ball. About the only time, he might watch a televised game was Christmas and New Year's Day or when a National Championship was being televised.

As with football, he played golf through his injuries. Hip surgery left him cripple, but he persisted in his love of the game. He adapted to a new swing so he could continue to play and continued to do so until he was no longer able to stand. Not to be stopped, he joined a swim team and made an impressive showing even though his water mobility was primarily through the use of his strong arms. His biggest contribution to his team however, was the motivation and inspiration that he gave to other team members.

DuPont credited him for developing a strategy for contract negotiation and the results were a credit to his analysis and suggestions. But more importantly, Abe was a friend to everyone. He was known for his fun-loving attitude and had many friends.

Welton Ralph Abell

From Wikipedia, the free encyclopedia

Colonel **Welton Ralph Abell** (May 17, 1922–April 26, 1998) was United States Marine Corps officer serving in the Korean War, as well as a former advertising executive. Abell was a recipient of the Navy's second-highest decoration — the Navy Cross — for combat valor in the Korean War.

Welton Ralph Abell	
May 17, 1922 – April 26, 1998 (aged 75)	
Nickname	"Ralph"
Place of birth	St. Louis, Missouri
Place of death	San Clemente, California
Place of burial	Arlington National Cemetery
Allegiance	United States of America
Service/branch	United States Marine Corps
Rank	Colonel
Commands held	2nd Battalion, 7th Marines
Battles/wars	Korean War *Battle of Inchon *Battle of Chosin Reservoir
Awards	Navy Cross
Other work	Advertising executive

Contents

- 1 Marine Corps service
    - 1.1 Navy Cross citation
- 2 Education and civilian career
- 3 Final days
- 4 Books
- 5 See also
- 6 External links
- 7 References

Marine Corps service

Abell enlisted into the Marine Corps on October 23, 1942 and in July 1943 was sent to the University of Notre Dame as a V-12 student. He was commissioned a second lieutenant in March 1945. He saw no action in World War II and in 1946 was awarded a degree in Journalism from the University of Missouri.[1] He was Marine Corps reserve first lieutenant when called to active duty in 1950. Serving with the 2nd Battalion, 7th Marines (2/7) in Korea, he suffered a painful shoulder wound during a heavy enemy counterattack at the Battle of Chosin Reservoir but refused medical attention and regrouped his depleted company to fight off an attempted encirclement. He led his men up a steep hillside in a blinding snowstorm. He had assumed command of Fox/2/7 after its company commander, Captain William Barber was evacuated from the battlefield for his defense of the Toktong Pass. In January 1951 he became the assistant operations officer of 7th Marines and remained in the billet until being sent home in June 1951.[2]

For these heroic actions, he was awarded the Navy Cross.

Navy Cross citation

WELTON RALPH ABELL
First Lieutenant
United States Marine Corps Reserve

> For extraordinary heroism in action against the enemy while serving with a Marine Infantry Battalion in Korea, from 6-10 December 1950. While serving as company commander of a marine rifle company Lieutenant Abell demonstrated outstanding qualities of personal leadership, bravery and resourcefulness

under most unfavorable circumstances. On 5 December 1950, he was serving as a member of a regimental staff. During the afternoon he was given command of a rifle company which for five days had been isolated and suffered heavy casualties. This company which consisted of sixty-four men and one officer had just completed a day's march through enemy territory in sub zero weather. During the night the company was augmented by one hundred officers and men from special units of the division. This constituted Lieutenant Abell's command the following morning when his company moved out at first light as part of the advance guard battalion for the division's move from Hagaru-ri to Koto-ri. Throughout the following twenty-two hours of continuous action in sub zero weather in overcoming successive strong enemy positions which blocked the road, Lieutenant Abell placed himself at the head of his troops and with complete disregard for his personal safety moved under intense enemy fire to areas where the fighting was the heaviest in order to personally direct fire and movement of the men who were inexperienced in infantry tactics. Early in the day all but two of the officers were either killed or critically wounded, thus rendering control more difficult. In the afternoon an enemy movement threatened his flank. After two runners had been wounded in trying to reach one of his squads with a message to shift their fire, Lieutenant Abell personally moved through intense enemy fire in order to dispose his men and direct their fire in such a manner as to block the enemy threat. Throughout this move Lieutenant Abell led by example and by his display of calm courage and confidence where the fighting was heaviest he inspired his men and gave them faith in both his ability and theirs. On 8 December he continued to demonstrate outstanding leadership in the battalion's advance guard action from Koto-ri. Assigned the mission of seizing and defending a hill he skillfully maneuvered his depleted company and in the late afternoon was ordered to take up a defensive position. While inspecting his lines and encouraging his men he was painfully wounded. In spite of this he continued to exercise command and remained with his company until a strong counterattack had been repulsed. Only then did he return to the aid station for treatment. His fearless action and outstanding achievement contributed materially to the accomplishment of his battalions mission. Lieutenant Abell's display of outstanding courage and devotion to duty were in keeping with the highest traditions of the United States Naval Service.

Navy Cross

Education and civilian career

In 1943, Abell was studying journalism and advertising at the University of Missouri in Columbia when he enlisted in the Marines. The service sent him to the University of Notre Dame for ROTC training.

After the war, he got his degree at Mizzou and went to work writing advertising copy for the Barry-Wehmiller Machinery Co. He moved to California in 1953 and worked in advertising. He retired in 1989.

Final days

Abell died on April 26, 1998 at age 75 of cancer at his home in San Clemente, California. As a Marine Corps Reserve colonel, he received a full-honors military burial at Arlington National Cemetery. He is buried in section 65, site 624.

In addition to his wife Margaret Minot Abell, survivors include two sons, Scott Abell of Rancho Santa Fe, California, and Michael Abell of San Diego, California ; two sisters, Betty Ullrich of Crestwood and Helen Schicker of Affton; and four grandchildren.

BILL BUSCH was one of the fraternity brothers at Wichita State who enlisted with John, Hollar, and Kessler in 1942. They were called up to go to V-!2 school at Notre Dame in July 1943. They went to boot camp at Parris Island together and Bill went to Quantico to Officer Candidate School (OCS). He saw action in Okinawa with the First Marine Division. After the war, he became a lawyer and owned an insurance company in Omaha, Nebraska. He was called back into service during the Korean War and served as a major in the Judge Advocates Office. Bill died in 2003.

DON JONES got a civil engineering degree but went back to school and started over in music. He taught at Emporia College, Kansas where he met Russ and married her after she graduated. Their son, Bryan is an engineer in Albuquerque, New Mexico. Daughter Sarah is at St. Olaf's in Wisconsin. Russ is now married to the ex=president of Grinnell College where Don was teaching when he died of cancer in 1969.

Don's sister Cletis was married to an Army Colonel who was killed . She died of a brain tumor and left four children. They were raised by Kenneth Jones, her brother, who still lives in Wellington. Don and Cletis' brother in law, Murray Dresbach lives in Washington State and has Alzheimer. He married Dorothy Jones who died of cancer some time ago. During the war, Murray worked in Savannah for Boeing.

Don's feats mentioned in John's Letter included a Silver Star for devising a way to blow up fortifications near Metz on the Maginot Line. Don also helped the engineers rebuild the Remagen Bridge. He served with combat engineers in Italy and was wounded in the fighting in Europe. Don ended up in the Army under Patton.

Note: The scan of the article from the Wellington Weekly News is not very readable. Here is the text:

PVT. DON JONES
A HERO IN METZ
Son of Mr. and Mrs. J. W. Jones of this City Given Recognition by A. P.

Metz. Nov. 20 1944. AP---Pvt... John (Don) Jones of Wellington, Ks., son of Mr. and Mrs.. J. W. Jones of 312 South Blaine was one of the combat engineers who yesterday braved shells, mortars and machine gun fire of the Germans without a chance to return the fire while rowing boats full of assault waves across the muddy, swirling Moselle river.

It was Sunday back behind Metz yesterday with scrubbed and Sunday dressed French attending church. A few Yankee doughboys went along. But inside Metz there were only the brave and dirty boys of the 95th division, mopping up remnants of German defenders and crunching forward with fixed bayonets toward the last of the organized resistance, across the Moselle. Company A, 20th engineers. Jones outfit, took the first wave across at noon, three engineers working the oars in each of a dozen boats, with a dozen doughboys ready to spring ashore from each boat and start shooting.

The German gunners opened up and the river around the boats was splashed with shells and mortars. Some of the men were hit, but the engineers, their rifles slung over their shoulders kept on rowing. Once ashore, the doughboys soon located the enemy gunners and supporting artillery cleaned them out.

Not long afterward, the word went back: "Call off the artillery. We got those positions now."

From the *Wellington Weekly News*, Monday, November 20, 1944.

Gunnar Hald

Hald joins Gould as Director

Gunnar Hald, an active realtor in Metroplex commercial properties since 1963 has joined the Dan Gould Co. as Director of Commercial Sales. Hald will continue to teach Real Estate courses at the University of Texas in Arlington on a limited basis.

A native of Minnesota, Gunnar served in the Marine Corps in the South Pacific during World War II. In 1948 Hald received his Law Degree from Notre Dame and in 1949 his Masters Degree in Science and Education from Notre Dame's Graduate School. After graduation, Hald handled warehouse leasing for Montgomery Ward's Chicago plant then moved to New York to work in the Real Estate Department for Mack Truck, Inc. While working in New York, Hald leased 33,000 square feet of the Empire State Building.

From 1958 to 1963, he was associated with the Champlin Oil Company in Fort Worth. Over 300 Service Stations sites were secured under his supervision. Hald's activities as an independent Commerical Realtor for the past fifteen years has been in leasing and the sale of locations to 7-11 Stores and a host of fast food resturants. And, throughout the Fort Worth-Dallas area, he has packaged and sold Shopping Center locations. Of great value to the Dan Gould Commercial Department will be Hald's vast experience in the leasing of office, retail and warehouse space.

HALD

GUNNAR CARL JENSEN HALD, 57, 2065 Fleur De Lis, Arlington. Passed away Friday. Survivors: Sons, Peter Hald, Austin, Tim Hald, Chris Hald, Fort Worth; one granddaughter; brother, Chris Hald, Oregon; sister, Miss Sophia Hald, Michigan. Stateroom services 12:30 p.m. Monday. Rev. Gary Lindley officiating. Arrangements Greenwood, 3100 White Settlement Rd. at University Dr. 336-0584.

CAPTAIN WILLIAM W. KESSLER, USMCR (041246)

William W. Kessler enlisted in the Marine Corps Reserve at Wichita, Kansas on 3 June 1942 and reported for active duty at Marine Barracks, Quantico, VA. on 12 September 1944. On 13 September 1944 he was appointed a Second Lieutenant (Temporary) to rank as such from that date and began duty as a student in the Reserve Officer School. He completed the Reserve Officer School on 27 November 1944 and following a period of leave he reported on 13 December 1944 to Camp Lejeune, NC. as a company officer in the 1st Training Battalion, Infantry Training Regiment, Training Command, Fleet Marine Force. On 9 March 1945, after having completed the Infantry Officer Course, Second Lieutenant Kessler was detached to the 54th Replacement Draft which was formed at Camp Lejeune. His duties, in addition to being a Platoon Leader, included those of Public Relations and Morale Officer. On 3 April the draft entrained for Camp Joseph H. Pendleton, Oceanside, CA. and arrived there on 8 April 1945.

The 54th Replacement Draft embarked from San Diego, CA. on 13 April 1945 aboard the U.S.S. Admiral C. F. Hughes which sailed on 14 April and arrived at Pearl Harbor, T.H. on 19 April. On 21 April the Admiral Hughes sailed from Pearl Harbor and arrived on 30 April at Guam, Marianas Islands, where the draft disembarked. Following advance staging at Guam the 54th Replacement Draft embarked on the S.S. Fairland on 20 May and sailed for Saipan, Marianas Islands, arriving on 21 May 1945. The draft continued on 23 May to Okinawa, Ryukyu Islands where it arrived and debarked on 27 May. Second Lieutenant Kessler was detached to 3d Battalion, 4th Marine Regiment, 6th Marine Division where he joined "K" Co. of that Battalion as a Platoon Leader in the forward echelon engaged in combat operations relative to the occupation of Okinawa Shima, Ryukyu Islands. He served in this assignment during the Okinawa Campaign, 30 May - 6 July 1945 and was twice wounded in action on 19 June 1945. He was not evacuated and following securing of Okinawa Shima, embarked with his unit on 7 July aboard the U.S.S. Arenac which sailed to Guam, Marianas Islands, arriving and disembarking on 14 July 1945.

As Second Platoon Leader, "K" Co., 3d Battalion, 4th Marine Regiment, 6th Marine Division he embarked with that unit on 15 August 1945 on the U.S.S. Mellette at Guam and sailed for Yokosuka Naval Base, Yokusuka, Japan. Upon arrival in Japan the unit participated in the initial landings and occupation of the Japanese homeland. On 17 January 1946 Second Lieutenant Kessler was detached and ordered to embark aboard the U.S.S. Haskell in Yokosuka, Japan for transport to the United States. Upon disembarking at Seattle, WA. on 2 February 1945 he was to report, after delay enroute and leave, to the Marine Corps Separation Center, Naval Training Center, Great Lakes, IL. He joined 2d Casual Company at the Separation Center on 18 February and on 19 March after returning from leave, his temporary appointment as a Second Lieutenant was terminated and he resumed his enlisted status. On the next day, 20 March 1945, he was appointed a Second Lieutenant in the Marine Corps Reserve with his original date of rank of 13 September 1944. Upon acceptance of this appointment on 25 March 1945, Second Lieutenant William W. Kessler,

U. S. Marine Corps Reserve was released to inactive duty and assigned to the General Service Unit rolls of the 9th Reserve District.

On 29 August 1946, the Officer-in-Charge, Midwestern Recruiting Division, St. Louis, MO. delivered to Second Lieutenant Kessler a Purple Heart medal and Gold Star in lieu of a second medal in recognition of wounds received during the June 1945 invasion and occupation of Okinawa Shima, Ryukyu Islands. Subsequently, while still a member of the 9th Reserve District, Kessler was promoted to First Lieutenant on 28 July 1947 with rank from that date. On 20 January 1948 First Lieutenant Kessler's permanent promotion was effected with the original date of rank assigned. He was transferred to the 8th Marine Corps Reserve District on 5 February 1948 as a result of his move of residence into the area of that District's responsibility.

With the outbreak of the Korean War (27 August 1951), First Lieutenant Kessler was recalled to active duty and ordered to Marine Corps Schools, Quantico, VA. There he was assigned the duties of Executive Officer, "C" Co., Headquarters Battalion, MCS. On 22 October 1951 he received word of his promotion to Captain in the Marine Corps Reserve. The commission which was dated 22 August 1951 established 1 January 1951 as his date of rank. Captain Kessler was transferred from "C" Co., Headquarters Battalion on 9 January 1952 to "B" Co., Headquarters Battalion for duty as a student under instruction in the 3d Special Junior Course. He satisfactorily completed the 3d Special Junior Course on 29 May 1952 and was transferred to The Basic School, MCS, still at Quantico, VA. There he became an instructor of general subjects in the school responsible for training the Marine Corps' newly commissioned Second Lieutenants. His additional duties during his period of duty with The Basic School included those of summary Court-Martial Officer. On 12 December 1952 Captain Kessler completed his tour of duty with The Basic School and was transferred to Casual Company, Headquarters Battalion, for processing and release from active duty. He departed MCS, Quantico, VA. on 17 December and upon arrival at Purcell, Oklahoma on 21 December 1952 was released from active duty. On that date he also rejoined the 8th Marine Corps Reserve District.

Captain William W. Kessler, U.S. Marine Corps Reserve served his country during two wars. His active duty during World War II in the Pacific included combat operations on Okinawa Shima, Ryukyu Islands and occupation of Japan at Yokosuka Naval Base, Yokosuka, Japan. During the Korean War he was a valuable instructor in The Basic School at Quantico, VA. where he imparted his combat achieved skills to new commissioned Marine Corps Second Lieutenants. His total active duty time was 2 years, 10 months and 7 days. In decorations and awards he is authorized the Purple Heart with Gold Star, Presidential Unit Citation, Asiatic Pacific Campaign Medal with one Bronze Star, Navy Occupation Medal (Pacific), World War II Victory Medal, National Defense Medal, and Marine Corps Reserve Ribbon.

HWH
30 April 1980

8:WWC:get
13 Dec 1952

FIRST ENDORSEMENT on CMC Release from active duty orders, WWKessler, etc.
of 4 Nov 1952

From: Commandant, Marine Corps Schools
To: Captain William W. KESSLER 041246/0302 USMCR

Subj: Release from active duty

Ref: (a) MarCorps Memo 107-51
(b) Almar #29
(c) Almar Act ConUS 022105Z 2 Nov 51

1. On 16 December 1952, you will stand detached from your present station and duties, will proceed in compliance with your basic orders, as modified by reference (b), to your home of record, or in lieu thereof, to such other place as you may desire to go. Upon date of arrival at your destination, but not later than 21 December 1952, you will stand relieved from active duty. The foregoing date is the constructive date of arrival home and is based on actual and necessary schedules which most nearly coincide with the possible time of your departure from this station by the mode of transportation selected by you.

2. Your unused leave to include constructive date of arrival at your destination is twenty-seven (27) days.

3. You have elected mileage to Purcell, Oklahoma, which is your home of record.

4. You have elected to travel to your destination by the following mode of transportation: Privately owned conveyance.

5. Settlement of pay and allowances for travel time will not be made until a certified copy of your orders, endorsed as stated in paragraph 3 of your basic orders, has been received by the disbursing officer.

6. In accordance with reference (c), you are authorized to perform the travel to your destination by privately owned conveyance.

C. B. CATES

Copy to:
CMC (DPA)   CO HqBn - 2
CMC (AFC)   DisbO
Qtrs Desk   LOCATOR (FILE)
8th MCRD

Certified True Copy
W.W. Kessler

Received these orders at MCS, Quantico, Virginia on 16 December 1952

William W. Kessler, Capt

APPENDIX VI. BRAIN SURGERY

BRAIN SURGERY

John began to have seizures from his brain injury in 1949. They were controlled by medication for awhile, but became more frequent. On the recommendation of his doctor in Corpus Christi, he elected to go to Montreal Neurological Hospital in Montreal, Canada in November 1949 for an operation they had originated to remove scar tissue causing seizures.[1] The surgery took approximately eight hours under local anesthetic.

The surgeons probed before each particle of the scarred brain tissue was removed to see what effect it would have. His only reaction was once when they asked him what he felt and he couldn't answer because one side of his mouth had contracted. Later he told me that they had found more shrapnel. I knew this was not true from the doctor's report, and we realized that he had relived the surgery he had in San Diego to remove shrapnel that remained after his first surgery.

John had no more seizures and was able to discontinue the medication he had been taking. It was a miracle for us not to have to live with the threat of a seizure. We paid for the surgery with the help of his hospitalization insurance with his company and for airfares to Montreal. The VA was no help whatsoever. The medical care for veterans until many years after the war was a farce. We were one of the lucky ones who had the resources to seek help elsewhere.

In 1958 before he had surgery, John had aphasia due to the seizures extending into his speech center for a day or two. Although his speech returned, he had difficulty thinking of the word he wanted for the rest of his life. If you didn't know his condition, it seemed only that he had slow speech from living in the South.

After the surgery, a tantalum plate was used to close the bone deficit in John's skull. Tantalum was discovered in 1802. It is used in many industrial and medical applications. Tantalum is the material of choice for surgical repairs of human bones such as the skull plate John received in Montreal. It is also used as foil or wires to connect torn nerves, and a woven gauze to bind up abdominal muscles. Tantalum and its alloys are resistance to corrosion and wear.

---

[1] Dr. Wilbur Penfield was a pioneer in brain surgery.

APPENDIX VII.

MY GRANDPA
A story his grandson Michael dictated it to his teacher who wrote it out for his school newspaper.

MY GRANDPA

My grandpa was injured in a war. He died in September. I miss him since he died. He got the purple heart. He died of cancer of the liver. I will always remember him. He is my hero.

Michael Lee Hyndman
Grade 1

CHRISTMAS

My sister and I got presents on Christmas. We opened them and played all day. We rode our new bikes. At night we were tired but happy. It was a good day

Edward Apolinar
Grade 1

A TRIP TO THE PARK

We are going to bring food to the park. My brother and I and all my family will come. We will eat and play on swings and go fishing. It will be a happy day.

Jennifer Barron
Grade 1

THE BEACH STORY

It was the first day of spring break. Me and my brother and my cousins were going to the beach today. It took us five hours to get there. When we got there we looked for sea shells. I found twelve. My cousins found twelve. My brother found thirteen. Then we had lunch. All of us had shrimp and for a drink a Sprite. It was fun that day.

Melissa Reed
Grade 1

APPENDIX VIII. WHITE HOUSE VISIT, 1985.

At a Reunion of Iwo Jima survivors in Washington, D. C. on the 40th anniversary of the invasion, they were invited to the White House to meet President Ronald Reagan. Each man was given a copy of the president's photograph and a copy of his remarks on the occasion.

To The Men of Iwo with best wishes,

Ronald Reagan

THE WHITE HOUSE

Office of the Press Secretary

For Immediate Release   February 19, 1985

REMARKS OF THE PRESIDENT
AT PHOTO OPPORTUNITY
WITH 28TH MARINE REGIMENT

The East Room

4:45 P.M. EST

THE PRESIDENT: Thank you very much. That's quite a reception for a horse cavalryman and a Navy flyboy. (Laughter.)

Well, at dawn, 40 years ago today, 450 United States Navy ships stood off a tiny island in the Pacific. Few Americans had heard of the place -- it measured 4-2/3 miles by 2-1/2 miles, ash-covered beaches and one extinct, unknown volcano. And at 7:00 a.m., 0700 hours to you, a command was passed to the ships: "Land the landing force."

No one, not even you, the Marines and the Navy corpsmen who stepped ashore from the Amtracs at two minutes after nine, knew that what you were about to do would forever enshrine the island, Iwo Jima, and the volcano, Mount Suribachi, in American history.

Today, Iwo Jima is remembered with other names like Saratoga, the Alamo, and Gettysburg. Remembered, not simply because Americans were again conspicuously gallant in battle, but because our sons were called upon to endure unspeakable hardship for the sake of freedom.

Every one of you present today, and all of you 40 years ago, have a special place in our nation's heart -- reserved only for the few in every generation called upon to sacrifice themselves so that a great nation's ideals of freedom and peace may live and prosper and endure. The manner of your performance -- as captured in Joe Rosenthal's photo of your flag-raising at Mount Suribachi -- remains a beacon, indeed, a birthright, for America's young people and for every future American.

The other day I came across a description of Iwo written by the then Private First Class Russell Werts. And it ended in the following note: ". . .our troopship started to pull away from Iwo and head for Guam. As I stood by the rail and watched the little island fade in the distance, a feeling of loneliness came over me. It was as if a part of me was left behind, as if an Iowa farm boy was waving goodbye. We would never meet again. Somewhere in that jagged jungle of rocks, he forever walked with the ghosts of Iwo. . ."

Well, I would like to say to Russell, and to each of you who willingly gave your youth to the nation, that you receive in kind a place in the American heart and the national memory that endures so long as this nation and the ideals for which it stands endure. We're very grateful to you.

And we're deeply honored to have you here today. The White House really belongs to the American people. And I couldn't help but reflect today that seldom in history has any President been in the company of more deserving Americans.

I hope that each of you enjoyed being here as much as Nancy and I am delighted to have you. And on behalf of all Americans, we salute today, you, the men of Iwo. God bless all of you. (Applause.)

BIBLIOGRAPHY

Allen, Robert. First Battalion, *28th Marines on Iwo Jima: White Crosses and Stars of David*. McFarland & Co. 1999

Allyn, John. *The Forty Seven Ronin*. Charles E. Tuttle, Co. 1970.

Bradley, James. *Flags of our Fathers*. Bantam Books. 2000.

Brown, Thomas, MD. *Battle Wounds of Iwo Jima*. Vantage Press. 2002.

Buell, Hal. *Uncommon Valor, Common Virtue*. Penguin Group. 2006.

Burrell. Robert S. *The Ghosts of Iwo Jima*. Texas A. & M. Press. 2006.

Clement, J. Fred. *The SCOS 400*. SOCS Classmates. 1996.

Caruso, Patrick. *Nightmare on Iwo*. Naval Institute Press. 2001.

Conner, Howard M. *The Spearhead. The WWII History of the Fifth Marine Division*. Infantry Journal Press. Washington, D.C. First Ed. 1950.

Dickensen, James. *We Few*. Naval Institute Press. 2001.

Haynes, Fred. *Lions of Iwo Jima*. Henry Holt Co. 2008.

Kessler, Lynn. *Never in Doubt*. Naval Institute Press. 1999.

Leckie, Robert. *Strong Men Armed*. Da Capo Press. 2006.

Lucas, Jack. *Indestructible*. Da Capo Press. 2006.

Muscarella, Anthony. *Iwo Jima. The Young Heroes*. Castle Books, 1989.

Newcomb, Richard. *Iwo Jima*. Holt, Rhinehart & Winston. 1966.

Overton, Richard. *God Isn't Here*. American Legacy Medias. 2004.

Penfield, Wilder. *Mystery of the Mind*. Princeton University Press. 1970.

Ross, Bill D. *Iwo Jima. Legacy of Valor*. Vanguard Press. 1985.

Schaffer, John and Frank. *Keeping Faith*. Carrol & Graf. 2002.

Snively, John. *The Last Lieutenant*. New American Library. 2006.

Thomey, Tedd. *Immortal Images,* Naval Institute Press. 1996.

Wheeler, Keith. *We Are the Wounded*. F. P. Dutton o. 1945.

Wheeler, Keith. *The Pacific is My Beat*. F. Dutton. 1943.

Wheeler, Richard. *Iwo Jima*. Harper & Row. 1983.

Wheeler, Richard *A Special Valor. U.S. Marines and the Pacific War*

Wright, Derrick The Battle for Iwo Jima. 1945. Sutton Publshing 1999.

WWII Magazine. *Iwo Jima, The Battle We Can't Forget*. Weider History Group. 2006

Official Histories

Garand, George W. and Strobridge, Truman. *History of the U.S. Marine Corp Operations in World War II. Western Pacific Operations*. Volume V. Iwo Jima. Pages 443-729.

Morison, Samuel Eliot. *Victory in the Pacific*. Part I. Iwo Jima. Pages 3-70. Little Brown and Company. Boston. 1961.

VHS and DVDs.

History Channel. *Iwo Jima., Hell's Volcano*.

Ed Swaney. *The Battle of Iwo Jima*

Oliver North. *War Stories. Iwo Jima*.

Iwo Jima Memoirs.

On February 19, 1990, John attended a memorial ceremony at a bay front park in Corpus Christi, Texas observing the 45th anniversary of the Iwo Jima Operation. A strong north wind came up and fellow Marines thought he needed extra cover, so they found a blanket in one of their cars. The next morning we opened the hometown paper (Caller-Times) and a photograph of John took up half of the front page. The Photo is the endpiece of this book

Iwo Jima victory remembered

12 honored at ceremony marking the capture of the island

By Alexander Kafka
STAFF WRITER

Corpus Christi's Sherrill Park is 45 years and half a world away from the World War II battles of Iwo Jima. Or is it?

"They start playing that music and you're there," Joseph Caldwell, 67, said, gesturing toward a loudspeaker blaring marching music. "It gets in your blood, and you never leave it behind."

Caldwell, who was a private first class with the 4th Marine Division on Iwo Jima, is one of a dozen Marines living in the Corpus Christi area who were honored yesterday in the second annual park ceremony commemorating the Pacific island's capture from the Japanese.

A big man with a brusque and friendly manner, Caldwell hasn't romanticized the fighting he took part in 4½ decades ago.

"We liked to kill them and they liked to kill us," is how he summed it up.

Please see Marines/B4

B4/Sunday, February 18, 1990
Corpus Christi Caller-Times

Marines FROM PAGE B1

He admits, with a smirk, to remembering nothing good of his days with a rifle battalion.

More than 6,000 men lost their lives in February and March 1945 in the fight to capture the eight-square-mile middle island of the three Volcano Islands. Of those men, 5,800 were in the 3rd, 4th and 5th Marine divisions.

Iwo Jima, the Sulphur Island, was of great strategic importance. The Japanese had used it as a fighter plane base to attack American bombers. When the island was taken by U.S. forces, it was used as an air strip for American fighter planes protecting bombers flying from Saipan and Tinian to Japan.

The United States controlled Iwo Jima until 1968, when the island was returned to Japan.

Abe Bazaman, 67, was in a 4th Division machine gun unit. Iwo Jima, for him, was two days long. The first day, he took a bullet in the shoulder; the second, both legs were hit by mortar shell shrapnel.

When he returned to the United States, Cpl. Bazaman stayed in the service, but his injuries kept him on limited duty and, in effect, he had "a permanent liberty pass with no money for liberty."

Wearing his full uniform, Bazaman sat yesterday to the right of the podium. During the national anthem, the Pledge of Allegiance and moments of silent prayer during the ceremony, he said he thought not only of his fallen comrades in the Pacific front, but also of his brother, who died fighting the Germans.

Col. Peter Perkins, commanding officer of the Marine Air Training Squadron of Corpus Christi, gave yesterday's keynote address.

"All too often," he said, "we forget that the freedoms we enjoy today were bought with (the) blood" of those who fell on Iwo Jima. Theirs, he said, was "heartbreaking progress, measured in inches, not yards .... Heroism was commonplace."

Second Lt. John Hyndman, 67, said he was flattered by the ceremony, but that even the mention of Iwo Jima gives him the jitters.

His "commonplace heroism" involved a shrapnel wound to the head that left him unconscious for a week and a half.

Also honored at yesterday's ceremony – organized by the Mayor's Committee for Veterans' Affairs and hosted by the Coastal Bend Detachment of the Marine Corps League – were Gilbert Graves, Daniel Hinojosa, Joe Roddy, W.W. Bodine, Pete Barrientes, Meade Warthen, Raul Escobar, and two Navy corpsmen – Leo Luna and Salome Soliz Jr. – who were attached to Marine divisions at Iwo Jima.

Except for Escobar, who is from Sinton, the men are Corpus Christi residents.

Madge Hyndman 1989.

Pfc. Eugene Hyndman US Army,

Gunter Barber and Lois Hyndman

John Hyndman, jr. 1968.　　　**John's Sons**　　　**Gerald Hyndman 1979.**

John　　　　　**Dorothy**　　　　　**Jerry**

Madge Hyndman and Her Children on Her 95th birthday, November 1989.

Back row, l. to .r: Michael Hyndman, Gerald A Hyndman, John Hyndman, jr. Gunter Barber, John Barber
Front Row, l. to r: Lisa Hyndman, Judith Hyndman, Lois Hyndman, Jeanne Barber, Krystal Hyndman

February 19, 1990.

INDEX

A, B
Abell, Ralph , 61, 206, 270
Abrams, Verlie, 61, 199, 267
Allen, Robert, iii, 207
Allyn, Jerre, iii, 118
Allyn, Jimmy 114
Allyn, John, 81, 114, 115
Allyn, Inez, 123
Allyn, John Perce, 114, 129
Altman, Harlan, 199
Aunt Dott, (Dorothy Murphy Wheeler), 18, 91, 185
Aunt Kit, (Mae Allyn Schipbach, 104
Aunt Mabel, 40, 43
Barber, Jeanne, 217
Barber, Gunter, 283, 284
Bonnie (Edna Mae Allyn Cobb), 18, 47, 143, 182
Bowman, Kendall, 162
Brachman, Bill, 162
Busch, Bill, 62, 129, 270, 129

C, D
Cady, Jack, 182
Callan, USS, 131
Chauncey, USS 188, 189
Casburn, Mabel, 40
Casburn, Cecil, 57, 76
Champeny, Majorie, 147
Clark, Bertha, 162
Clement, J, Fred, iii, 3, 231, 281
Cobb, Alan,18
Cobb, Edna May, 18
Cobb, Paul, 18
Counsell, Juanita, 44,194
Dickens, USS, vi, 159
Dickensen, James, 2, 281
Dresbach, Murray, 145

E, F, G
Eby, Walt, 205
Felt, Mary Margaret, iii, 188
Garner, John Frank, 22, 25, 180
Granell, Bill, 1643 190, 192
Goodrum, Vernon Edgar, 157

H
Hald, Gunnar, 62, 106, 273
Hald, Tamara, iii

H
Hall, Gunnar, 62, 106,271
Haynes, Maj. Gen. Fred, 281
Helms, Frank, 102, 128,147, 183
Hill, Mary, 201
Hinbaugh, Lou, iii, 184, 234
Hollar, Don, iii, 6, 7, 55, 62, 68, 103, 105, 2701
Houson, Don, 101
Hutchcroft, Lester "(Bill," iii, 101, 103, 136. 165, 232
Hvidsten, Ralph, iii, 16, 35
Hyndman, Dorothy, iii, 2, 81, 84, 86, 126, 285
Hyndman, Eugene, 283
Hyndman, Jerry (Col. Gerald), 9, 12, 90, 162, 284
Hyndman, John,, Jr, 284 , 285
Hyndman, Krystal, 285
Hyndman, Lisa, 285
Hyndman, Lois Williams, i, 110, 186, 283, 285
Hyndman, Madge, 118, 119, 121-1127, 283, 284
Hyndman, Michael, 285

I, J, K
Icaza, Frank, 183
Irby, Orel, 101
Johnsons, 209-212
Jones, Cletis, 273
Jones, Don, 15, 16, 86, 100, 142, 145, 272
Jones, Dunbar, 113
Johnson, Bill, 137, 209-212
Johnson, H. L., 113
Johnson, William Parks, iii, 113
Kessler, Bill and Muriel. iii, iv, 27, 62, 274-276
King, Ernest, Admiral, 175
Kwajelein, USS, vi, 184

L, M, N, O, P, Q, R
Lauterbach, Neal, 158
Mayfield, Kansas, iv, 4
Moore, Captain, 208
Moore, Keith, 187
Moore, Mary Margaret Felt, 17=87
Morris, Carolyn, 14
Murphy, Bob, 91
Murphy, Marilyn,182
Murray, John, iii, 67, 70
Odor, Doris, 51, 65
Penfield, Wilbur, 278, 280
Quiring, Boydine, 39
Rancho Santa Fe, vi, 112, 198, 204

287

R
Reagan, Ronald, 279
Rogers, Harold, 18
Rogers. Dorothy, 216, 284
Romig, Bill, 15, 140, 146
Ronin, Forty Seven, 115
Routh, D., 187
Rush, Mrs., 14
Schaefer, Robert, 215
SOCS 400, iii, 2, 3, 87, 96, 231, 2801
Steinke, Gene, 128
Tout, Jim, iii, 184, 1945 214-215

U, V, W, X, Y, Z
Trewitt, Margaret, iii, 213
V-12, 2, 3
Van Deventer, Judy, 137
Veronee, Marvin, iii
Van Doren, Ann Cowan, iii
Wallace, Joanne, 40
Wellington, Kansas, iv, 18, 67, 191, 214
West, Mary Ann, 9
Wheeler, Dorothy Murphy, 90
Wheeler, Keith, 182, 184
Wood, W. A. Major, 253

Note: Many of the names of John's friends and shipmates are mentioned over and over in his letters. This index does not list the page number of every mention of a name. For example, Don Hollar was with John through V-12, Parris Island, and Lejeune. He is mentioned in many of letters from these stations and frequently thereafter.

John Spencer Hyndman, Sr.
Arlington Grave Site, 221
Biography, iv
Brain Surgery 277
Corpus Christi, 282
End Piece, 286
Dates of Service, v
Medals and Ribbons, 223-224
Taps, 216
Train to Pendleton, 110